Göttinger Wirtschaftsinformatik
Herausgeber: J. Biethahn† · L. M. Kolbe · M. Schumann

Band 104

Sromona Chatterjee

Computer Vision and Machine Learning in Sustainable Mobility: The Case of Road Surface Defects

CUVILLIER VERLAG

Herausgeber

Prof. Dr. J. Biethahn† Prof. Dr. L. M. Kolbe Prof. Dr. M. Schumann

Georg-August-Universität
Wirtschaftsinformatik
Platz der Göttinger Sieben 5
37073 Göttingen

Bibliografische Information der Deutschen Nationalbibliothek
Die Deutsche Nationalbibliothek verzeichnet diese Publikation in der Deutschen Nationalbibliografie; detaillierte bibliografische Daten sind im Internet über http://dnb.d-nb.de abrufbar.
1. Aufl. - Göttingen : Cuvillier, 2020
Zugl.: Göttingen, Univ., Diss., 2020

Nonnenstieg 8, 37075 Göttingen
Telefon: 0551-54724-0
Telefax: 0551-54724-21

1. Auflage, 2020
Gedruckt auf umweltfreundlichem, säurefreiem Papier aus nachhaltiger Forstwirtschaft.

ISBN 978-3-7369-7258-2
eISBN 978-3-7369-6258-3

Computer Vision and Machine Learning in Sustainable Mobility: The Case of Road Surface Defects

Dissertation

zur Erlangung des wirtschaftswissenschaftlichen Doktorgrades der Wirtschaftswissenschaftlichen Fakultät der Georg-August-Universität Göttingen

Sromona Chatterjee
aus Kolkata, India

Göttingen, 2020

Betreuungsausschuss

Erstbetreur:	Prof. Dr. Lutz M. Kolbe
Zweitbetreuer:	Prof. Dr.-Ing. Mohit Kumar
Drittbetreuer:	Prof. Dr. Matthias Schumann

Abstract

Road maintenance has traditionally been a time consuming, expensive, and manual process. Timely maintenance of roads helps in lowering rehabilitation costs, accidents, environmental pollution, while facilitating increased connectivity, trade, and growth. Lately, easily acquirable front-view scene images are observed to be used for infrastructure management and road maintenance as they provide quicker, low-cost, and flexible solutions. Such scene images can easily be acquired using standard commodity cameras. In this dissertation, machine learning based approaches have been developed to analyze front-view scene images for detecting cracks automatically on road surfaces across different locations and under various conditions. This work thus contributes toward automated approaches to detect different kinds of cracks on road surfaces, thereby proposing a low-cost solution to road maintenance practices. As a result, different components are developed in this work which are sketched together to form a Decision Support System for the task of crack detection. In this study primarily three algorithmic approaches have been developed. Firstly, an unsupervised graph-based hierarchical clustering technique for road area segmentation has been developed, thus helping in detecting the road area in scene images. Secondly, a classifier and superpixel based supervised learning approach consisting of automatically and systematically identifying relevant features for detecting superpixels containing cracks has been developed. Thirdly, an unsupervised learning approach consisting of Gamma Mixture Fuzzy Model based clustering technique and keypoint matching mechanisms have been designed in this work for detecting which road pixels are crack pixels in images. Finally, this study integrates the findings and approaches to propose a Decision Support System for crack detection on road surfaces of easily acquirable front-view scene images. Evaluations performed on an experimentally collected diverse front-view scene image dataset show promising results for crack detection using the developed approaches in this work.

Die Straßeninstandhaltung ist traditionell ein zeitaufwändiger, teurer und manueller Prozess. Die rechtzeitige Instandhaltung von Straßen trägt dazu bei, Sanierungskosten, Unfälle und Umweltverschmutzung zu senken und gleichzeitig die Anschlussmöglichkeiten, den Handel und das Wachstum zu fördern. In letzter Zeit werden leicht zu beschaffende Szenenbilder aus der Vorderansicht für die Straßeninstandhaltung verwendet. billigere, schnellere und flexible Lösungen für das Infrastrukturmanagement anzubieten. Solche Szenenbilder können leicht mit handelsüblichen Kameras aufgenommen werden. In dieser Dissertation wurden auf maschinellem Lernen basierende Ansätze entwickelt, um Szenenbilder aus der Vorderansicht zu analysieren, um Risse auf Straßenoberflächen an verschiedenen Orten und unter verschiedenen Bedingungen automatisch zu erkennen. Diese Arbeit trägt somit zu automatisierten Ansätzen bei, um verschiedene Arten von Rissen auf Straßenoberflächen zu erkennen. Dabei werden verschiedene Komponenten entwickelt, die zu einem Entscheidungsunterstützungssystem für die Aufgabe der Risserkennung zusammengeschrieben werden. In dieser Dissertation wurden im Wesentlichen drei algorithmische Ansätze entwickelt. Erstens wurde eine unüberwachte graphenbasierte hierarchische Clustering-Technik zur Straßenbereichssegmentierung entwickelt, die bei der Erkennung des Straßenbereichs in Szenenbildern hilft. Zweitens wurde ein auf Klassifikatoren und Superpixeln basierender Ansatz des überwachten Lernens entwickelt, der darin besteht, automatisch und systematisch relevante Merkmale zur Erkennung von Superpixeln mit Rissen zu identifizieren. Drittens wurde in dieser Arbeit ein unbeaufsichtigter Lernansatz entwickelt, der aus einer auf dem Gamma Mixture Fuzzy Model basierenden Clustering-Technik und Schlüsselpunkt-Matching-Mechanismen besteht, um zu erkennen, welche Straßenpixel in Bildern Risse enthalten. Schließlich integriert diese Studie die Ergebnisse und Ansätze, um ein Entscheidungsunterstützungssystem für die Rissdetektion auf Straßenoberflächen von leicht zu erfassenden Bildern aus der Vorderansicht vorzuschlagen. Auswertungen auf einem experimentell gesammelten Bilddatensatz, der aus verschiedenen Straßenoberflächen und -zustände zeigen vielversprechende Ergebnisse für die Risserkennung mit dem entwickelte Ansätze in dieser Arbeit.

Acknowledgment

I would like to take this opportunity to express my special gratitude and thank my doctoral adviser, Prof. Dr. Lutz M. Kolbe, for giving me the opportunity to work on this interesting dissertation topic. I am deeply grateful to him for providing the motivating environment to develop my own research ideas. I am deeply thankful to him for his insightful comments, guidance, and incredible support. My heartfelt appreciation and thank goes to Prof. Dr.-Ing. Mohit Kumar for the research collaborations, encouragement, and constructive feedback which were immensely helpful. He generously gave me time for the discussions, for which I am deeply grateful. I would also like to thank Prof. Dr. Matthias Schumann for being part of my thesis committee and for all the support.

Moreover, I thank all my colleagues at the Chair of Information Management during my time there for their help, fruitful discussions, and for providing a great working environment: Carolin, Schahin, Patrick, Yachao, Benjamin, Ilja, Jan, Gerrit, Patryk, Björn, Benedikt, Daniel (Hodapp), Daniel (Leonhardt), Everlin, Andre, David, Fabian, Muhammad, Simon, Markus, Sebastian, Tim, Stephan, Bernd. Thanks Carolin and Yachao, had a great time sharing office with you. I would also like to thank my co-authors Björn, Schahin, Benedikt, Sascha of various papers for their valuable inputs.

Finally, this work would not be possible without the continuous support and encouragement of my family. Thanks Papa, Ma, my sister Debalina, and my little niece Tanusha. I am deeply grateful to my husband Yugendra for helping me in every possible way and for encouraging me to push my limits. I would also like to specially thank my friends Rima, Sunil, Oliva for their support, and all of my friends who have helped me in various ways throughout the journey.

Thank you very much!

Contents

Acronyms

2-D: Two-dimensional
3-D: Three-dimensional

AdaBoost: Adaptive Boosting
ANN: Artificial Neural Network
API: Application Programming Interface

CNN: Convolutional Neural Network
CLAHE: Contrast Limited Adaptive Histogram Equalization

DSR: Design Science Research
DSS: Decision Support System

FCN: Fully Convolutional Network

GMFM: Gamma Mixture Fuzzy Model
GPS: Global Positioning System
GLCM: Gray Level Co-occurrence Matrix
GB: Gradient Boosting
GIS: Geographic IS

HD: High Definition
HoG: Histogram of Oriented Gradients
HSV: Hue, Saturation, Value Color Space

IS: Information Systems

K-NN: K-Nearest Neighbors
KL-divergence: Kullback-Leibler divergence

L-SVM: Linear Support Vector Machine
LBP: Local Binary Patterns

ML: Machine Learning

PMS: Pavement Management System
PCI: Pavement Condition Index

RF: Random Forest
RGB: Red, Green, Blue Color Space

SIFT: Scale Invariant Feature Transform
SURF: Speeded Up Robust Features
SVM: Support Vector Machine

UAV: Unmanned Aerial Vehicle

VoG: Variance-of-Gabor

List of Figures

List of Tables

Chapter 1: Introduction

1.1 Motivation

Research in the area of pavement and infrastructure evaluation with automation techniques has been an active topic since the last several years (Chambon and Moliard 2011; Koch et al. 2015; Eisenbach et al. 2017). It constitutes of detection, evaluation and assessment of different pavement conditions such as, cracks, potholes, spalling, joint rupture, skid resistance, smoothness (BASt 2008; Miller et al. 1993; PMIS 2011; Zhang 2009). Pavement Management System (PMS) plays an important role in the maintenance of pavement networks and scheduling periodical maintenance to avoid incurring long term costs and road accidents (PMIS 2011; Hoeller 2012). This work uses advanced computer vision and machine learning (ML) techniques to analyze easily acquirable 2-D natural front-view scene images for crack related defect detection on roads, thereby helping in road surface evaluation.

In today's time, a huge increase in the urban population has created a manyfold demand on public infrastructures such as roads, tunnels, bridges. By 2050, urban population in the world will be around 66% (Chatterjee et al. 2018b; UN-DESA 2016). This creates a massive strain on infrastructures due to heavy traffic, movement of people, and the need for more connectivity. As an example, Koch and Brilakis (2014) noted that in Germany municipal roads cover 65% (400,000 km) of the entire road network, and their condition has deteriorated over the last years. In 2014 a comprehensive policy report released by the European Union noted significant backlog in road maintenance, requiring large investments for road rehabilitation and repairs (Gleave 2014). The report also pointed out that bad road conditions and soaring maintenance costs lead to a reduction in trade, an increase in accidents, high vehicle operating costs, an increase in CO_2 emission and pollution. Pollution could increase not only due to more fuel consumption because of bad roads, but also from a longer period of construction works. Consequently, delayed monitoring and maintenance give rise to a higher cost of rehabilitation. The impact of road maintenance expenditure can be seen in Figure 1.1. Therefore, it can be seen that timely and cost-effective monitoring of pavements is highly necessary to increase sustainability across all dimensions- social, economic, and environment (Chatterjee 2018b; Kahn 1995).

Traditionally, road monitoring and surface distress detection are predominantly done manually or by specialized vehicles fitted with costly sensors (Chatterjee et al. 2018a; Eisenbach et al. 2017; FHWA 2016; PMIS 2011; Radopoulou et al. 2016). Municipalities and certified

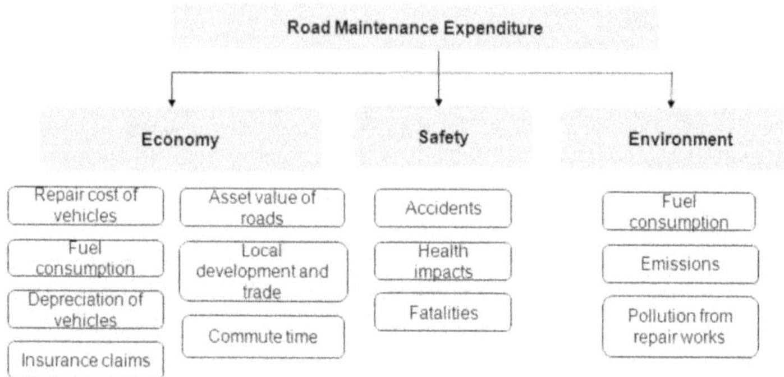

Figure 1.1: Impacts of road maintenance expenditure (taken and modified from Gleave (2014)).

service agencies inspect roads visually, or they take images to inspect them manually or in semi-automatic ways afterward. However, manual approaches are laborious and suffer from non-uniform, subjective, and delayed results (Chatterjee et al. 2018b). On the other hand, specialized vehicles are equipped with line scanner cameras or downward-facing cameras to take images of road surfaces, costly sensors, lasers, multiple cameras, artificial lighting, etc. These make such vehicles larger and unfit for narrower roads, lanes, or bike-paths, as well as highly expensive. The cost of such vehicles could be around $800,000 (Radopoulou et al. 2016). This makes them unaffordable and infrequently used by most municipalities. In some of the cases, aerial vehicles with imaging capabilities are also used (Dobson et al. 2014; MnDOT, 2018; Zakeri et al. 2016).

The ubiquitous nature of digital devices around us has given rise to unprecedented data traces (Galliers et al. 2015; Yoo 2010), thus enabling us to infer the world like never before (Yoo et al. 2012). Nowadays, Big Data enabled changes can be felt in all walks of our life catering to social interactions, economy, personalized services, to name a few. This has shown how causal relationships can be derived from data (Agarwal and Dhar 2014). This explosion of data, along with powerful analytics and computing facilities, has lately given rise to enhanced capabilities for management and decision-making (Agarwal and Dhar 2014; Kitchin 2014a; Rabari and Storper 2014).

Usage of everyday devices like smartphones or cars could thus be employed for road maintenance to offset the high cost of specialized vehicles and image acquisition. Lately, few efforts are seen to acquire front-view images using simple commodity cameras, like cameras mounted on cars, service vehicles, or smartphone cameras for road surface analysis (Chatterjee et al.

2018a; Mertz 2011; Tedesschi and Benedetto 2016; Varadharajan et al. 2014). However, to date most crack detection techniques for road surfaces use downward-view images acquired with special setups (Eisenback et al. 2017; Varadharajan et al. 2014). Figure 1.3 (A) shows a setup for front-view image data acquisition that is used in this work. Such kinds of acquisitions are much cheaper, easier, flexible, and faster. Data from different sources could be acquired and integrated. However, such capabilities are not yet fully harnessed (Chatterjee et al. 2018b). To get tangible real-world understanding from the massive data around us, we need to intelligently process the data for obtaining valuable insights (Goes 2014; Guenther et al. 2017). However, with more generalized data, data processing techniques to extract meaning from it become also highly challenging.

Regarding the algorithmic approaches that are portrayed in the literature, most crack and such defect detection approaches are highly image-processing based and use techniques related to thresholding, edge detection, segmentation, morphological operations, histograms, or statistical properties like, standard deviation (Koch et al. 2015; Mohan and Poobal 2017; Sinha and Fieguth 2006). A segmentation and fuzzy c-means clustering based approach is seen in Noh et al. (2017). Additionally, several image features in combination with Support Vector Machine (SVM) are seen also in many works (Eisenbach et al. 2017; Varadharajan et al. 2014). Lately, deep learning approaches are applied for pavement surfaces (Eisenbach et al. 2017; Gopalkrishnan 2018). In Zhang et al. (2016) a deep Convolutional Neural Network (CNN) is used for crack detection on asphalt roads. Pauly et al. (2017) also use CNN for crack detection using image patches. In Silvia and Licena (2018), a CNN, along with transfer learning using VGG-16 network, have been used for crack detection on concrete surfaces. Several techniques could also be found in defect detection for other infrastructures like sewer pipes (Su and Yang 2014) or quality inspection in steel parts (Soukup and Huber-Mörk 2014).

In general, the last years have seen the affirmation of either image-processing or of the use of ML requiring a lot of training data for pavement surface monitoring (Chatterjee et al. 2018b; Eisenbach et al. 2017; Koch et al. 2015; Li et al. 2014; Mohan and Poobal 2017). Moreover, some employ image-processing at the initial steps prior to the usage of ML techniques like, Artificial Neural Network (ANN), SVM (Li et al. 2014; Wu et al. 2016). As an example, in Wu et al. (2016) binarization and a novel morphology based operation are performed prior to the use of ANN for final crack detection. Further, most of the works use downward-view images. Lately, efforts are seen to use complete front-view scene images, similar to the type of images used in this work, for the purpose of crack and defect detection on road surfaces (Maeda et al. 2018; Radopoulou et al. 2016; Varadharajan et al. 2014). This work uses front-view scene images collected under normal daylight, as shown in Figure 1.3. Front-view images suffer from various challenges, such as lack of focused view of road surfaces, presence of external scene elements (e.g. building, vehicles, road signs, manholes), illumination scenarios and shadows, varied surface conditions and materials, lighter cracks, and different crack types (Chatterjee et al. 2018a; Varadharajan et al. 2014). Nevertheless, front-view images give more coverage area, flexibility, and scalability.

Intelligent Decision Support Systems (DSSs) that incorporate advanced data-driven approaches (Abella et al. 2017) and simple 2-D front-view scene images for automatically detecting and evaluating pavement surface defects (such as cracks) could enhance overall automation and effectiveness of a PMS (Chatterjee et al. 2018b). A combination of data analytics and cheaper measures to acquire data could help to increase the safety and timely maintenance of pavements. From these perspectives, the motivation of this dissertation is to develop computer vision and ML-based techniques to analyze 2-D front-view scene images for crack and related defect detection on pavement surfaces. This work handles different kinds of cracks such as single cracks, distributed multiple cracks, or network cracks. Cracks are one of the first defects to occur, and if not attended on time can lead to more severe defects (BASt 2008). This work further integrates the findings to propose a DSS for effective detection of road surface damages like cracks.

Thus, this research is motivated by both algorithmic development and practical aspects. Considering the algorithmic viewpoint, this work proposes two perspectives for crack and related defect detection on varied road surfaces: an ML-based classifier and a keypoint matching mechanism. Inspired by image matching applications, a keypoint matching approach has been developed in this work to detect cracks and defective pixels. Furthermore, it has been proposed in this work that Gamma mixture based clustering, fuzzified image feature descriptors, and texture features with ensemble ML approaches could better model the cracks. This stems from the observation that cracks are not easily distinguishable from the background and are often sparse. This work further provides an unsupervised learning approach using hierarchical clustering for road area detection and segmentation from the scene images. The images belong to various scene settings, such as rural and urban. Crack and defect detection algorithms are applied to the segmented road area. The developed crack detection algorithmic approaches in this work take into consideration the kind of image data available, challenges of such front-view image data, and how the data can be processed using classifier and keypoint matching techniques. The developed techniques do not depend on noisy image-processing based approaches and use ML, systematic image feature selection process, Gamma mixture model, and fuzzy-theoretic based analytical models to detect defective areas and pixels in images. The approaches have been developed in order to achieve more flexibility and adaptability.

On the other hand, from the viewpoint of practitioners and sustainability in infrastructure management, this work proposes ML-based techniques for crack and defect detection using simple and easily acquirable front-view scene images. Thus, human interventions could be greatly reduced for effective road monitoring using the proposed automated approaches in this dissertation. Usage of easily acquirable scene images helps in making road monitoring cost-effective and less time consuming. This, in turn, would increase road safety and road lifecycle, as well as reduce the occurrence of accidents and pollution. Finally, as part of this work, a prototype of computer vision and ML-based intelligent DSS for road surface evaluation using front-view images has been developed. The DSS has been designed using Design Science Research (DSR) approach in a modular manner to integrate the findings of the developed algorithmic approaches and viewpoints of different stakeholders. Such a DSS could thus help to achieve more automated, inexpensive, flexible, scalable, and timely road surface inspection practices.

1.2 Research Questions

In this section, the research questions that are dealt with in this dissertation are detailed. A block diagram, as shown in Figure 1.2, is presented showing how the research questions are connected. As discussed in the above section, image-processing based techniques are highly noisy. Manual effort is required to annotate training images for classifiers, which can also be subjective and time consuming. It is also seen that various crack detection approaches suffer when applied to different locations for the training and testing phases (Gavilan et al. 2011). Therefore, it is important to know how to characterize these cracks in flexible ways to achieve scalable and adaptable road maintenance practices. At the same time, alternative approaches to image-processing, feature-based classification, or an immense amount of labeled training data are also required for effective pavement surface evaluation. Additionally, the design of an intelligent and suitable DSS for road surface monitoring with interpretable outputs and construction is also of high necessity.

In general, it has been observed that cracks have special properties that make them challenging to be detected. Firstly, cracks are not as easily distinguishable as other objects like buildings, vehicles. Lighter and distributed cracks also increase the difficulty. Secondly, the number of defective or crack pixels is always much lower than non-defective ones in images, pointing towards a heavy-tailed distribution of gradient values. Crack pixels are generally darker than the non-crack ones. Figure 1.3 (D) shows a distribution of pixel intensity values in gray-scale colorspace. Thirdly, cracks or such defective pixels could be detected at a patch level (i.e. region level or superpixel) or at a pixel level, as shown in Figure 1.3 (F - G). On top of these, front-view

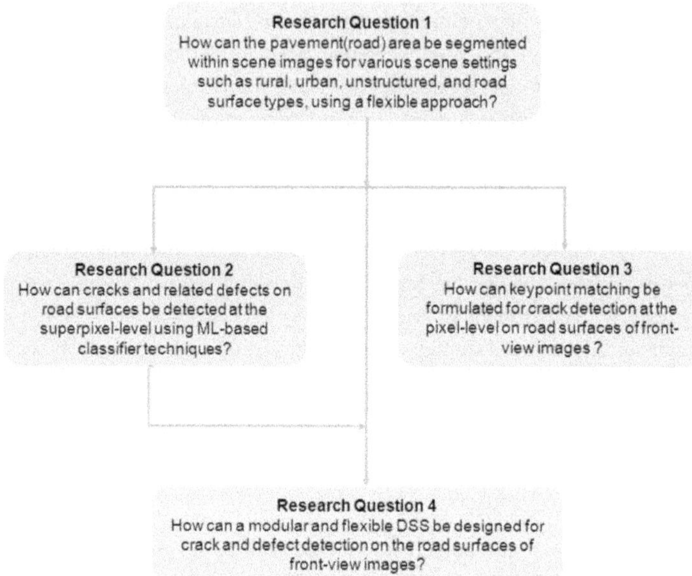

Figure 1.2: Relationship between different research questions.

scene images taken under normal daylight also lack a closer view of road surfaces and may suffer from various illumination and surface textures, different crack and defect types, as in Figure 1.3. Such observations motivate the formulation of the following research questions.

1.2.1 Road Area Segmentation and Data Preparation

Figure 1.3 (A) shows how data is collected for this work. The 2-D scene images are collected under normal daylight from the driver's viewpoint. Simple high definition cameras are mounted on pedelecs/ e-bikes for the data collection. Thus, in order to prepare the data for crack detection on road surfaces, the road surface must firstly be detected in the scene images.

Different road segmentation algorithms are found in the literature based on techniques related to seed points (Kong et al. 2010; Zhou and Iagnemma 2010), deep learning and semantic segmentation (Alvarez et al. 2012; Brust et al. 2015) and camera based intrinsic features (Hoiem et al. 2005). Vanishing point estimation is another commonly used approach that is followed (Moghadam et al. 2012). However, vanishing point related techniques many times include lane

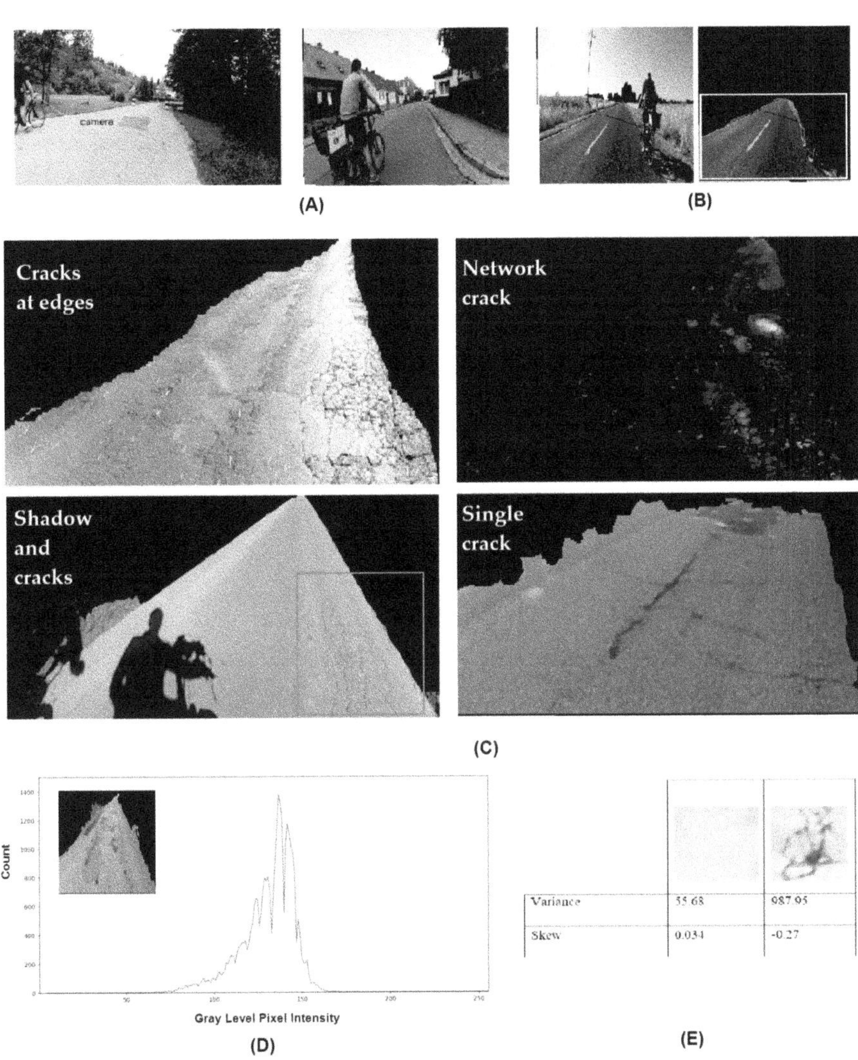
camera
(A)
(B)
Cracks at edges
Network crack
Shadow and cracks
Single crack
(C)
Count
Gray Level Pixel Intensity
(D)
Variance
55.68
987.95
Skew
0.034
-0.27
(E)

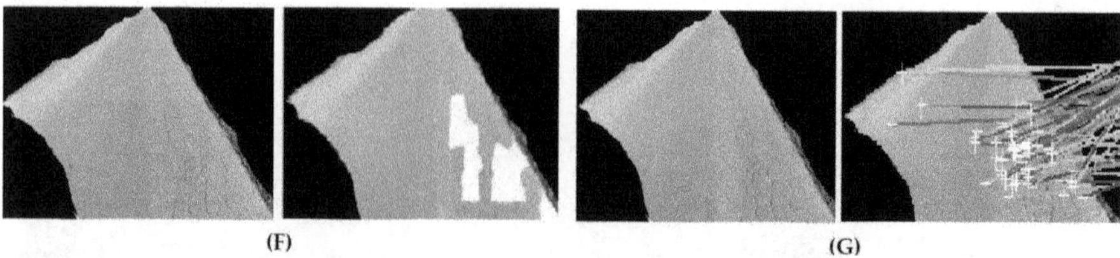

Figure 1.3: (A) data collection setup using a mounted camera on a pedelec. (B) Front-view scene image and the corresponding road surface image. Road surface images are obtained from scene images after applying the road segmentation approach. Bounding box shows the region-of-interest. (C) Example road surfaces with defects and crack-types that are handled in this work. (D) Characteristics of images containing defects: (left) Histogram of the gray-level intensity pixel values for an image containing cracks and defects. The intensity image in RGB colorspace is shown in the inset. (right) Statistical proprieties of defective and non-defective image patches. (F) Superpixel level crack detection. (G) Pixel level crack detection. Crack areas or pixels are marked in white.

markings or camera features; thereby making it less flexible or not applicable to rural roads where lane markings are not present. On the other hand, supervised learning based approaches mostly require a lot of manually labeled training data. Approaches related to 3-D segmentation is also seen in the publications (Hillel et al. 2014). In this work, the aim is to segment the road for 2-D scene images that include various scene settings (rural, urban, and unstructured) and road surface types (paved, unpaved); hence an adaptable approach is required that can handle different settings. So, the first research question that is answered in this work is the following:

> $ResearchQuestion1$: *How can the pavement (road) area be segmented within scene images for various scene settings such as rural, urban, unstructured, and road surface types, using a flexible approach?*

$ResearchQuestion1$ helps to remove the scene elements, such as buildings, vehicles, sky, people; thereby detecting only the road surface. This helps to handle front-view images more effectively for crack detection, as external scene elements would create more uncertainties if not removed.

Accordingly, an unsupervised learning approach based on hierarchical clustering has been developed in this work. Additionally, shadows (such as from buildings, trees) could be identified as part of the algorithm, so that they do not interfere at the later stages of crack detection. Here, external information such as camera characteristics, lane markings, road shape or boundaries are not considered. Furthermore, the number of clusters is also not required to be given. Hence, $ResearchQuestion1$ helps to come up with an adaptable and flexible approach of road area segmentation for various scene settings and road surface types. Once the road has been segmented, cracks and defects could be detected on the road surfaces.

1.2.2 Classifier Based Defect Detection on Road Surfaces at the Superpixel Level

To identify cracks and related defects on the road surfaces of front-view images using state-of-the-art ML classifiers, it has been observed in the literature that a systematic study is required to ascertain what are the most relevant image features for such tasks (Chatterjee et al. 2018a). Image features for understanding objects or regions in images could be based on shape, color, texture, histogram-based features, geometric properties, to name a few. As cracks are not always easily distinguishable due to various surface conditions, texture, illumination, as seen in Figure 1.3 (B - C, F), it is required to understand suitable feature types and frameworks. Furthermore, suitability of the kind of ML approaches, such as ensemble learning, Artificial Neural Network (ANN), for the task also needs to be investigated. This motivates the second research question as follows:

> *ResearchQuestion2: How can cracks and related defects on the road surfaces of front-view images be detected at the superpixel level using ML-based classifier techniques?*

The sub-research questions that are handled within *ResearchQuestion2* are the following:

> *ResearchQuestion2.1: How state-of-the-art ML classifiers can be applied for crack and related defect detection?*
> *ResearchQuestion2.2: What are the most relevant image features for crack detection at the superpixel level, so as to make the cracks more distinguishable?*

Here, *ResearchQuestion2* helps to answer the research goal of using superpixel and ML classifiers for crack detection on the road surfaces. Superpixel is a group of pixels and has unique characteristics (Achanta et al. 2012). For example, a superpixel containing cracks has more variance (variance could be calculated using the gray-level pixel intensities within the supeprixel) than the one without crack, as shown in Figure 1.3 (E). Crack pixels are generally more darker than non-crack ones, thus a considerable difference in intensity values are there. Hence, the research question aims to find the most relevant feature types suitable for the task at hand. Furthermore, the research question helps to ascertain suitability of different state-of-the-art ML classifiers and does not use noisy image-processing techniques for the task of crack detection at the superpixel level.

1.2.3 Keypoint Matching Based Defect Detection on Road Surfaces at the Pixel Level

Apart from recognizing cracks at the superpixel level, pixel level recognition is a step ahead. For recognizing different crack shapes, types (e.g. single cracks or network) and properties at later stages, it is highly useful to detect cracks and such defects at the pixel level.

Furthermore, supervised learning approaches require a lot of labeled training data, and can face challenges to handle lighter cracks and varied road texture types (e.g. when the surface contains different road texture types at different locations). Labeling could suffer from non-uniformity and human bias. Moreover, it is seen that the density of crack pixels in an image is much less than that of non-crack pixels. Figure 1.3 (D) shows the distribution of pixel intensity values (in gray-scale) of an image containing defects. It is also seen that the distribution of gradient values (as cracks can be inferred as edges) in such images is highly heavy-tailed and this characteristic can be used to build an alternative approach for crack detection. Thus, the third research question in this work is summarized as follows:

> $ResearchQuestion3$: *How can keypoint matching be formulated for crack detection at the pixel level on road surfaces of front-view images?*

The sub-research questions that are handled within $ResearchQuestion3$ are the following:

> $ResearchQuestion3.1$: *How can keypoints be generated in images for crack detection, considering density of defective crack pixels are much less in any image?*
> $ResearchQuestion3.2$: *How can keypoints be encoded with descriptors for crack detection, so as to make the descriptors more discriminative?*
> $ResearchQuestion3.3$: *What is the matching criteria to ascertain matched keypoints across images for crack detection?*

Here, noisy techniques like image-processing are not used for crack and defect detection at the pixel level, unlike most followed methods. This research question aims to use an analytical model consisting of fuzzy image feature descriptors and a keypoint matching approach for the first time in order to detect cracks on road surfaces. Keypoints in images are interesting points or regions, such as edges or corners, and local image features could be defined at such keypoints (Lowe 2014). In this way, objects or regions in images could be represented as a collection of keypoints. This approach is seen in image matching problems, where objects are matched across images based on the properties of the detected keypoints (Kumar et al. 2016, 2019). So, keypoints encoded with descriptors can be matched between two images to see how similar they are.

Thus, this third research question aims to generate keypoints and encode defective pixels (i.e. keypoints) by employing descriptors that make them more distinguishable than non-defective ones, as crack pixels are not highly distinguishable. Furthermore, this approach does not require training images or histogram based descriptors. Studies have shown that using fuzzy-theoretic based descriptors result in better image matching criteria than histogram based descriptors; motivating the usage of fuzzy-theoretic based approach for this research question (Kumar et al. 2016, 2019). So, for the task at hand, the aim of this research question is to come up with appropriate methods for generating keypoints considering the heavy-tailed distribution of the gradient values of the pixels, fuzzy descriptors to define the keypoints, and a matching criteria to finally denote which keypoints can be nominated as real defective (crack) pixels.

1.2.4 A Vision-based Decision Support System for Road Surface Defect Detection

Different DSS and Information Systems (IS) for infrastructure management can be found in the literature. Following the comprehensive study in Chatterjee et al. (2018b), such systems may cater to tasks like maintenance and monitoring, planning, road safety, guidelines for pavement condition, data management, data integration, data viewing, to name a few. However, it has been seen in the literature that fully automated pavement condition index rating is required, as pavement evaluation is still largely manual in nature. Further, system level design of related IS is also a necessity. Moreover, it has been noticed that there is a high need to understand how different actors, processes, analytical approaches, and data from varied sources can be integrated into an intelligent DSS. Thus, the third research question in this work is as follows:

> *ResearchQuestion4: How can a modular and flexible DSS be designed for crack and defect detection on the road surfaces of front-view images?*

This last research question aims to design and evaluate a ML-based intelligent DSS for road defect detection and monitoring. Front-view scene image and video data, along with GPS data, are used for the developed DSS. It integrates developed algorithmic approaches, stakeholder's viewpoints, understandable outputs, and visualizations.

1.3 Structure of the Dissertation

1.3.1 Publications Included in the Dissertation

An overview of the publications included in this dissertation is provided in Table 1.1. The table includes the chapters, title of the original publication, name of the outlet, current status of the publication and the author's contribution.

Chapter No.	Title	Outlet	Rating	Status	Author's Contribution
2	Understanding the Scene Data: Pavement Area Grouping in Images	Proceedings of the International Conference on Information Systems (ICIS) 2017, Seoul, South Korea	VHB Rating A	Published	90 %
3	Intelligent Road Maintenance: A Machine Learning Approach for Surface Defect Detection	Proceedings of the European Conference on Information Systems (ECIS) 2018, Portsmouth, UK	VHB Rating B	Published	85 %
4	Defect Detection on Road Surfaces Using Fuzzy Image Descriptors and Keypoint Matching	Engineering Applications of Artificial Intelligence	Impact Factor 4.2	Submitted	85 %
5	Smart Infrastructure Monitoring: Development of a Decision Support System for Vision-Based Road Crack Detection	Proceedings of the International Conference on Information Systems (ICIS) 2018, San Francisco, USA	VHB Rating A	Published	70 %

Table 1.1: Overview of the publications included in this dissertation.

1.3.2 Connection between Chapters, Research Questions and Developed Approaches

An overview of how the included publications (i.e. chapter 2 to chapter 5) in this dissertation are related to the four research questions, as explained in section 1.2, is shown in Figure 1.4.

Further, the relationship between research questions, developed approaches, and chapters has been schematically shown in Figure 1.5. In this work, primarily four approaches have been developed to answer the research questions and they are described below.

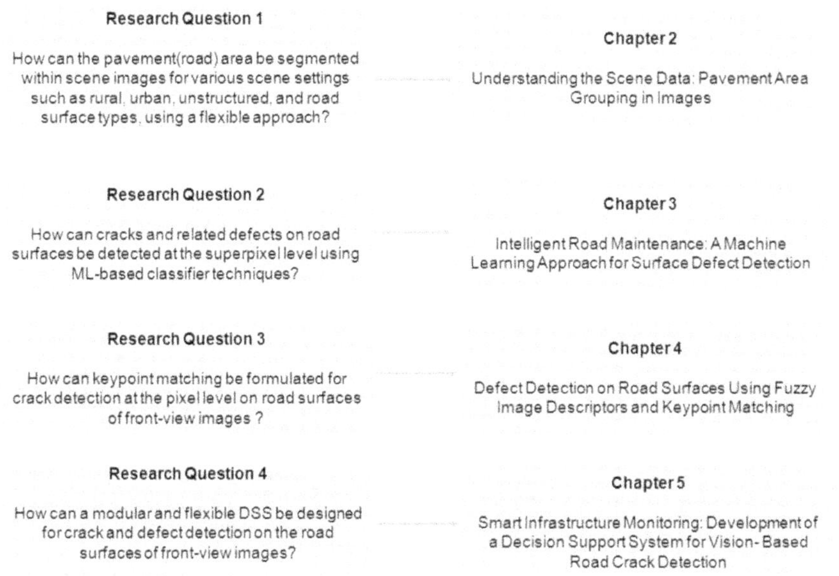

Figure 1.4: Relationship between research questions and chapters.

1. *Road Segmentation Using Hierarchical Clustering Based Approach:*

   Firstly, an unsupervised road segmentation algorithm is proposed for different scene types (urban, rural, unstructured) and road surfaces to segment the road area from the complete front-view scene image. Figure 1.3 (B) shows an example of a scene image and the corresponding road image. Crack and defect detection is done on this road area. This step helps to prepare the data for the next steps of defect detection and removes various scene elements such as building, vehicles. This has been covered in chapter 2 using the publication "Understanding the Scene Data: Pavement Area Grouping in Images". Thus, chapter 2 answers $ResearchQuestion1$.

   The developed algorithmic approach for segmenting the road area in an image, as given in chapter 2, is based on hierarchical clustering. The technique is a graph-based hierarchical clustering approach where similar superpixels in an image are clustered. Color, texture, and histogram based feature descriptors are used. Features such as Local Binary Patterns (LBP), Histogram of Oriented Gradients (HoG), Gray Level Co-occurance Matrix (GLCM), and pixel locations have been used. In the approach, similarity between superpixels and image areas is obtained using a Gaussian kernel-based hybrid distance metric containing Euclidean and Bhattacharya distances. Such similarity measures, along with the Hungarian algorithm and pairwise assignment, are used to group and merge the regions in an iterative manner. The developed approach has been successfully compared with base classifiers such as SVM, Gaussian Naive Bayes, AdaBoost and K-Nearest Neighbors (K-NN).

2. *Superpixel Level Crack and Defect Detection Based on State-of-the-art Machine Learning Classifiers and Feature Selection:*

   Secondly, a superpixel and classifier based approach is developed for crack and related defect detection using front-view scene images. As cracks are not easily distinguishable as other objects such as buildings or vehicles, most relevant image features for crack superpixels are identified as part of this work. This has been covered in chapter 3 using the publication "Intelligent Road Maintenance: A Machine Learning Approach for Surface Defect Detection". Further, the approach detailed in chapter 2 has been first used to segment the road area from the front-view scene images, and then cracks are detected on it. This is detailed in chapter 3. Thus, chapter 3 answers $ResearchQuestion2$.

   The developed algorithmic approach of chapter 3 identifies suitable image features for the task of crack detection. State-of-the-art feature extraction algorithms, such as GLCM, statistical measures of variance and skewness have been used, and a new feature variant called Variance-of-Gabor (VoG) using the Gabor filters has been defined. They have been identified by tuning the parameters of different feature extraction algorithms in a systematic manner according to ML-classifier's performance. This led to a systematic feature engineering and feature selection approach for the task at hand. Furthermore, an approach on how state-of-the-art ML-based classifiers can be applied for crack detection at the superpixel level on front-view images has also been developed. Supervised ML classifiers such as Gradient Boosting (GB), Random Forest (RF), ANN, SVM have been used and compared for the task at hand.

3. *Pixel Level Crack and Defect Detection Using an Approach Based on Keypoint Matching, Fuzzy Descriptors, and Gamma Mixture Fuzzy Model:*

   Thirdly, a keypoint matching method across two images (one reference image and another one is query image) is developed for crack and related defect detection on road surfaces of front-view scene images. The approach has been influenced by image matching, whereby keypoints are matched across the reference crack image and the query image to find similarities among them. This has been covered in chapter 4 using the publication "Defect Detection on Road Surfaces Using Fuzzy Image Descriptors and Keypoint Matching". Further, the methodological approach of chapter 2 has been used for road segmentation, and after that keypoint matching approach has been used for defect detection on such road surfaces. This is detailed in chapter 4. Thus, chapter 4 answers $ResearchQuestion3$.

The developed algorithmic approach of chapter 4 primarily has three steps. Firstly, the keypoints are generated using a fuzzy-theoretic approach called Gamma Mixture Fuzzy Model (GMFM) (Kumar et al. 2016). Gradient values in the image are assumed to be a mixture of two Gamma distributions- one depicting edges (cracks) and another depicting non-edges (non-cracks). Accordingly, GMFM is adapted in this work to cluster the pixels into two clusters- edges (cracks or defects) and non-edges (non-cracks). The cluster with pixels having a higher magnitude of gradient is taken as "probable crack" and defective pixels. These probable crack pixels are taken as keypoints. So, GMFM is used to generate edge-based keypoints. Secondly, after the keypoints are generated, discriminative fuzzy descriptors are used to encode these keypoints. Thirdly, keypoints between the reference crack image and the query image are matched to see which keypoints are similar and can be nominated as "real" crack pixels. The matching metric has been developed using Kullback-Leibler divergence between two Dirichlet distributions. The developed approach is compared with state-of-the-art feature descriptor based matching algorithm such as Scale Invariant Feature Transform (SIFT). The fuzzy-theoretic based approach helped to handle uncertainties and noise in an effective manner for crack detection. It also helped to handle lighter and edge cracks, as well as road surface textures that are highly shaded and complex.

The approach in chapter 4 contrasts the classifier or image-processing based approaches that are mostly found in the literature for crack and related defect detection. Thus, labeled training data and noisy image-processing techniques are not required. This makes the system less susceptible to bias. The developed approach consists of an unsupervised ML method that uses GMFM-based clustering, along with keypoint matching, to detect crack pixels in images.

4. *A Vision Based Decision Support System- DSS for Road Crack Defect Detection:*

   Fourthly, this work integrates the algorithmic approaches and the findings to develop a vision-based intelligent DSS for defect detection on road surfaces. The Design Science Research (DSR) (Gregor and Hevner 2013) has been additionally used for this purpose. This is covered in chapter 5 using the publication "Smart Infrastructure Monitoring: Development of a Decision Support System for Vision-Based Road Crack Detection". Chapter 5 answers $ResearchQuestion4$. The algorithmic approaches of chapter 2 and chapter 3 have been used for designing the DSS and is described in chapter 5.

The DSS has been developed to have the properties of being modular, flexible, and satisfying the following requirements: robustness, automation, performance, adaptability, integrative and understandable. The DSS contains the following modules: road detection module, parameter selection, and training module, crack detection module, crack marking module, pavement rating module, and a mapping module. 2-D front-view scene image/ video and GPS data have been used as primary inputs to the system. Further, users can input parameters to control the ML-based algorithms, in order to achieve increased flexibility. Figure 1.5 shows the primary inputs and outputs of the DSS.

Figure 1.5: Contextual relationship between different developed algorithmic approaches and research questions: Every block marked with "Approach for Research Question" contains the corresponding algorithmic and research approach that has been developed to answer the question. The diagram schematically shows how the developed approaches are related, flow of data, and outputs of the approaches.

1.4 Positioning of the Work in Information Systems Research

Within Information Systems (IS) this dissertation contributes toward decision support systems (Banker and Kaufmann 2004). In this work, the developed algorithmic approaches, along with the insights drawn from design science research, form the basis of the designed DSS. The developed approaches are ML-based and use simple 2-D front-view scene images for automatic crack and related defect detection on pavement surfaces. The GPS information is used in addition for mapping the road images to a physical location.

Thus, such approaches can enhance automation in decision-making for PMSs; indicating towards data-driven innovations in management and decision-making (Abbasi et al. 2016; Abella et al. 2017; Galliers et al. 2015). Moreover, it has been seen that the percentage of cracks is an important metric for ascertaining the overall pavement condition index (PCI) within a PMS, as per standard practices (Straube 2015). Accordingly, the DSS in the work uses the percentage of detected cracks for classifying pavements with immediate attention requirement (high risk), medium-level damages (medium risk), low-level damages (low risk). Hence, this work also contributes toward enhanced automation for PCI generation and PMSs by using easily available massive amounts of video and image data (Ong et al. 2014; PMIS 2011). Such information, along with the localization of detected cracks on images and GPS information, could be fed to the municipalities or certified service agencies for more comprehensive pavement condition analysis. Thus, processing front-view scene images using ML and data-driven approaches could serve as a first-hand road surface damage analysis platform. Such a platform could provide quicker evaluations and controlling of damage propagation, while, expensive and invasive methods could be employed to selected scenarios based on requirements.

Additionally, such data-driven intelligent DSS could also be used to develop smart alert systems for citizens in order for them to avoid the roads in bad conditions. This could also help in sustainable urban planning practices. In this way, capabilities for offering smart services could be enhanced (Fink 2010). Public service vehicles (Henfridsson and Lindgreen 2005; Mertz 2011) and citizens could also be employed to gather front-view image or video data. Further, with the advent of advanced autonomous facilities in vehicles of the future, gathered image data could be autonomously processed for road surface evaluation and optimal journey path selection. Hence, with such a wide range of possibilities of intelligent, adaptable, crowdsourced, and decentralized solutions, improved infrastructure, public asset, and route management could be achieved (Laubis et al. 2017, 2018). In this way, the ubiquitous and pervasive nature of digital technologies around us (Yoo 2010), as well as the gathered Big Data, can be translated into value for providing transformative insights and management capabilities (Kitchin 2014b, 2016). This shows that using the insights of this dissertation, portability and interconnectivity- two of the important aspects of Big Data for creating value in organizations, could be greatly impacted in the context of road monitoring organizations (Günther et al. 2017).

Hence, the usage of everyday digital devices to acquire easily available front-view image data, along with suitable, adaptable, and scalable approaches based on intelligent data analytics to leverage the data, has various advantages. Many pillars of smart city, smart services, infrastructure management, and road maintenance organizational activities could be realized for a better quality of life (Kitchin 2014b). As a result, different aspects of the smart city ecosystem (Khatoun and Zeadally 2016) like smart mobility for selecting safer and efficient routes, smart governance, smart growth and living, and sustainable practices could be positively impacted and realized.

Furthermore, using intelligent and automated solutions to process easily available data for faster evaluation of road surfaces, as done in this work, helps in achieving timely and cost-effective maintenance. Therefore, the cost for rehabilitation, vehicle operation, movement of goods and people, and periodic maintenance could be drastically reduced (Gleave 2014). Timely maintenance would also help to reduce delays, traffic, and accidents. This consequently enhances road safety (Stilgoe 2017) and overall trade. It can also be seen that untimely maintenance leads to road condition degradation that leads to an extended period of road maintenance and higher fuel consumption, contributing to higher CO_2 emission (Gleave 2014). Timely maintenance using automated solutions could also help to curb such environmental degradation to a greater extent. As a result, the developed DSS for road monitoring could positively affect environmental sustainability (Gholami et al. 2016). Thus, this dissertation also contributes to the research stream of Green IS (Watson et al. 2010). This is because of the fact that suitable IS artifacts provide practical and explainable research outcomes while creating sustainable research approaches (Chatterjee et al. 2018b; Melville 2010; vom Brocke et al. 2013). Finally, it can be seen that by following intelligent and automated approaches for road asset maintenance, social, economic, and environmental sustainability could be positively impacted.

1.5 Anticipated Contributions

From the viewpoint of practical, as well as academic contributions, the following benefits could be realized using the approaches developed in this dissertation:

1. *Road inspection and related scientific methods for quality check:*

   From the viewpoint of research and academic literature, this dissertation contributes toward the development of scientific methods for surface quality checks, especially in the context of pavement surface damages. Cracks and such defects are in essence anomalies against a relatively non-defective background. The algorithmic approaches developed in this work could provide insights to the researchers about processing front-view images for pavement crack and surface damage detection. It also provides insights on relevant image features and ML algorithm types for classification purposes.

Furthermore, the proposed approach of crack detection in this work using fuzzified features, clustering technique using a mixture of Gamma distributions, and KL-divergence between two Dirichlet distributions, provide insights to the researchers about how key-point matching between two images could be used for damage detection on surfaces in an unsupervised manner. This could especially be helpful in scenarios where data labeling is labor intensive. This also shows applicability of the image matching perspective for the task of crack detection on pavement surfaces.

Finally, the development of the complete end-to-end pipeline of processing front-view images for the task of crack detection could provide a constructive idea for handling such data and create value.

2. *Road monitoring organizations and practitioners:*

   Using the developed algorithmic approaches and the DSS, certified organizations or municipalities could device effective strategies to use easily acquirable front-view image and videos for road surface inspection and crack detection purposes. The DSS is designed to have modular, extendable, and interpretable properties.

   First-hand analysis of road surfaces could be performed using relatively cheaper options, as in this work, before more costly or invasive solutions are required. This would help to reduce maintenance costs and time. Due to the use of cheaply acquirable front-view image data and advanced data analytics, the frequency of maintenance can be increased as opposed to the status-quo of using expensive specialized vehicles and systems. Automated decision-making would also reduce subjective analysis and bias. Various innovative, decentralized, and crowdsourced approaches could be devised for transforming and automating the monitoring and decision-making processes. This directly impacts and increases the lifecycle of roads and trade on one hand, while reducing accidents on the other hand.

   Additionally, the comparison between different crack detection approaches in this work could be used by the practitioners to ascertain the suitability of an algorithm, depending on data-types and various scenarios.

Chapter 2: Understanding the Scene Data- Pavement Area Grouping in Images

Title	Understanding the Scene Data: Pavement Area Grouping in Images
Authors	Sromona Chatterjee[1], Björn Hildebrandt[1], Lutz M. Kolbe[1] [1] Chair of Information Management, University of Göttingen, Platz der Göttingen Sieben 5, 37073 Göttingen, Germany * Corresponding author: sromona.chatterjee@wiwi.uni-goettingen.de
Outlet	Proceedings of the International Conference on Information Systems (ICIS), December 2017, Seoul, South Korea
Abstract	Modern societies are clearly en route towards digitalization. Natural scene images particularly could provide many value added applications and services. In this paper, we address the challenges that arise with pavement detection in rural, urban, and unstructured scenes. We use an approach combining region similarity, split and merge, and pairwise assignment, to merge image regions according to a homogeneity criteria, and group pavement regions in images. Homogeneity criteria is based on color and texture feature types. In successive steps a distance matrix based on varying kernel is created. The approach is numerically simple, yet retains the ability to merge similar regions. Assignment with Hungarian method is used to achieve hierarchical region merging. As a result, pavement area grouping could be handled. Evaluations on relevant datasets show that our approach allows successful merging and recognition of image regions belonging to the pavement area for various scenes and surface types.
Keywords	Pavement detection, region grouping, pairwise assignment, digital innovation

Table 2.1: Fact sheet for chapter 2.

2.1 Introduction

Modern societies are clearly en route towards digitalization (Yoo 2010). Digital technologies such as sensors and connectivity devices are integrated into everyday artifacts such as phones or cars (Yoo 2010), transforming them into connected ubiquitous computing environments (Henfridsson and Lindgren 2005). Hence, the use of pervasive digital technologies combined with the emergence of digital infrastructures (Tilson et al. 2010) produce massive amounts of data traces that allow for investigating causal relations in real world contexts (Yoo et al. 2012). For instance, video and image data recorded by the front camera of cars provide a precise representation of the street scene that could be used for various purposes such as navigation (Moghadam et al. 2012), as well as for other fields of application like, urban planning (Tang and Sun 2012; Yang and Lin 2013).

Venter and Stein (2012) state that images and videos form almost "80 percent of all the public and/or corporate unstructured big data". Natural scene images of urban and rural regions, being one of the most valuable sources of big data, could be used for various valued-added applications and services in real world. Traditionally, large efforts are needed by the road authorities or service providers in order to collect necessary data for infrastructure maintenance and planning purposes (BASt 2008; MnDOT 2009). With pervasive digital technologies (Yoo 2010), scene images can now be easily acquired using phones, street cameras, car cameras, unmanned aerial vehicle (UAV) (Dobson et al. 2013). These technological advances are thus creating "brand new data points" (Menychtas et al. 2011; Rabari and Storper 2014) for various developmental purposes. However, the immense availability of street scene image data (Ong et al. 2014) remains ineffective without application of appropriate methods, which are required to extract valuable information, enable automated decision making, and to provide valuable service offerings and capabilities.

One way of processing the scene image for advanced applications and services is by detecting the pavement area within an image. Pavement detection is an ongoing research field and is a crucial step for applications across domains like, road infrastructure management (Schreiber et al.2014), road/ pavement surface condition analysis to assess cracks, potholes, patches, ruts (Koch et al. 2015), and autonomous driver assistant systems (Hillel et al. 2014). Figure 2.1 shows some of the application areas. For example, subjective results from humans and costly systems for pavement analysis lead to non-uniform maintenance and higher backlog, environment degradation, accidents; along with untimely response toward rehabilitation tasks (Gleave 2014). In the need to develop cheaper and automated solutions and to have full road and scene view, 2D digital image analysis are increasingly preferred for pavement management (Chambon and Moliard 2011; Dobson et al. 2014; Hosin and Suseon 2006). Big data is seen to provide new opportunities not only to improve management of assets, but also to reduce environmental impact of CO_2 emissions by successfully identifying defected pavement areas (Louhghalam et al. 2017). This effect is seen to achieve even if only 1.5 percent of damaged areas are attended; signifying the effects a society could get by processing such immense data across economic, social, and ecological dimensions. Technological innovation is the key to address important challenges of cities, and make solutions scalable (Khatoun and Zeadally 2016). Same images could be used for various tasks like, surface analysis, road marking and scene analysis, urban planning, and preventive maintenance (Gleave 2014; Yang and Lin 2013). However, this big data from various sources possess challenges on how to analyze and integrate them (Goes 2014). For example, it is important to make automated analysis of pavement in 2-D scene images adaptable to diverse environmental conditions, as well as independent of data acquisition systems. In this way, once pavement area is detected, further applications could be developed using it, as in Figure 2.1, without being hindered by the external factors in the scene. Thus, intelligent pavement detection could lead to cheaper, automated, scalable, and timely solutions. Hence, to create value by processing different types of scene images in a more adaptable manner, to reuse the data for many application areas, and to use the data platform for service development, we present here an approach for pavement area extraction from 2-D images.

Recognizing the pavement area within single images is a challenging task and various approaches like, seed-area based detection (Kong et al. 2010), camera feature based specific techniques, or deep learning with Convolutional Neural Network (CNN) (Brust et al. 2015) are used. However, for pavement area detection within an image which is required for further surface analysis and to understand rural/ unstructured/ urban conditions, several challenges are still observed when utilizing existing methodologies: 1) Pavement detection methods are often different for rural and urban settings. For example, methods depending on structured information of lane markers, road boundaries, and vanishing point at the horizon (where lanes converge) are not applicable to different types of scene. In rural or unstructured or within-city areas lane markers are not available. 2) It is not always easy to annotate a large and diverse training set by ascertaining different environment conditions, shadow areas, and surface types. Human annotations could often be subject to noisy labeling, owing to the tediousness of the job. Moreover, in the need of having increased intelligence and higher adaptability, using less of human effort and bias could be preferred. Further, it is useful that major shadow areas are recognized for later analysis. Thus, in this work we handle the task of pavement detection using a combination of unsupervised and ranking-based approaches. The presented approach here could deal with different pavement surface types (paved, graveled, pedestrian lanes, brick paths) and scene settings (rural, urban, bike paths, unstructured). Furthermore, the diverse scene categories and surface types that we handle are marked in Figure 2.8 (Set 1). Hence, the research questions that we intend to answer here are:

> *RQ1: How can we extract the pavement area from a natural scene high definition images for different scene settings like, rural/ unstructured/ urban, using an adaptable approach; on which various surface analysis could be performed later?*
> *RQ2: How can we extract the pavement area from a natural scene image under normal day lighting for different pavement shapes and surface types like, paved, graveled, pedestrian lanes?*

The research approach is shown in Figure 2.2. Unlike many existing methods we do not rely on external camera information or structured information like, lane markers, within a scene; thus making our approach more scalable and adaptable. In our work we take complete scene images as input, and output the recognized pavement area, as shown in Figure 2.1, using image-processing, hierarchical clustering, and pairwise assignment approaches. Connected graphs are used as an underlying data structure. The remainder of the paper is organized as follows: in the next section we state the related works regarding pavement detection, followed by a description of the methodology used consisting of our data collection method, the features used, and the developed approach for pavement area extraction using region similarity and merging techniques. Finally, we present our results, discussion and the conclusion.

2.2 Related Work

In general, identifying pavement in an image is a complex task because of varying conditions such as: 1) camera viewpoint, 2) non-uniform lighting, 3) shadows, 4) pavement geometries and shapes, 4) different scene backgrounds, and 5) pavement surface types. Furthermore, for analyzing an image, width $\times$ height $\times$ channels data points (with channels= 3 for a colored image) are needed to be processed. Processing methods rely mostly on region based (Qin et al. 2010), edge detection based, or texture based methods (Moghadam et al. 2012). Apart from urban areas, for scenes where there are no strong pavement and non-pavement demarcations as in rural/ unmarked settings, the problem further becomes challenging.

In a prior research rural roads are handled using Fuzzy Support Vector machines (Zhou and Iagnemma 2010), but here connected roads are assumed and seed points within the image are taken as positive or negative examples for training. Another work utilizes vanishing point estimation, weighted voting system, and Gabor filters for road direction estimation to detect drivable road under extreme unstructured condition such as desert roads (Moghadam et al.

Figure 2.1: Extracted pavement area from images. Original images in the first row, and their corresponding pavement image in the second row. Pavement images could be used to understand many conditions like, cracks, potholes, broken area, patches, parking places and other road markings.

2012). Fritsch et al. (2014) give an approach based on SPRAY features for detecting road area for unmarked urban and rural settings. However, it required to have lane markings at the outer side boundary of the pavement area for first steps. Other than rural settings, urban scenes also possess additional major challenges like, diverse traffic conditions and less difference between pavement and non-pavement colors in overall scene (due to buildings, etc.). Various methods for urban scenes based on Conditional Random Field (CRF) (Passani et al. 2014), vanishing point (Miksik 2012), ground plane estimation from cameras (Hoiem et al. 2005) or complex pixel based deep learning using CNN are seen in the literature (Brust et al. 2015). Methods involving stereo vision, 3D segmentation, LIDAR, and using sensor inputs are also seen to be used for understanding road scenes (Hillel et al. 2014). A 3D reconstruction method using multiple camera images with Markov Random Field (MRF) is used in (Cherian et al. 2009) to estimate the depth of pixels and understand co-planarity. Approaches relying on geometries of road boundaries, lane-markings or such structured information are also seen. Support Vector Machine (SVM) is seen to be used in (Zhou et al. 2010) for self-supervised learning using texture and color features. However, supervised learning based techniques require considerable amount of annotated training data to handle various environment conditions. On the other hand, structure based techniques related to lane markings have difficulties in adapting to different scene settings of rural and urban. Lately, semantic segmentation approaches using deep learning on scene images to detect important objects like, road, building, sky, could also be

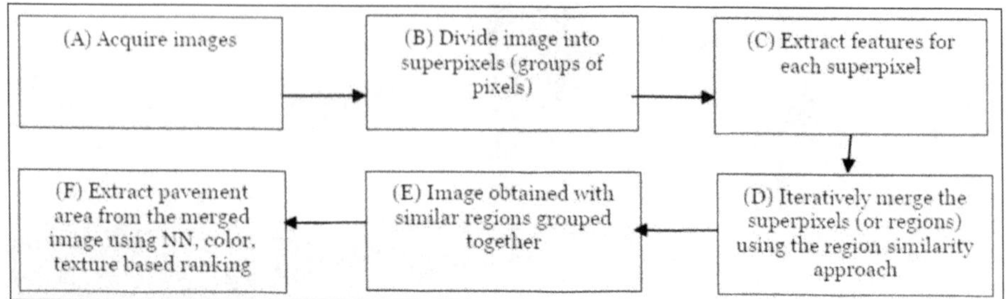

Figure 2.2: Research approach for pavement area grouping and detection in natural scene images.

found. A semantic pixel level region segmentation approach using CNN based deep learning can be found in (Alvarez et al. 2012) where road surfaces are labeled by learning a weighted combination of features at different scales. Although not for pavement detection, (Liu et al. 2013) gives an interesting region grouping approach for image segmentation using internal patch statistics.

Our approach, as shown in Figure 2.2, uses color and texture as feature types and connected graphs as data structure to segment the image into homogeneous regions. The novelty of this approach lies in obtaining the similarity between image regions using a mixture of kernel based distance metrics, followed by pairwise assignment for the iterative merging and clustering. Kernels with Euclidean and Bhattacharyya distances in combination are used to handle different feature types. Finally, we use linear assignment using Hungarian algorithm to identify those closest pairwise graphs that should be merged, for a growing region. Hungarian algorithm based linear assignment can be used for attributed graph matching scenarios (Jouili et al. 2009) and can be adapted as a hierarchical clustering technique (Goldberger and Tassa 2008). This larger merged pavement region, obtained after segmenting the image by grouping pavement regions, can then be easily detected within the scene. Some of the results using our region-matching approach are show in Figure 2.6 - Figure 2.8. The developed approach helps us to group the pavement regions, unlike many previous methods, without additional information like; 1) its shape or surface texture type, 2) pavement boundaries, 3) lane markings, 4) predefined number of clusters for hierarchical clustering. The learning and merging of image parts are done in an unsupervised manner, while the final pavement detection is done by using a ranking- based and a decision tree-like approach. Also, we do not provide any predefined number of initial groups or required number of clusters, unlike traditional clustering methods like that of spectral clustering or k-means. In this way, we utilize minimal input information to automate pavement detection for rural and urban settings under different conditions and surface texture types of paved, graveled, pedestrian lanes, brick paths. In the next section we describe our data collection method.

2.3 Data Collection and Preparation

We collected videos and images (and GPS values) of natural scenes in Germany covering almost 2500 km of roadway. We collected the data over a period of 1 year by mounting high definition cameras with GPS capabilities on pedelecs/ e-bikes. Figure 2.1 show examples of our collected data and the view captured. The images are obtained from the video clips and are of 1242×720 resolution. Out of this dataset for evaluation purposes and comparing with ground truth, we selected 300 images covering different scenarios under normal daylight like, different scene types (bike paths, sidewalks, as well as urban within-city settings, rural, and unstructured scene), graveled/ paved surface texture types, and broken surfaces. Additionally, we also used KITTI (Fritsch et al. 2013) benchmark test images on urban marked (um-road) scenes for evaluating our approach. The um-road test dataset consists of 96 two-way road images in urban marked (having lane markers) settings. Images in this dataset belong to varied environmental conditions (Fritsch et al. 2013). To prepare the data, we firstly resize the images to one-fourth of its size using Gaussian pyramid (Burt 1981). So, for an image resolution of 1242×375, like for KITTI dataset, 311×94×3 data points are processed. For larger resolutions, like 1242×720, we process 311×180×3 data points. For very large resolutions, lower-three fourth could also only be processed further to reduce the data points. We process the smaller sized images and later we scale it up to the original size (using mask), so we don't lose any image details for pavement surfaces. Moreover, we estimated the parameters for our approach on a separate image set consisting of 65 images, which we refer as development dataset. Out of this, 45 were taken from KITTI um-road's training dataset and 20 from our collected dataset. The original training set of KITTI has 95 images but we used only 45 of it to create our development (training) dataset for estimating the parameters. In the following sections we describe the feature extraction, and the image region merging approach.

2.4 Feature Extraction

To group the image pixels into initial guesses of regions (Figure 2.4, first picture), we divide the image into n superpixels/ initial regions to decrease the number of data points to process.

We extract features for these n regions. So, the regions are now encoded in terms of feature space. Overtime, we iteratively merge the superpixels to form bigger regions, until the scene is divided into few major regions. These bigger regions represent recognizable scene elements like, sky, grass, pavement, parts of building, etc. Thus, the scene is segmented in such a way, such that pavement region stays unique and can be easily detected. Merging is done based on how similar the regions are. Here, similarity and/or homogeneity between regions is defined in terms of color and texture. Table 2.2 shows the list of features extracted for every superpixel. Though it is very difficult to identify features of varied elements (like, buildings, sky, grass, trees, roads, side-walks, shadows, humans, vehicles, etc.) in a scene, features here are selected based on the following two criteria– maximizing separation among different major scene objects, and keeping the group of different image parts belonging to pavement and its shadows as unique regions. Hence, the following features are used in this work: HSV (Hue, Saturation, Value/ Intensity) and RGB (Red, Green, and Blue) color spaces are used to give color features, whereas Gray Level Co-occurrence Matrix (GLCM) statistical properties and Local Binary Patterns (LBP) histogram are used as texture descriptors. Histogram of Oriented Gradients (HoG) is also used as a feature descriptor to give the information about edges and corners in an image.

Color	H-S Color histogram, μ_R, μ_G, μ_B, μ_{RGB}, μ_H, μ_S, μ_V, std_R, std_G, std_B
Texture	LBP histogram GLCM homogeneity (numeric) GLCM entropy (numeric) GLCM energy (numeric) GLCM correlation (numeric)
Edge	Histogram of Oriented Gradients
Geometric	Region (x,y) location

Table 2.2: List of extracted features.

2.4.1 Color, Texture, and Histogram of Oriented Gradients Features

Among many features studied for road detection, the discriminative property of different color channels and spaces, like, RGB, HSV, LAB, and Grayscale has been observed in (Alvarez et al. 2014). In this work, we primarily use HSV and RGB, while for shadow identification we additionally use LAB. Figure 2.3 shows the mapping between HSV and RGB color spaces. Here, $M1 = max(R, G, B)$ and $M2 = min(R, G, B)$. HSV is more invariant to lighting and perceptually closer to human vision system, and thus it is primarily used in this work. In HSV color space, hue gives the dominant color, saturation gives a measure of purity of color within it, and value gives the color intensity and is often closer to normal grayscale value ranging between 0 (black) and 255 (white). Color histogram of every superpixel with 100 bins for H and S channels are used here as features. V channel is omitted in the histogram, as H-S combination gave the best configuration. μ_H, μ_S, mean of each of the H, and S channel of an image region, are also obtained for each superpixel. Similarly, the means of the R, G, B color space, μ_R, μ_G, μ_B, are also obtained. Also, $\mu_{RGB} = \frac{R+G+B}{3}$ is obtained for every superpixel. Standard deviations of R, G and B channels, i.e.; std_R, std_B, std_G are also used as features.

Local Binary Patterns (LBP) (Ojala and Pietikainen 1996) is used here as one of the texture features due to its ability to identify flat textured regions and its suitability to detect pavement (Passani et al. 2014). Furthermore, LBP is selected for having important characteristics like; rotation and scale invariance, robustness towards noise and illumination (Silva et al. 2015). Here, LBP is calculated on each of the grayscale superpixel, giving a 75 bin LBP histogram for each of the superpixels. It is calculated on grayscale image due to better performance than on other image channels. It is calculated within a radius r for each of the pixel's neighborhood, with p neighboring points. The central pixel is then given a LBP code. Histogram of Oriented Gradients (HoG) (Dalal and Triggs 2005) is also used here to get a feature vector giving information on strong edges and corners in the image. The HoG is obtained after the horizontal and vertical gradients are calculated on the image regions. An image with HoG calculated for every 6×6 cell of pixels with 31 orientations can be seen in Figure 2.3 (right side, last image). Here, for every superpixel we calculate a HoG descriptor with the said configuration on the grayscale image. Grey Level Co-occurrence Matrix (GLCM) (Conners et al. 1984; Haralick 1979) gives second order statistical properties of an image region and are also used as texture features. They are calculated here on the grayscale image. Here, four types of properties: homogeneity (g_h), entropy (g_{e1}), energy (g_{e2}), and correlation (g_c); are used as features for each superpixel. These features are in equations (2.1 – 2.5):

$$g_h(\theta, d_o) = \sum_{i,j} \frac{1}{1-(i-j)^2} p(i,j), \tag{2.1}$$

$$g_{e1}(\theta, d_o) = -\sum_{i,j} \log(p(i,j)) p(i,j), \tag{2.2}$$

$$g_{e2}(\theta, d_o) = \sum_{i,j} p(i,j)^2, \tag{2.3}$$

$$g_c(\theta, d_o) = \sum_{i,j} \frac{(i-\mu_i)(j-\mu_j)}{\sigma_i \sigma_j} p(i,j), \tag{2.4}$$

$$g_{contrast}(\theta, d_o) = \sum_{i,j} p(i,j)(i-j)^2, \tag{2.5}$$

where, $p(i, j)$ denotes the probability of the change from graylevel i to j at a distance do and direction θ. GLCM is parameterized by (do, θ) i.e. for a given angle θ (determining spatial relationship direction) and an offset do (determining neighbor pixels). The number of graylevel is taken as 253 for GLCM. However, it is not rotation and scale invariant, unlike LBP. To handle this, each features for a given offset (do = 2, 5, 7) is calculated separately for each of four angles ($\theta = 0°$, $45°$, $90°$, $135°$) and then averaged.

Figure 2.3: Left: Converting a RGB to HSV by transforming each pixel value. Right: First row– RGB and its HSV image. Second row– image in only H and S channel. Third row– Image in grayscale channel and its HoG image. Lower three-fourth of the images are shown.

2.5 Region Based Merging

Initially the image is over-segmented into n superpixels using Simple Linear Iterative Clustering (SLIC) method (Achanta et al. 2012). SLIC is used because of its simple yet robust behavior. It clusters pixels in 5-D feature space with three color values and (x, y) location of pixels. Once the superpixels are generated, features are extracted for them as discussed in the above section. Afterwards, a Regional Adjacency Graph (G) is defined on the connected superpixels, as shown in Figure 2.4 (second picture). Two merging steps are performed using the extracted features:

initial region growing and iterative region merging, as described below. In the initial region growing step the superpixels are merged to form regions, while in the iterative merging step these regions are further merged to finally segment the image containing the pavement area as grouped regions. A connected graph is used as the underlying data structure for these next steps, containing superpixels as nodes and region descriptors (or feature vectors) as node attributes. In Figure 2.2 this section belongs to the fourth block, numbered "D", within the overall research approach.

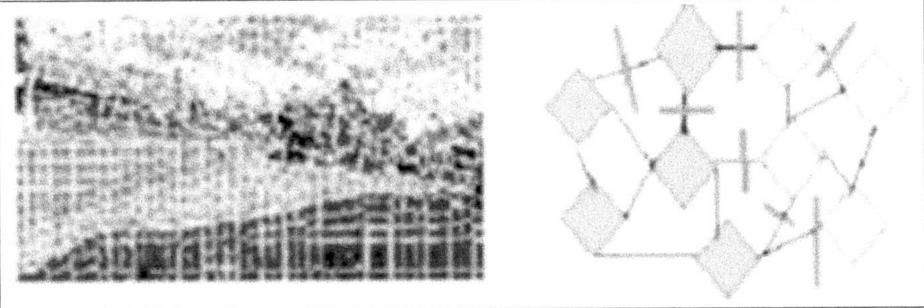

Figure 2.4: (Left) n superpixels (as nodes) and regional adjacency graph on an image. (Right) Multiple threshold cut (light blue lines) with a signal-to-noise ratio value on the graph, giving initial regions to start.

2.5.1 Initial Region Growing

In this step, initial merging and splitting actions have been performed on G, which is the initial regional adjacency graph of the superpixels. G is divided into regions $G_1, G_2 \cdots G_m$ with multiple threshold cut on it, as shown in Figure 2.4. To start with, every nth superpixel node is associated with an attribute vector F_n, as shown in equation (2.6). F_n is defined as following: $F1$ in equation (2.6) denotes the color features consisting of the means of the three color channels together, individual mean R, G, B values, and the standard deviations of the three channels. $F2$ consists of the individual mean of H, S, and V channel values. Further, $F3 = [g_h, g_{e1}, g_{e2}, g_c]$ denotes GLCM texture features of the superpixels and $F4$ contains the H-S color histogram as features. $F5$ denotes its LBP texture features. $F6$ denotes the HoG features.

$$F_n = [F1_n, F2_n, F3_n, F4_n, F5_n, F6_n]. \tag{2.6}$$

$$F1_n = [\mu_{RGB_n}, \mu_{R_n}, \mu_{G_n}, \mu_{B_n}, std_{R_n}, std_{G_n}, std_{B_n}]. \tag{2.7}$$

$$F2_n = [\mu_{H_n}, \mu_{S_n}, \mu_{V_n}]. \tag{2.8}$$

Splitting of G is performed based on two criteria. Any two neighbor superpixel node color attributes, say $F1_{n1}$ and $F1_{n2}$, are firstly checked if they have a high correlation of ≥ 0.9. After this, the predicate logic $cut(n1, n2)$ in equation (2.9) is checked. It follows a simple signal to noise ratio on μ_H, μ_S, μ_{RGB} of a superpixel node. ϵ is used to perform the division when neighbors have similar color values and is taken as 0.001. When the predicate logic in equation (2.9) evaluates to true (left side $\geq \delta$ for each of the conditions, following a logical and operation), neighboring superpixel nodes are merged into a region. Otherwise, a threshold cut occurs between these superpixels. The splitting process therefore generates larger regions, $G_1, G_2 \cdots G_m$, having similar color features. The merging process at this step thus follows a fast greedy approach. Figure 2.4 shows such an operation. In this figure, ash colored boxes on the right shows a formed region, while magenta colored box shows a single border region superpixel. Once the initial regions, G_m, are obtained from G, there are still some un-merged nodes of G left behind which are not part of any regional groups. Such single nodes are assigned to one of the regions along its border. Out of all the border regions, the one having a border superpixel m_b closest to the single node is used for merging. Closeness is obtained from the squared Bhattacharyya distance between normalized F_4 color histograms with b bins, and the squared Euclidean distance between F_3 statistical properties of the nodes, as given in equation (2.10).

$$\begin{aligned} cut(n_1, n_2) : 10\log_{10} \frac{\mu_{H_{n_2}}}{|\mu_{H_{n_1}} - \mu_{H_{n_2}}| + \epsilon} \geq \delta \wedge 10\log_{10} \frac{\mu_{S_{n_2}}}{|\mu_{S_{n_1}} - \mu_{S_{n_2}}| + \epsilon} \geq \delta \wedge \\ 10\log_{10} \frac{\mu_{RGB_{n_2}}}{|\mu_{RGB_{n_1}} - \mu_{RGB_{n_2}}| + \epsilon} \geq \delta \end{aligned} \tag{2.9}$$

$$d(n, G_m) = 2(1 - \sum_{k=1}^{b} \sqrt{F4_m(k) F4_{m_b}(k)}) + ||F3_n - F3_{m_b}||^2. \tag{2.10}$$

2.5.2 Iterative Merging Procedure

In the iterative merging step the generated regions, m, from the above step are further merged. It uses kernel based distances and linear assignment method. At this step, merging takes place at the larger region level, unlike the last step where merging happened at the superpixel node level. Following equation (2.6), new feature vector is defined at the region level and is given in equation (2.11).

$$F_m = [F4_m, F5_m, F6_m]. \tag{2.11}$$

$F4$ gives the H-S color histogram, $F5$ the LBP histogram, and $F6$ the HoG feature histogram. All histograms are normalized. The histograms of the regions are obtained by concatenating node-level histogram of all nodes that are there with a region. Location $L = (x, y)$ giving the standardized position of the central node in the regional graph is also used.

Distance Between Regions

Once the region features, F_m, are obtained, Gaussian kernels are defined. The final distance formulation $d(G_i, G_j)$ between any two region G_i and G_j,

$$d(G_i, G_j) = 1 - exp(-\frac{||L_i - L_j||^2 + 2{d_2}^2 + 2{d_3}^2 + 2{d_4}^2}{2\sigma^2}), \tag{2.12}$$

with $i, j \in [1 \ldots m]$ is given in the equation (2.12).

$$d(F4_i, F4_j) = \sqrt{(1 - \sum_{k=1}^{b} \sqrt{F4_i(k) F4_j(k)})}, \tag{2.13}$$

$$d(F5_i, F5_j) = \sqrt{(1 - \sum_{k=1}^{b} \sqrt{F5_i(k) F5_j(k)})}, \tag{2.14}$$

$$d(F6_i, F6_j) = \sqrt{(1 - \sum_{k=1}^{b} \sqrt{F6_i(k) F6_j(k)})}, \tag{2.15}$$

where, $d2 = d(F4_i, F4_j)$, $d3 = d(F5_i, F5_j)$, and $d4 = d(F6_i, F_{6_j})$. It can be noted that while L follows squared Euclidean based metric for the Gaussian kernel, $F4_m, F5_m, F6_m$ follow Bhattacharyya distance based metric. Bhattacharyya distance metric is used as it is geometrically most similar to the Euclidean, and provides robust distance between distributions for the task at hand. Furthermore, it is observed that the Euclidean distance between two long feature vectors with flattened histograms doesn't give satisfactory merging results due to high dimensions when used with pairwise linear assignment. The combined metric also gave better results than using Kullback-Leibler divergence. Hence, four different attribute types are handled in the way described by the equations (2.12 - 2.15) for obtaining the final pairwise distances between regions. Finally, the scale parameter, σ^2, in $d(G_i, G_j)$ can be successfully used as a guiding element for merging similar regions. This further helped to deal with high dimensional feature space. All pairwise distances are between 0 and 1 and are then stored as a distance matrix D, a non-negative, symmetrical, $m \times m$ matrix.

Recommendation Phase

In this phase, distance matrix, D, obtained using above metrics is used for recommending the regions that should be merged. The diagonal of D is biased to avoid self-recommendations. Figure 2.5 shows such an example matrix. In this iterative merging process the entries and size of D are modified in the successive steps. This happens as new distances are obtained from the equation (2.12), and also by varying the scale parameter, σ^2, of the kernel when graphs are merged. The cost function is defined over the distance matrix as $\sum D_{ij}$ being a linear combination of the distances and it is minimized for finding the closest graph matches. To obtain the matches from D in order to give which graphs/ regions should be merged, the problem is handled using matrix operations for linear assignment. Hungarian method (Kuhn 1955) is used for such assignments and the steps for the algorithm are as follows: 1) Firstly, row operations are performed on the D matrix for each row by subtracting each cell value from a minimum entry in that row. So that each row has at least a zero entry, and that cell is marked. Now, if at this stage every row and column combination has exactly one zero, then the assignment is finished, otherwise the next steps are repeated. 2) The next steps check all rows and columns of D so that they are covered. This continues until each row and each column in the matrix has exactly one marked zero. These cell positions are taken as the matches. In this way, recommendations for closest matches are obtained.

–	0.9	0.3	0.6	0.7
0.9	–			
0.3		–		
			–	
				–

Figure 2.5: A symmetric distance matrix D. It is the input to the Hungarian algorithm for finding the matches between image regions.

Selection From Recommended Matches and Final Merging Phase

Once the recommendations are obtained using the Hungarian method, it must be noted that Hungarian method always recommends for each graph/ region a match after optimization using the matrix D, i.e. the number of regions or graphs $\#(G_m)$ are reduced to $\#(G_m)/2$ after every run. Hence, an additional check is required if the recommended matches between graphs from Hungarian method, say G_i and G_j, can be finally merged following region homogeneity criteria. To check the homogeneity criteria at this stage we use a predicate based on color for the regions to be merged. We use the predicate logic developed in (Hassani et al. 2008) for multi-channel image and check it between recommended matched (graphs) prior to the merging using the predicate: $merge(G_i, G_j) \; : \; max_{c\in(r,g,b)}|\bar{C}_i - \bar{C}_j| \leq M\sqrt{(\frac{1}{2})ln(\frac{2}{\alpha})}\sqrt{\frac{|G_i|+|G_j|}{|G_i||G_j|+\epsilon}}$. The nodes selected for checking this condition are obtained using closeness centrality on the graphs. Here, α is the open parameter with a very low value and is fixed to 0.01 in this work. M is maximum of any channel, $|\bar{C}_i - \bar{C}_j|$ is obtained as the largest color difference between the respective color channels of regions. $|G_i|$ and $|G_j|$ give the area of the regions. When the predicate logic $merge(G_i, G_j)$ evaluates to true (left side $\leq$ right side), then the recommended regions are merged, otherwise the merging does not happen. The merge predicate logic is checked for R, G, and B channels and also for the saturation (S) channel of the regions. It has been seen that the predicate is helpful only at the later stages of the iterative merging, when the recommended closest graphs are already merged to give much larger homogeneous regions. The nodes selected within the graphs for the edge creation, as needed for merging, are obtained using closeness centrality to maintain the representation. In this way, recommended graphs from Hungarian method are ascertained for final merging in every integrative merging step. In every successive merging step, the σ^2 of equation (2.12) guides the merging. We decrease σ^2 stepwise in every run of the iterative merging. So, we start σ^2 as say, with value i, and decrease it by d in successive runs. This affects those scene images which contain varied objects. As it decreases, the separation among regions in feature space increases, and nearest neighbors are increasingly searched. As clustering progresses, all the inter-cluster distances (as in Figure 2.5) moves very close to 1, signifying all the clusters are highly separated. Such recommendation and selection phase constitutes a single merging step within the iterative merging procedure. This process continues until the number of formed regions, which can be seen as merged larger superpixels or clusters, remain unchanged and σ^2 >0. Thus, the approach primarily has two parameters that influences the merging: δ and σ^2. The complete merging steps can be seen in Table 2.3. At the end of the merging, a segmented image with merged pavement regions is obtained, as in Figure 2.6 (d). On obtaining the merged images, we now finish block numbered "E" in Figure 2.2 within the steps of our research approach.

Steps of the developed approach for region merging based on region similarity:
1) Over segment the image into n superpixels and Regional Adjacency Graph (G) is formed with superpixels as nodes
2) Extract features for each superpixel
3) Split G into regions using graph cut and δ with equation (2.9)
4) Merge left out superpixel nodes to a border region with equation (2.10) 5) For every region: (a) Region based features are formed, as in equation (2.11) (b) Pairwise distances between regions obtained using equations (2.12 - 2.15) (c) Merge the regions using Hungarian algorithm for assignments
6) Repeat step 5 iteratively using new distances and varying σ^2 until convergence is achieved

Table 2.3: Steps of the developed approach.

2.6 Implementation Environment

We developed an application based on our approach given in Table 2.3, using Python 2.7 as the platform, and OpenCV 2.4.11 (Open Source Computer Vision) library. Some of the useful libraries that we also used are SciPy, scikit-image, scikit-learn for linear assignment, clustering and classifying methods, and NetworkX for handling the graph-based data structure of the image regions in the image. It helped to have different node attributes (feature vectors) and edge attributes (color differences) for our graph structure.

2.7 Results

The results in this section demonstrate how the developed procedure is used for region merging, as required for pavement detection. We used our own dataset collected as previously described, as well as KITTI (Fritsch et al. 2013) benchmark um-road test dataset images which consists of 96 images for evaluations. We evaluated on 300 images from our collected dataset covering rural, unstructured, and urban conditions. We ascertained all the parameters separately on the development data, as stated earlier in the Data Collection section, and performed the final testing on the test images of our collected data as well as on KITTI um-road test data. Figure 2.6 – Figure 2.8 show the results obtained. Evaluations on the datasets are given in Table 2.4, and a F1-measure of 87.86 percent has been achieved on average across scene settings.

We set the hyper-parameters (δ, σ^2) for our developed approach in the Table 2.3 as stated here. Out of these, σ^2 is the most important. In equation (2.9), δ is easier to set and is tested for values in the range of 11 to 20 (after 16 over-segmentation may take place) following the standard signal-to-noise ratio values. δ= 14 should be taken for all the images under darker conditions, and δ= 11 for the rest. We roughly estimate the darker condition of a scene automatically from overall grayscale histogram peaks of the image. If the peak happens below the grayscale intensity value of 30, then the scene is considered to be under darker or shaded conditions. n superpixels is selected according to the original image resolution. n = 470 for 311$\times$94 images, while for darker conditions n = 560. For larger 311$\times$180 images n = 580. The scale parameter, σ^2, in equation (2.12) guides the iterative merging and starts with an initial value (say, i) and then we decrease it by d in all the successive runs, while maintaining it at the end. Figure 2.6 (F) shows how changed (i, d) for σ^2 affects the merging. Both the merging converges at around 6 to 7 updates, with (0.9, 0.05) showing slightly smoother merging (right hand corner bluish area). Higher values were taken here as an example to show that pavement stays uniquely merged, even if other elements in the scene get over-merged, showing robustness of our approach. Value for σ^2 has been experimentally seen to be influenced by the contextual information of the scene type being rural, unstructured, urban, or highway under light or dark conditions. For example, for scenes under darker condition larger d of 0.25 could be taken giving quicker convergence. Some of the successful combinations are (i = 0.3 or 0.9, d= 0.05), (i = 0.5, d =0.1), (i = 0.6 or 0.9, d =0.15). If σ^2 is too low it can result in over-segmentation. On the other hand, if its value is relatively high it can result in under-segmentation. Here, (i, d) is set to (0.6, 0.15) for all the evaluations.

2.7.1 Pavement Region Merging

Figure 2.6 shows final pavement region merging steps. The curve here shows the formed merged regions at the end of every run in the iterative merging step. The starting number of regions, 170 in this case, is obtained after the initial steps of region growing using equations (2.9 - 2.10). The regions are homogeneous with respect to the properties of the image parts belonging to the pavement region. As a result, merged regions of the pavement, and also a neighbor relation among different adjacent regions are obtained. Figure 2.8 (set 1) shows additional images for different pavement surfaces and settings.

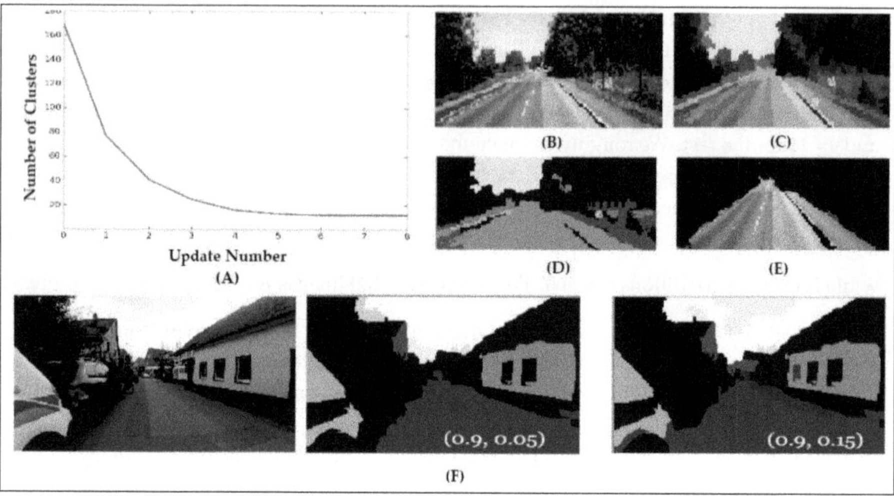

Figure 2.6: Merged regions obtained using region similarity. (A) The curve shows the merging steps. (B) The original image. (C) The image at an intermediate merging step. (D)The image after final merging. (E) The detected pavement area of the image for further analysis. (F) Merging showing effect of different σ^2 values.

2.7.2 Pavement Region Detection and Extraction

As seen in Figure 2.6 and Figure 2.8, once the regions are merged, we detect the merged region satisfying the criteria stated here as the final pavement. These results clearly show that post merging, the pavement area could be detected as they are grouped into a larger pavement region, in spite of intra-pavement surface differences and varied scene settings. Within the overall research approach, this sub-section is the last step and falls under the block numbered "F" in Figure 2.2. Here, we use a combination of simple ranking-based, texture-based, and Nearest Neighbor (NN) methods to detect/ extract the grouped pavement regions. We start with having a reference image set of 30 images to ascertain two factors: possible pavement geometric positions in any natural scene (left-centered, right-centered, and central-centered pavement position) and possible pavement color combinations (mixture of hue (H), and saturation (S)). The reference set does not contain any test data and is a sub-part of the training data. We employ the following basic spatial prior knowledge: full pavement area is always in the lower two-third of the image. This basic assumption helps us to reduce the search space. We then detect the pavement using following criteria on the merged regions:

1) Potential pavement regions have the following thresholds on their R, G, B values: $\frac{|G-R|}{G} \leq a1$, $\frac{|B-G|}{B} \leq a2$, $\frac{|G-R|}{G} - \frac{|B-G|}{B} \leq a3$, and the grayscale intensity ($gray_i$) value $\geq$ a4 Here, if $a1, a2 \leq 0.40$, then a3 = 0.25, else a3 = 0.50. a4 is taken as 15. These values follow that pavement area generally is grayish in color and because we detect a bigger merged region (not a pixel), so we could average the color present in the whole image regions. After this, we rank the merged regions and select the one with the highest rank as pavement.

2) The guiding approach for the ranking is that the potential pavement region would mostly occupy major area in the image, and it would be one of the most homogeneous (lowest contrasted) region in the image. Contrast C of the GLCM for merged regions, giving the texture information, are obtained with equation (2.5).

3) Position P of merged regions are obtained from the rectangular bounding around it, giving the four coordinates. We then find the Nearest Neighbor (NN) of P and its H and S colors in the reference image set, and get the respective distances d between each image region and its nearest neighbor in this set. Finally, we rank each region according to its contrast C and distance d values. The minimum C gets highest rank, and same for the d. Both the ranks, C and d, are combined to get the final rank R_m for each merged region. Highest ranked regions are checked and are detected as the final pavement region. Neighboring regions to this detected pavement area are also checked for similar criteria. If the detected pavement area has the intensity $gray_i \leq 60$, then the neighbors are checked as the low intensity shows it may be a shadow region.

4) We handle major shadows here, i.e., shadows that cover a significant area of the pavement like that of trees or buildings, and recognize shadow using the following conditions in the neighborhood of the non- shadowed detected pavement region. Once, shadow is merged into a separate group as shown in Figure 2.8 (Set 4 – Set 5), we detect the shadow using color alignment (Guo et al. 2013) and its H-channel properties. Shadow regions (s) always are less in grayscale intensity value, and each of the R, G, B values are also less than the non-shadow (ns) counter-part. Further, in Hue color space, $H_s >> H_{ns}$ and in LAB color space the ratio $(\frac{L+1}{A+1})_s < (\frac{L+1}{A+1})_{ns}$ (Li et al. 2016) for shadow and non-shadow parts. Shadow regions also hold the property of $|\frac{|G-R|}{G}| - |\frac{|B-G|}{B}| \leq 0.15$. Furthermore, the s and ns regions on the pavement have comparable color ratios in the normalized $R = \frac{R}{R+G+B}, G = \frac{G}{R+G+B}, B = \frac{B}{R+G+B}$ color space, i.e. $r1 = \frac{B}{G}, r2 = \frac{G}{R}$ is maintained. Thus, using these comparative properties, we detect the shadow area in an image.

Thus, basic color properties and the GLCM contrast helps us to detect and extract the pavement area in an image independent of strict color or texture requirement, once merging is completed, as it searches most homogeneous region in the lower two-third of the image. The NN helps here to substantiate the pavement position in an image. Reasonable thresholds on basic color properties have been used to avoid common green color components like, grass. Varying the kernel scale parameter, σ^2, in equation (2.12) helped us to merge shadows into a distinct region, as in Figure 2.8 (Set 5), so that they do not get merged with other nearby darker areas and maintain the borders. Moreover, it was noticed as the detected dataset increases, it could be implicitly used for ascertaining pavement color's Nearest Neighbor using histogram intersection. At the end, post processing of filling small holes in the detected region has been used. We finally used Hough Line Transform on the detected pavement region to ascertain straight lines. This refines the result and roughly demarcates between road and off-road areas, as shown in Figure 2.7 (I) (A, second image). We take only those lines which are on the left and right of the mid-point of the detected pavement area; to demarcate the left and right pavement edges. However, in shadowed conditions it didn't improve the result much. In this way, the detected pavement region, along with its probable shadow area, are extracted.

2.7.3 Evaluations

We performed the evaluation using the standard method of precision (P), recall (R), and F1-measure (Fritsch et al. 2013) against ground truth. We also report accuracy (Acc). The results are given in Table 2.4 and Table 2.5. Ground truth of pavement areas were manually marked in original test images, as shown in Figure 2.7 (I), and are compared with the detected pavement area obtained by applying our approach and other methods. Evaluation measures that have been used are defined as follows:

$$P = \frac{TP}{TP+FP}, R = \frac{TP}{TP+FN}, F1 = 2\frac{P.R}{P+R}, Acc = \frac{TP+TN}{TP+TN+FP+FN}.$$

Here, TP denotes true positives with respect to the ground truth, as marked in Figure 2.7. FP denotes false positive (detecting non-pavement area as pavement), FN denotes false negative (detecting pavement area as non-pavement area). F1-measure gives the trade-off between the two using the harmonic mean of precision and recall. All evaluations are performed with respect to the ground truth on a pixel basis.

It is seen from Table 2.4 and Table 2.5 that we compare our approach with common methods like, AdaBoost, K-Nearest Neighbor (K-NN) classifier, Gaussian Naïve Byes (NB) and Support Vector Machine (SVM). We trained these supervised methods using the extracted features, as given in the section Feature Extraction, for each superpixel from annotated training images and then test their performance against the said datasets. We selected AdaBoost as a typical example of an ensemble learning method, whereas NB serves as a simple method without needing any parameter tuning. The hyper-parameters of these methods are selected using grid search

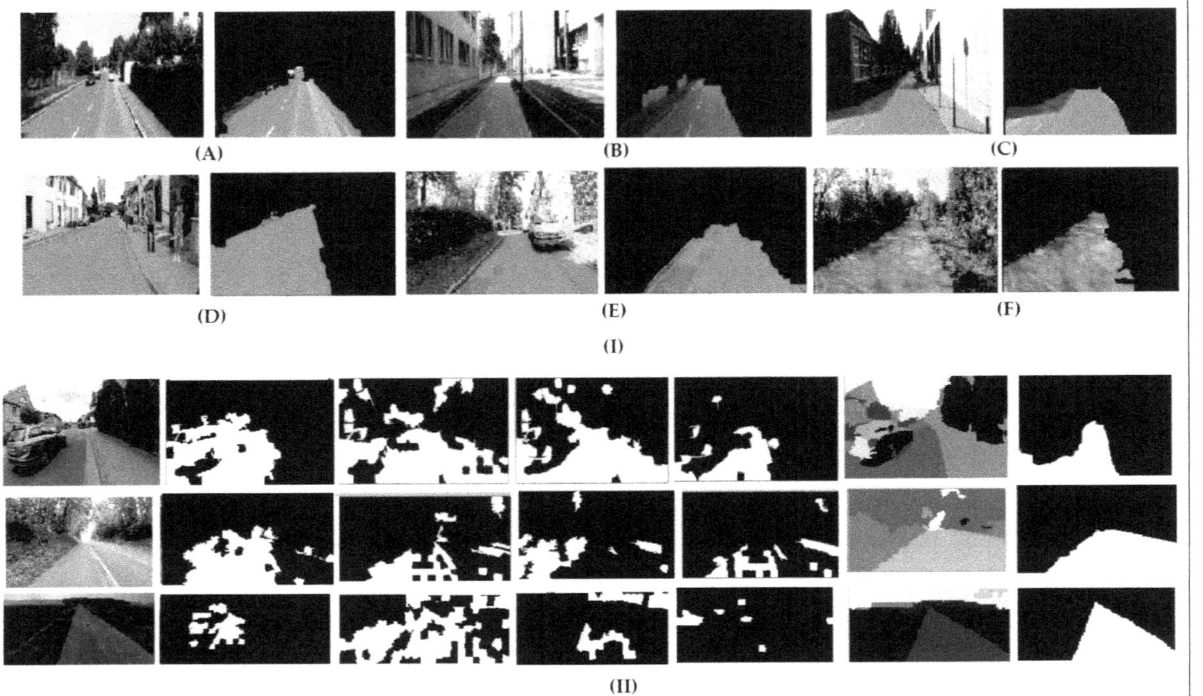

Figure 2.7: (I) Ground truth is marked with red color in all the images, illustrating the process used for evaluations. Every set shows original image annotated with ground truth, and extracted pavement area after detection with true positives (also in red) and false positives (blue). (A) additionally shows refining of the result using Hough lines (left line marked with blue, and right line marked with green). (B - F) give examples of shadowed scenes, and unmarked urban or unstructured scenes. Red denotes true positives. Blue denotes false positives. Missed part shows false negatives. (II) Examples of predictions from different methods. Detected pavement area is shown as masks. First column shows original images, second column shows detection using AdaBoost, third with K-NN, fourth with NB, fifth with SVM. Sixth column gives the result of final merging using our approach, and the last column shows the detected area using our approach.

Method name	Datasets	No.of Images	P (%)	R (%)	F1 (%)
Our Approach	**Collected data** (rural/ unstructured scenes)	200	**90.24**	**92.08**	**91.14**
	Collected data (mixed of rural/ urban)	100	**85.23**	**89.12**	**87.13**
	KITTI (um-road)	96	**82.60**	**88.23**	**85.32**
	Average over the full dataset	396 (total)	**86.02 (avg.)**	**89.81 (avg.)**	**87.86 (avg.)**
AdaBoost	Collected data (rural/ unstructured scenes)	200	72.81	71.69	72.50
	Collected data (mixed of rural/ urban)	100	78.67	63.93	70.50
	KITTI (um-road)	96	61.71	90.29	73.13
K-NN	Collected data (rural/ unstructured scenes)	200	61.62	71.61	66.35
	Collected data (mixed of rural/ urban)	100	65.15	64.72	61.35
	KITTI (um-road)	96	46.90	90.90	62.23
Gaussian Naive Bayes	Collected data (rural/ unstructured scenes)	200	60.53	61.61	61.14
	Collected data (mixed of rural/ urban)	100	65.53	66.17	66.00
	KITTI (um-road)	96	45.06	78.24	58.01
SVM	Collected data (rural/ unstructured scenes)	200	76.61	45.33	57.39
	Collected data (mixed of rural/ urban)	100	71.12	46.77	56.37
	KITTI (um-road)	96	57.57	75.23	65.13

Table 2.4: Evaluation and comparison of the developed approach on different scene datasets.

and cross-validation, and the ones giving the best performance are selected for final testing. Number of estimators are set to 200 for AdaBoost with Decision Tree Classifier, giving the best performance. Number of neighbors for K-NN has been taken as 5, with after 15 showing degraded performance, and Manhattan distance is considered. The penalty parameter for SVM with RBF kernel has been searched between 0.001 and 1000, with 0.1 giving the best results followed by 100. AdaBoost is seen to perform better within the above said methods, being second to our approach. Simple post-processing like, considering only lower two-third of the image,

Method name	Datasets	No.of Images	P (%)	R (%)	F1 (%)
Our Approach	Paved surfaces	306	86.23	89.51	87.23
	Graveled and unpaved	90	88.24	92.18	90.33
AdaBoost	Paved surfaces	306	71.66	73.21	72.36
	Graveled and unpaved	90	74.25	62.90	68.41
Gaussian Naive Bayes	Paved surfaces	306	58.56	65.30	62.17
	Graveled and unpaved	90	59.99	52.56	55.80
SVM	Paved surfaces	306	67.58	55.99	61.53
	Graveled and unpaved	90	69.58	39.03	49.37

Table 2.5: Evaluation and comparison of the developed approach on different pavement surface datasets.

has been applied. However, as the neighboring information is not there for these methods it's hard to apply simple post-processes further. Furthermore, it can be seen that precision, recall, and F1 are more representative measures than accuracy for pavement detection tasks (Fritsch et al. 2013) as true negatives could be more easily detected. Further, Figure 2.7 (II) shows visual comparison between our approach and the other methods. Our approach shows to be adapted to different scene and lighting settings, giving consistent results across situations than others. Additionally, Figure 2.8 shows more results of our approach.

2.8 Discussion

The increased integration of digital technologies into everyday artefacts (Yoo 2010) gives rise to an unprecedented level of connectivity and produces large amounts of data that, for the first time, allow us to study causal relations in real world contexts. However, in order to provide value added services, we need methods to process large amounts of data and derive valuable information from them. In this work, we successfully developed an approach for pavement area merging in rural/ unstructured or urban scene type images and for different pavement surface texture types like, paved or graveled. We used a numerically simpler approach and grouped the pavement regions in images. Figure 2.8 shows different illumination conditions,

Figure 2.8: Detection and extraction of the pavement region in images. Images are best viewed in color. Merged regions are colored in their mean color, or with distinct colors for better visualization if the mean colors are too close. (Set 1) shows merged regions for different scene settings and surfaces, written on the original images. (Set 2) shows pavement detection for unstructured rural scenes. (Set 3) shows pavement detection under different illumination and lighting conditions. (Set 4) shows pavement detection for urban scene settings. (Set 5) shows merging and detection for rural scenes and unmarked pavement conditions.

shadow settings, scene types, and surface types handled by our approach.

The region merging approach for pavement detection in this work implies robust behavior in HSV color space and it's effective combined use with LBP and HoG features for matching different image areas. We used a split and merge approach, by starting with a simple signal-to-noise ratio notion on mean colors to obtain initial homogeneous regions from the superpixels. Thereafter, we used an iterative merging procedure consisting of a mixture of Euclidean and Bhattacharyya distances, pairwise assignment with the Hungarian algorithm, and a Gaussian kernel with varying scale parameter. This helped us to handle different scene and surface types. Once, the merged regions are formed, pavement is generally one of the most homogeneous region in the lower two-third of the scene. We could thus generate rich training and/or datasets automatically for different developmental purposes. The evaluations are given in Table 2.4. It shows that we achieved a high recall of 92.08 percent and 88.23 percent for rural/ unstructured and urban settings, respectively. Similarly, we achieved a precision of 90.24 percent and 82.60 percent for rural/ unstructured and urban settings, respectively. Finally, we achieved a high F1-measure with 91.14 percent and 85.32 percent on average for both the rural or unstructured and urban scene types, respectively.

We handled different surface texture types and unstructured scenes in this work without using a large training set. Regarding the benchmark dataset, KITTI-um test data, we achieved a high precision and a recall of 82.6 percent and 88.23 percent, respectively. We noticed that many of the works report their evaluations from bird's eye viewpoint space, and we did the evaluations in the perspective image space. The two spaces can have little difference on the final results, like, considering few of the pixels on the lane boundary or at long-end. So, for comparative purposes and qualitative analysis we can see that in (Passani et al. 2014) a precision and a recall of 78.03 percent and 66.79 percent were achieved, respectively, in the view space for the urban scenes using Conditional Random Field on miniaturized scene images. In (Vitor et al. 2013) the authors reported 50.21 percent of precision and 83.91 percent of recall for the benchmark data using image segmentation and Artificial Neural Network. To provide a direct comparison between our approach and other common approaches, we selected AdaBoost (a typical ensemble method), SVM, K-NN, and Gaussian Naive Bayes, as given in Table 2.4 and Table 2.5. The results in Table 2.4 and Table 2.5 clearly show that our approach outperforms these methods by a large margin on the F1-measure, as also seen in Figure 2.7 (II). We could thus see that our approach has a good performance, while handling many scene types, and not only urban. Furthermore, in our approach we didn't give any initial number of required clusters or groups for the merging process and performed it in an unsupervised manner, implying that the approach could be adapted and useful for detecting most-dominant homogeneous areas in an image. We tested it on a limited number of indoor images to detect the floor areas and got encouraging results, and hence aim to extend the approach also for indoor environments in the future.

Once the pavement area is detected in images, it could be used for multi-various tasks, such as to obtain and analyze: 1) road/ bridge surface visual characteristics like, surface defects, cracks, patches, potholes, and other infrastructure defects, 2) lane markers or dividers, 3) drivable lane, pedestrian lanes, 4) condition of speed limit signs on roads for safety, 5) major broken areas, 6) other infrastructure knowledge like, presence of manholes, patch joining, etc., 7) traffic light positioning placement as per road markers for increasing safety, 8) historical data pool, 9) navigation requirements in rural or unstructured condition; to name a few. For all such applications, detecting the pavement area in a scene is the first and a crucial step for further processes being built on top of it. So, if the first step could be handled for diverse scenes, then the effects of further processes could also be maximized, tested, enhanced, and applied to various situations.

As an example for road-marker analysis, in (Schreiber et al. 2014) the authors detected road markings (like, 30, 50, BUS, STOP) for 2D images using image warping, Optical Character Recognition (OCR), and SVM, after probable road surface area is estimated using vanishing point. However, vanishing point may not always be applicable to detect the road in various scene categories like, rural or within-city urban roads, that don't have lane markers. As another example for surface analysis, in (Varadharajan et al. 2014) the road surface is first detected in a scene using camera-based technique, prior to crack detection on surfaces. However, if scene images are acquired without prior knowledge of camera height or from various sources to use the ubiquitous nature of cameras, then the detection method will suffer. In comparison, our method is independent of such camera or lane based assumptions. Once pavement is detected, machine learning approaches like, Neural Network (Li et al. 2014), Multiple Instance Learning (Varadharajan et al. 2014), could be used for defect detection. Thus, our approach (as the first step for such applications) could be used in various conditions on which further processes like, the marker analysis or surface analysis, could be applied and extended to diverse scenes. Our approach is thus useful for adaptability across different scene settings (rural, unstructured, and urban), pavement shapes, and surface types (paved, graveled, pedestrian lanes); and gives flexibility to process not only consecutive, but also single images.

Hence, our approach to detect pavement from 2-D scene images helps for many cases in the following ways: 1) We didn't use any structured information like, lane markers (Beyeler et al. 2014) because pavement vs non-pavement demarcations are not strong in rural/ unstructured/ within-city settings, camera specific characteristics, or vanishing point estimation techniques (Miksik 2012); making our approach independent of such scene and data-acquisition specific constraints. 2) It helps to extend standalone processes of further steps get integrated for developing many applications and services across diverse scene and surface settings, as our approach is adaptable. 3) It also helps further processes build on top of the pavement detection module get less intercepted by various objects in a scene, thus enhancing these processes, as the pavement area is detected for diverse conditions and is used as input to the next steps. 4) Moreover, our approach helps to identify major shadow and non-shadow areas when the pavement is detected (Figure 2.8, Set4 - Set 5). Detecting shadow in advance before the next steps (for example to detect defects on surfaces) would enhance these processes as shadow and non-shadow areas could be handled separately; considering that shadow is one of the major problem for surface analysis (Koch et al. 2015). 5) Thus, the pavement images (with only pavement area) could provide the basis for developing flexible techniques using data-driven approaches (Abella et al. 2017; Louhghalam et al. 2017). This could increase automation in decision making and attend the open issue of diverse data unavailability for various developmental purposes across agencies/ service providers (Koch et al. 2015). 6) Finally, it helps in making solutions more scalable, adaptable, less subjective, and cheaper; with the ability to be applied in diverse cases.

Additionally, automated analysis of pavement area in an image could be used to provide relevant information and alert services to citizens in less time. Citizens could get information on pavement conditions (quality of the surface) which could affect their journey time and vehicle operating cost. Such information could also help people to select an appropriate driving or biking route. Alert system giving information on areas with major broken surface conditions could also be designed. Hence, various such applications could be developed using extracted pavement images with reduced data points to process for decision making, and planning. Processing huge amount of street scene image data with adaptable methods thus could influence generation of new services for increased digitalization in the society.

2.8.1 Limitations and Future Work

The presented approach here showed that major pavement regions could be comparatively easily detected using basic criteria, when merged together to form larger regions, as pixel level values are averaged. So, our future research would aim to combine a boosting approach that might enhance the results and help to handle under-merged areas, using the growing dataset as the number of images processed increases overtime. Our approach however suffers at the far-end point near the horizon, as can be seen in Figure 2.7 (B - C) and Figure 2.8 (Set 5, second image), when compared with the ground truth. This is due to either having strong saturated pavement area or scattered shadow area at the far end. Such conditions caused over-merging or the area could not be detected. Relatively better results were observed for such far-end merging conditions if the images were processed at a larger resolution. In future research, we would like to handle it using an additional edge map over the image to ascertain the far-end area in this respect. Additionally, since we have successfully detected the pavement areas from the images, future work would be directed toward developing methods for pavement surface condition analysis, like, for assessing cracks, patches, and potholes. We also invite others to trail our approach of pavement detection for building processes on top of it for various analysis works, and share their experiences for continuous development.

2.9 Conclusion

In this work, we presented a region based similarity approach to merge pavement area pixels in scene images, so that they form a larger region and could be detected. We successfully handled different pavement surface types like, paved, graveled, brick paths, and different scene types like, rural, urban. The approach also helped us to detect pavement areas in unstructured scenes which lack lane marker information. We evaluated the results on our collected dataset, as well on a benchmark dataset, and achieved a high F1-measure of 87.86 percent on average. We used a split and merge approach by starting with a simple signal-to-noise ratio notion on the super-pixel colors. Thereafter, we performed iterative merging and pairwise assignment using Hungarian algorithm, Bhattacharyya distance based metrics, and a Gaussian kernel. In successive steps of the merging, the scale parameter of the kernel is varied. As a result, other information like, shape, is not required for pavement detection. Once the merged regions are formed, pavement is generally one of the most homogeneous region in the scene. This work also shows how the approach could be used for merging larger homogeneous regions within a scene in an unsupervised manner, without knowing the number of regions required beforehand. To further enhance our approach, as future work we aim to integrate an edge map knowledge and perform pavement surface condition analysis tasks.

Chapter 3: Intelligent Road Maintenance- A Machine Learning Approach for Surface Defect Detection

Title	Intelligent Road Maintenance- A Machine Learning Approach for Surface Defect Detection
Authors	Sromona Chatterjee[1], Pouya Saeedfar[1], Schahin Tofangchi[1], Lutz M. Kolbe[1] [1] University of Göttingen, Platz der Göttingen Sieben 5, 37073 Göttingen, Germany ∗ Corresponding author: sromona.chatterjee@wiwi.uni-goettingen.de
Outlet	Proceedings of the European Conference on Information Systems (ECIS), June 2018, Portsmouth, UK
Abstract	The emergence of increased sources for Big Data through consumer recording devices gives rise to a new basis for the management and governance of public infrastructures and policy design. Road maintenance and detection of road surface defects, such as cracks, have traditionally been a time consuming and manual process. Lately, increased automation using easily acquirable front-view digital natural scene images is seen to be an alternative for taking timely maintenance decisions; reducing accidents and operating cost and increasing public safety. In this paper, we propose a machine learning based approach to handle the challenge of crack and related defect detection on road surfaces using front-view images captured from driver's viewpoint under diverse conditions. We use a superpixel based method to first process the road images into smaller coherent image regions. These superpixels are then classified into crack and non-crack regions. Various texture-based features are combined for the classification model. Classifiers such as Gradient Boosting, Artificial Neural Network, Random Forest and Linear Support Vector Machines are evaluated for the task. Evaluations on real datasets show that the approach successfully handles different road surface conditions and crack-types, while locating the defective regions in the scene images.
Keywords	Road surface image analysis, crack detection, surface defect detection, machine learning

Table 3.1: Fact sheet for chapter 3.

3.1 Introduction

The processes of digitalization and datafication have been affecting various aspects of society (Kitchin 2014a), including research practices (Abbasi et al. 2016; Shmueli and Koppius 2011) and decision making in business environments (Abbasi et al. 2016). With ubiquitous recording devices increasingly becoming sources for big data (Yoo 2010), data-driven management and governance of public infrastructures and policy design has emerged (Rabari and Storper 2014). The resulting ubiquitous rich image data enables the use of analytics to gain insights into situations and processes in public areas, such as planning and road maintenance (Tang and Sun 2012; Yang and Lin 2013). Consequently, we identify research opportunities regarding the development of analytic based solutions that can leverage visual data to support public planning decisions. Therefore, we present an ML-based approach in this paper for processing 2-D road and scene images to automatically detect cracks and related surface defects. The images that we use in this study are captured using commodity cameras mounted on pedelecs and e-bikes. We propose that an intelligent road surface defect detection system can improve the effectiveness of maintenance and decrease manual labor associated with the inspection of road conditions.

Roads are the vital infrastructure and asset for economic growth, at the same time it also requires periodic checks and maintenance which are time and resource intensive. A comprehensive re-search by Gleave (2014) studied the effect of the untimely maintenance of roads on different factors such as: (1) increased maintenance costs, (2) vehicle operating costs, (3) environmental degradation from CO_2 emissions, fuel consumption and pollution from difficult rehabilitation works, (4) increased safety issues related to accidents and health impacts. Automation in road defect and distress detection is an ongoing research area and is crucial for road infrastructure management as it detects surface conditions such as cracks, potholes, patches (Koch et al. 2015; MnDOT 2009). However, automated decision making in public infrastructure management of roads or bridges are yet to be realized on a large scale. They are still predominantly surveyed and assessed manually or in a semi-automatic manner to a great extent (Chambon and Moliard 2011; Gavilan et al. 2011; Radopoulou et al. 2016). Distress detection is currently done by manual visual detection, through large specialized vehicles or robotic carts to cover for the as-pects of data acquisition and processing (BASt 2008; MnDOT 2009; Prasanna 2012; Zalama et al. 2013) and by citizen reports. However, such specialized vehicles are much larger in size and come fitted with multiple cameras, artificial lighting, friction sensors, laser profilers, radars, etc., making them costly (could be around $800,000 (Radopoulou et al. 2016)) – unaffordable for most road authorities or agencies and used infrequently. This results in major maintenance back-logs (Gleave, 2014) and an inability to run on inner-city roads, narrower roads, bike paths and sidewalks.

To discuss more on the objectives that could be achieved through increased automation using the power of data, we can look at the findings in Gleave (2014). Based on their study of the roads in European countries, poor pavements and road surface leads to a 34% and 12% increase in the fuel consumption of light vehicles and heavy vehicles, respectively, leading to higher CO_2 emissions. Furthermore, deficient road surface could also increase the vehicle maintenance cost by 129% for heavy vehicles and 185% for light vehicles. In addition, poor road surfaces de-crease the life of the vehicle tires by approximately 10% for heavy vehicles and 66% for light vehicles. Further, poor road conditions are directly responsible for increased accidents, affecting public security and safety. Automated systems providing timely monitoring could thus contribute toward enhanced environmental sustainability (Gholami et al. 2016; Melville 2010). Thus, the need for a cost-efficient, scalable, flexible and intelligent system that can inspect roads for defects from simple images with reduced human intervention is undebatable.

We see that digital image analysis based road maintenance provides cheaper solutions and better resistance to movements than sensors (Chambon and Moliard 2011; Yang and Lin 2013). Given the increased usage of surrounded digital technologies and cameras, or aerial vehicles (Zakeri et al. 2016), scene images are easily acquirable nowadays by consumer devices (Henfridsson and Lindgren 2005; Yoo 2010). In turn, this requires robust processing for intelligent decision making. Hence, this research deals with the automatic detection of cracks, the most common form of surface defects, and related surface degradation from scene images using ML techniques.

However, to the best of our knowledge, most 2-D image-based approaches work with the images taken by cameras from a close distance facing downwards directly towards the road (allowing an easier control of external conditions. Artificial lighting is also often used for image acquisition). Moreover, most of the approaches for crack detection are image-processing and segmentation based, with very limited usage of ML for detailed analysis (Koch et al. 2015; Mohan and Poobal 2017; Varadharajan et al. 2014). Such image-processing based methods are particularly sensitive to noise like thresholds and cannot be directly applied to different locations (Gavilan et al. 2011). On the contrary, images captured from the driver's front viewpoint under normal daylight presents the challenges of varied illumination and surface conditions, lack of closer or focused view on image regions, cracks and defects occupying only smaller area in the whole image, and the presence of scene and surface elements (cars, road markings, buildings, grass, etc.). In-spite of these, they are much easily acquirable and have more coverage of the area to be inspected for quick first-hand analysis, thereby reducing future search spaces. However, there is a lack of a systematic insight related to: (1) most relevant features to be used and the ML approach to follow, (2) developing similar techniques for handling different crack-types such as single, network, cracks near edges, block cracks and related degraded surface areas (BaSt 2008), (3) avoiding noisy thresholding based techniques, (4) handling front-view images for a majority of the detection and defect localization in images. Thus, in order to achieve increased automation for intelligent infrastructure management, we aim to attend the below research questions in this work:

> *RQ1: What are the most relevant feature types that can be used and selected using ML based classifier's performance, in order to detect surface cracks and related degraded surface areas on roads from the scene images captured through a driver's front-faced camera's viewpoint?*
> *RQ2: How can state-of-the-art ML techniques be applied to crack and defect detection using front-view scene images for handling different crack-types, locations and surface conditions?*

Figure 3.1 shows examples of images handled by us and our approach for data collection. Unlike many existing methods, we use front-view scene images which are more cluttered and less structured. We do not use the commonly followed edge detection, thresholding or segmentation based methods, thereby making our work challenging. We take complete scene images as input and output the recognized crack and degraded surface area on roads as shown in Figure 3.3 (C). We use extracted features from superpixels and supervised ML-based classifiers for the task at hand. Moreover, we use the classifier performance for tuning the parameters of different feature extraction algorithms. Figure 3.2 shows the approach that we follow in this study. The remainder of this paper is organized as follows: in next sections we state the related works, data collection and data preparation processes, the features used and the classifier design for road surface defect detection. Finally, we present our evaluations and the discussion.

3.2 Related Work

Some of the common automatic visual inspection methodologies for road surface evaluations are based on radar, laser, accelerometer or vibration, 3-D reconstruction, remote sensing and 2-D image-based techniques (BASt 2008; Koch et al. 2015; MnDOT 2009; Salari 2012; Staniek 2014; Zakeri et al. 2016). These approaches have both advantages and disadvantages, with approaches other than image-based ones being more expensive as they require more equipment and computation. However, image-based techniques pose many challenges for increased automation such as varied viewpoint, lighting, shadows, texture, surface-types, less or more distress coverage area within images. The techniques for 2-D road surface crack detection could be broadly classified into either more image-processing based(Mohan and Poobal 2017)or a com-

Figure 3.1: (Left- most) Our approach for data collection using a simple HD camera mounted on a pedelac taking scene images from front viewpoint. Rest of the images show examples of pre-processed road images that are used in our approach. Few types of cracks are shown.

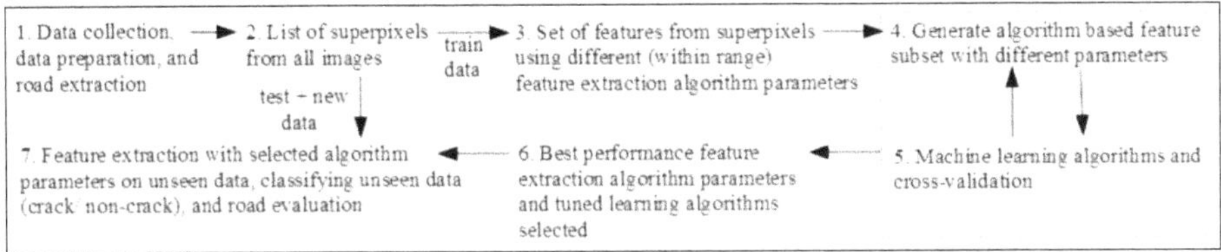

Figure 3.2: ML-based crack and defect detection approach for road condition evaluation and categorization using labeled superpixels and scene images.

bination of image-processing and ML (Koch et al. 2015). Further, these detection techniques could be classified into either using downward view-images or front-view images.

One of the common approaches in road or pavement defect evaluation is seen to be based on thresholding techniques, binarization, mathematical morphology (Teomete et al. 2005). Most image-processing based approaches assume that crack pixels are darker than non-crack pixels and use different thresholding or histogram based techniques (Mohan and Poobal 2017) depending on it. Statistical measure based approach using variance and standard deviation solely is also be seen in many works (Sinha and Fieguth 2006, Huidrom et al. 2013). A matrix operation based approach using residuals, followed by probabilistic and thresholding techniques, is used by Day et al. (2012) for analyzing durability cracking. Edge detection based systems using local curves, along with their combination with SVM, is also seen (Prasanna et al. 2012). A good overview of parametric and non-parametric ML approaches for crack detection is presented in Oliveira and Correia (2009) and the authors used mean and standard deviation as features. Li et al. (2014) used features such as rectangle area around cracked area and cracking rate (i.e. number of defect pixels in an image) with ANN for crack-type recognition (longitudinal, transverse, linear and network cracks). However, for crack detection or extraction it used Otsu's and other thresholding approaches as the first step. In Rababahh et al. (2005) thresholding based crack detection was followed by crack classification using Hough space features and edge detection, Genetic Algorithm, Self-Organizing Maps and Multilayer Perceptron; with Multilayer Perceptron outperforming the rest. An adaptive seed based approach is also seen to be used where pavement type is first classified using SVM prior to crack detection (Gavilán et al. 2011). Features are extracted here based on histogram shape descriptor that gives difference between crack and non-crack objects, and classifying them using SVM, after morphology is used. Line scan cameras were used in it. A Wavelet Transform based approach is seen in Nejad and Zekeri (2011) that uses Dynamic Neural Network and gives good results for network cracks (cluster of cracks). A Deep Learning based approach using Convolutional Neural Network (CNN) can also be seen in the literature (Pauly et al. 2017; Ruoxing et al. 2018; Zhang et al. 2016). An AdaBoost based system using Gabor filter features like, frequency, was also used for classifying cracks in into transverse or longitudinal types by Zalama et al. (2014). Wu et al. (2016) showed an ANN based approach for crack recognition, where the crack extraction and grouping is done using thresholding and morphology. As it is seen, most studies used downward-view images (with closer view) or specialized vehicle acquisition method. Furthermore, ML is seen to be used more for crack-type (like, linear, network, etc. using coverage area properties) classification (Li et al. 2014) or recognition, after considerable image-processing based approaches such as thresholding or morphology have been employed as the main step for crack detection or extraction (Koch et al. 2015; Moon and Kim 2011); making them sensitive toward noise.

On the contrary, few recent studies show growing interest in using ML extensively for crack or defect detection using front-view images, which are similar to the image types we use in this work (Varadharajan et al. 2014). In Radopoulou et al. (2016), the camera was placed much lower, closer to the license plate and the authors used the Wavelet Transform and Semantic Texton Forest ML approaches to analyze the data. Varadharajan et al. (2014) presented a Multiple Instance Learning based SVM technique for crack detection using a combination of Local Binary Pattern (LBP) texture, position and color giving 138 features, with the camera placed on the car's windshield. The approach in it helped handle subjective and weakly labeled images produced by people. However, the model missed distributed or lighter cracks and displayed similar and brightly lit surface conditions. As can be seen, the features used in various such approaches does not have easy discriminating abilities (Pauly et al. 2017). Gavilan et al. (2011) stated that location dependent results is a bottleneck in crack detection. Further, a lack of benchmark or publicly available datasets (Koch et al. 2015), along with difficult and costly image acquisition systems (Radopoulou et al. 2016), make the progress in automation slower. Thus, for an improved road surface management and increased digitalization, one should aim to procure HD images in an easier way and make digital image data availability more reachable. Using digital images for most of the major first-hand surface analysis will enhance road quality and reduce search space for follow-up intensive analysis. Furthermore, the development of intelligent techniques for handling various defects across different locations and conditions, instead of using more surface conditions and location specific approaches for enabling cross-applications has become a necessity.

3.3 Data Collection and Preparation

In this work, we collected high definition natural scene videos and images, along with their GPS values, in Germany over a period of 1 year by mounting a camera on pedelecs and e-bikes. We collected around 75 videos, each being 40 minute long, giving a large repository of images. We obtained images of 1242×720 resolution from the video clips.The images that we selected in this work belong to varied scenes such as rural and urban, varied road width and varied times such as morning and afternoon.They were all taken under normal daylight. As we process scene images taken from such front-view cameras, we first extract our region-of-interest in the scene image, i.e. road area needs to be extracted, as shown in Figure 3.3, for preparing the data for crack detection. From now on, we use the term "scene image" to refer the complete captured scene, while "road image" refers to the image with only extracted road area. The steps of pre-processing are as follows: (1) Road area extraction to generate “road images” from “scene images”. (2) Segmenting the road image into superpixels (groups of pixels) from which features are to be extracted. (3) CLAHE usage. Data preparation is shown in Figure 3.2 (steps 1 and 2). Figure 3.3 shows different aspects of our data preparation.

3.3.1 Generating Road Images from Scene Images

A scene contains various elements like, cars, buildings, trees, etc. and needs to be removed before the road area is extracted and used for surface defect detection. In this work, we used the approach in Chatterjee et al. (2017) to extract the road area region from the complete scene. We selected this approach as it helped us achieve the following: (1) The method is applicable to a wide range of scene types such as, rural and urban. So, we can use the same algorithm for

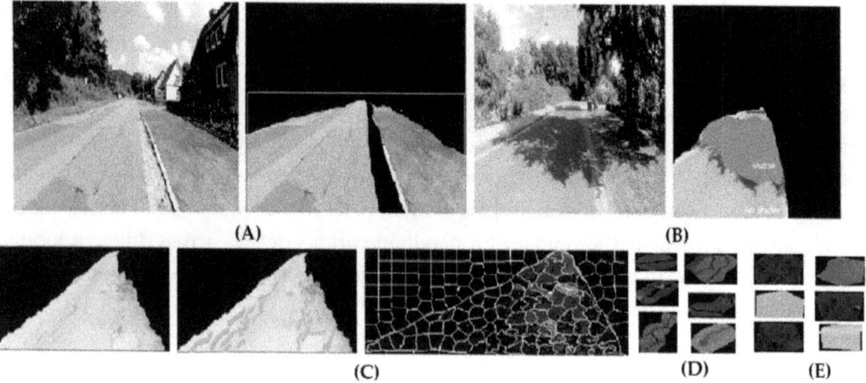

Figure 3.3: Data preparation: (A) Generated road images and region of interest (box) from scene images. (B) Basic shadow handling (shadow area in gray color). (C) Annotated cracks on the image and SLIC superpixels (in yellow) over road images. Background superpixels with black color are avoided. (D) Sample superpixels belonging to crack category. (E) Sample superpixels belonging to non-crack category.

different scene types that we handle in this work. (2) The algorithm detects the major shadow areas that could be avoided or handled accordingly, thus reducing false positives in the crack or surface defect detection step. The used approach is based on the Gaussian kernel based hybrid distance metric, linear optimization with Hungarian Algorithm and pairwise assignment from a distance matrix for hierarchical clustering. Once the road area is clustered, it is extracted as the road image as shown in Figure 3.3 (A-B).

3.3.2 Pre-processing of Road Images and Superpixel Generation

Once the road images are generated by extracting the road area from scene images, we used Hough lines to demarcate the road-side edges. Such lines are thus not considered as cracks in later stages. Following this, we resized the road images to 300×150 size and then divided the image into s_n (here, $s_n = 150$) superpixels, to group similar pixels. We used Simple Linear Iterative Clustering (SLIC) (Achanta et al. 2012) to generate the superpixels by clustering the red, green, blue color values of the pixels, along with their (x, y) location values.Furthermore, followed by the superpixel segmentation of each image, each of the superpixel undergoes histogram equalization. General histogram equalization (Gonzales and Woods 2002) provides the possibility to enhance the contrast of an image. An image with enhanced contrast is a much better input for a feature extraction algorithm. General histogram equalization might suffer losses due to over-brightness or over-darkness. To solve the information loss in general transformation we used Contrast Limited Adaptive Histogram Equalization (CLAHE) (Zuiderveld 1994). CLAHE transforms the image by calculating the histogram of each region instead of one histogram over the whole image. In this work, the original image is divided into smaller blocks called "tiles" having the size of 8×8. Then these blocks are histogram equalized. Thus, no data has been lost by extreme general histogram transformation, yet the crack region's color intensity has improved.

3.3.3 Final Road Image Dataset for Defect Detection

As our approach is based on supervised learning, it is a requirement to train the classifier models with samples. In our case, each sample is one superpixel, i.e. groups of pixels, as in Figure 3.3 (D-E). We selected 30 manually annotated images under diverse conditions. Every image is divided into s_n superpixels. Each superpixel sample belongs to one of the two categories- crack (positive) and non-crack (negative)at the broadest level. In this work, a dataset of images under diverse lighting and surface conditions have been used for annotation, as required for training and ground truth comparison. Figure 3.3 (C, second image) shows an example of an annotated image. Out of the superpixels those with black color values are not used as they are the background, as shown in Figure 3.3 (C). For every remaining valid superpixel, features are extracted and are labeled as crack (output as 1) or non-crack (output as 0) for the training. So, the regions are now encoded in terms of the feature space and we have a task of binary classification to be solved. It should be noted that the sample dataset is highly unbalanced, i.e., for every image, there are more superpixels which are non-crack than crack. One way of solving this is to generate more such data samples or superpixels belonging to diverse crack conditions. However, this requires more annotated images. Another way could be to drop some non-crack samples as many of them might have similar features. Accordingly, we balance our data by dropping similar non-crack samples and finally selected 1215 samples (containing samples for non-crack to crack in $50 : 50$ ratio). Out of these, we used 1000 samples for training and 215 samples for testing and comparison to the annotated ground truth. We also report successful crack defect detection on 80additional test images (i.e. 8828 more non-black valid test superpixel samples) with varied conditions and crack-types.

3.4 Problem Formulation

Each superpixel is a data point and we characterize it by a feature vector x. We denote the set of all feature vectors by X. Here, $x = [x1, x2, \cdots, x_m]$ with m being the total number of features per data point. For training, marked superpixels have a label $y \in Y$, where, $Y = \{0, 1\}$. The aim of the research is to find a ML approach with the combination of input features and the model, $f : X \rightarrow Y$, which maximizes the overall accuracy. The learned function, f, is the classifier which is then used to predict the label of unseen data into either class 1 (superpixel with positive condition having crack or defect) or class 0 (superpixel with negative condition having no crack or defect). In the next section we state how the features are tuned (using steps 3-5 of Figure 3.2) and selected by the classifier's accuracy.

We use the following four classifiers in this work- Gradient Boosting (GB) (Friedman 1999), Random Forest (RF) (Breiman 2001), Artificial Neural Network (ANN) (Roja 1996), and Linear Support Vector Machine (L-SVM) (Cortes and Vapnik 1995). They are shortly described here. GB and RF are typical examples of ensemble learning. For ensemble classifiers, in general, weak learners are used to form a strong learner. RF works in a parallel manner using independent classifiers following a bagging approach, while GB works sequentially following a boosting approach. Compared to RF, gradient boosted trees makes use of very small decision trees (tree stumps) (Hastie et al. 2009). The ground truth in GB is modeled by incrementally adding more trees where each tree tries to minimize the loss function evaluated on the previous model. On the other hand, RF uses many classification trees and it chooses majority vote concept to classify an object aggregating the result of these trees. ANN mimics the biological neuron characteristics and gives the non-linear function approximation. It typically consists of multiple layers with nodes known as input layers for receiving signals and data, hidden layers, and output layer that provide final results. The layers are inter-connected and weights are learned to adjust the flow of input signals across layers for minimizing the error. Binary SVM classifier works on the concept of decision hyperplane that separates a set of objects within two different classes by maximizing the margin between them. The objects lying on the margin hyperplanes are called support vectors.

3.5 Feature Extraction

Following our research approach in Figure 3.2, we use extracted features from image regions, i.e. superpixels, to classify them as regions containing defect or no defect. Features are the image descriptors which help encode regions. The texture and edge features could be intuitively understood to be more relevant than other kind of features, as cracks are inherently regions of anomalies or discontinuities. We experimented with state-of-the-art features,such as statistical measures, Grey Level Co-occurrence Matrix (GLCM) (Haralick 1979), Gabor (Daugman 1985; Gabor 1946), Histogram of Oriented Gradients (HoG) (Dalal and Triggs 2005), Local Binary Patterns (LBP) (Silva et al. 2015), different color channel (Gonzales and Woods 2002) variants and histograms (e.g. HSV, RGB, LSV),as well as, Sobel and Canny edge features (Canny 1986; Gonzales and Woods 2002). Selection of these algorithms was motivated by their varied use in the literature and that a crack in essence is an edge or a typical change in gradient. Using classifier's accuracy metric and incremental subset feature selection process (steps 3-5 in Figure 3.2), we selected the following 40 features for each of the superpixels: variance, skewness, 6 GLCM features and 32 features from a newly defined feature variant called Variance-of-Gabor (VoG).

To start discussing the features, variance and skewness are calculated using the flattened array of grayscale pixel values, say G_x, within a superpixel S. This array contains $\#(G_x)$ elements. In grayscale, every image pixel gets a weighted average of $0.29R + 0.56G + 0.11B$ from its R, G, B individual colors. Variance simply measures the spread or variability in the data and skewness measures the asymmetry or imbalance within the data distribution, which in this case could be defined for a superpixel as: $Var(S) = \frac{1}{\#(G_x)}) \sum_{i=1}^{\#(G_x)} (G_{x_i} - \bar{G_x})^2$. Similarly, $Skew(S)$ is obtained.

Apart from these, we also use GLCM second-order statistical properties of an image region (superpixel in our case) as texture features. Unlike first-order properties like variance, GLCM properties or features consider spatial relationship between neighboring pixels. The GLCM matrix is calculated on the grayscale image and six features of homogeneity (g_h), angular second moment (g_{asm}), energy (g_{e2}), correlation (g_c), contrast ($g_{contrast}$) and dissimilarity (g_d) are extracted from each of the superpixel as in equations (3.1 – 3.5). Energy g_{e2} is square of g_{asm}. The GLCM matrix is derived from frequency of each reference pixel and the neighboring one.

$$g_h(\theta, d_o) = \sum_{i,j} \frac{1}{1-(i-j)^2} p(i,j), \tag{3.1}$$

$$g_{e2}(\theta, d_o) = \sum_{i,j} p(i,j)^2, \tag{3.2}$$

$$g_c(\theta, d_o) = \sum_{i,j} \frac{(i-\mu_i)(j-\mu_j)}{\sigma_i \sigma_j} p(i,j), \tag{3.3}$$

$$g_{contrast}(\theta, d_o) = \sum_{i,j} p(i,j)(i-j)^2, \tag{3.4}$$

$$g_d(\theta, d_o) = |i-j|p(i,j), \tag{3.5}$$

where, the probability of change from graylevel i to j at a distance d_o and directional angle θ is given by $p(i,j)$. Distance should be small to consider closer pixels. Moreover, using the feature importance ranking of the RF classifiers, these features could be ranked as follows: correlation, homogeneity, contrast, dissimilarity, energy and angular second moment. GLCM is parameterized by (d_o, θ) i.e. angle θ (giving direction for the spatial relationship) and an offset d_o (neighbour pixels to be considered). The number of graylevel is taken as 256. Here, $\theta = 0°, 45°, 90°, 135°$ and $d_o = 1, 2, 3, \cdots, 8$ are the used ranges for the parameters for tuning using the classifier's accuracy metric to select their best combination of (d_o, θ). Figure 3.4 provides example of the effect of parameter tuning on final ANN classifier's accuracy.

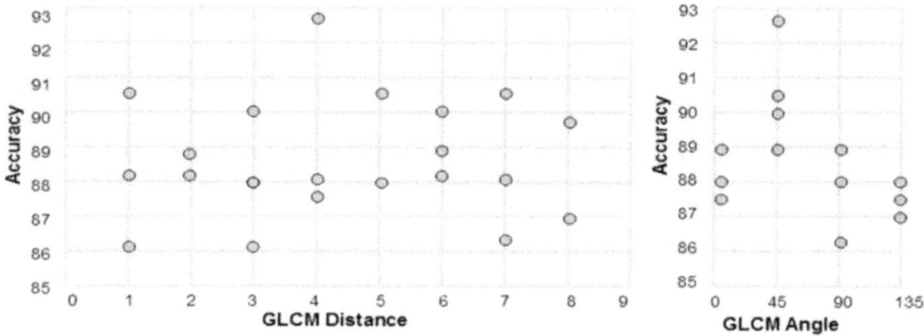

Figure 3.4: Effect of GLCM parameters on ANN classifier's performance. Seven percent variation can be seen in accuracy (in percent) depending on GLCM parameters. For each value of x-axis, multiple dots show accuracy for it when combined with other parameters.

3.5.1 Variance-of-Gabor (VoG) features

Gabor filter based approaches are widely applied for a variety of computer vision use cases such as object detection, texture analysis, edge detections, to name a few, owing to their similarity to human visual system characteristics. When Gabor filters are overlaid on an image, useful edge and texture features could be extracted as the filters respond to pixel positions where a major change in texture or edge takes place. Gabor filter is built as a product of Gaussian and sinusoid functions. The parameters of it are: α(controls the orientation of the filters), k (Gabor filter kernel size), σ (the scale parameter of the Gaussian function), λ (controls the wavelength of the Gabor filter sinusoids) in pixels. α is one of the most important parameters and for each of the α, a filter is produced, thus giving a series of filter bank. α also determines the angular response of the Gabor filter. For instance, $\alpha = 0°$ indicates that the Gabor filter only responds to horizontal features. Here, α is taken in the range of $0°$ to $180°$ (to avoid symmetry and directional redundancy) and 32 filter orientations are defined at an equal interval of $5.625°$ in order to get the features at different angles. Thus, $\alpha = [\alpha, \alpha_{i+1}, \cdots, \alpha_{i+31}]$ with $i = 1$ and $\alpha_{i+1} - \alpha_i = 5.625°$. At the end, a filtered image is generated for each of the α orientation, as in Figure 3.5.

We define Variance-of-Gabor (VoG) features of any superpixel following equation (3.6). Thus, for every superpixel having b Gabor filter bank, i.e. orientations for the θ, a VoG feature set of size b is obtained using the corresponding Gabor filtered images as follows:

$$VoG(S) = [Var(G_1), \cdots, Var(G_b)]. \tag{3.6}$$

Here, S is the superpixel and G_i is the ith Gabor filtered image with $i = 1 \cdots b$. $Var(G_i)$ is the variance of the ith Gabor image. We take $b = 32$ as it gives the best performance. For generating VoG features, we need to generate Gabor filtered images of the superpixels for each of the α using the filter parameters: k, σ, λ, ϕ. We automatically tune k, σ and λ using classifier's accuracy metric and obtain α with 32 orientations, $k = 11$, $\sigma = 15$, $\lambda = 10$, $\phi = 0$ for generating 32 VoG features. It has been noticed that larger σ and λ fade away the edges and make the filtered image blurred. As an example, Figure 3.6 show the tuning process for two of these parameters, σ and λ.

Figure 3.5: Sample Gabor filtered images of a superpixel for each corresponding orientation.

In order to tune the parameters of the feature extraction algorithms we used, i.e., GLCM and Gabor filter, we first took algorithm-specific feature subsets with different parameters and tuned the parameters using classifier's accuracy, as shown in steps 3 – 5 of Figure 3.2. Once the tuned parameters of feature extraction algorithms are obtained, the classifier's hyperparameters are extensively tuned using the complete feature set. Here, 10 fold cross-validation has been used

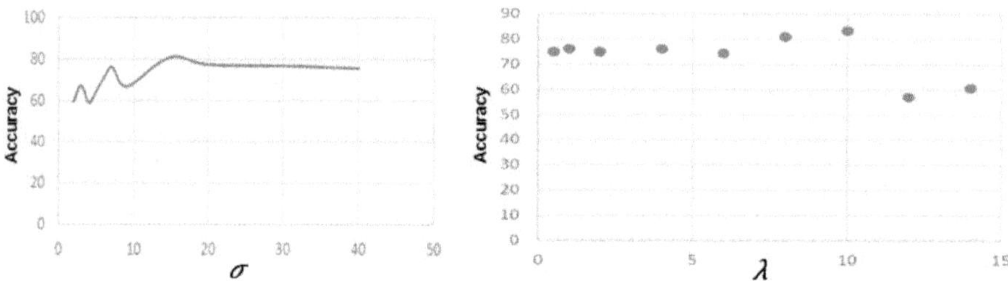

Figure 3.6: Parameter tuning of the Gabor filter for VoG features using classifier's performance.

for all the tuning. Finally, we have well-tuned 40 features, as given in Table 3.2, for each superpixel. The development platform in this work is Python 2.7 and we used libraries of OpenCV 3.3.0, SciPy, scikit-image and scikit-learn.

Variance, skewness, 32 VoG features with $k = 11$, $\sigma = 15$, $\lambda = 10$ for Gabor filter and 6 GLCM features (g_c, g_h, $g_{contrast}$, g_d, g_{asm}, g_{e2}) with best combination of (d_o, θ) as $\theta = 45°$, $d_o = 5$.

Table 3.2: List of features extracted from each superpixel using the tuned parameters.

3.6 Evaluations

We used here precision (P), recall (R), F1-measure for comparing the four classifiers as follows: $P = \frac{TP}{TP+FP}$, $R = \frac{TP}{TP+FN}$, $F1 = 2\frac{P.R}{P+R}$, $Accuracy = \frac{TP+TN}{TP+TN+FP+FN}$. Here, TP gives true positives (crack detected as crack), TN gives true negatives (non-crack detected as non-crack), FP gives false positive (detecting non-crack area as crack), FN gives false negative (detecting crack as non-crack). All evaluations are at the superpixel level.In total, we used 1000 data points for training, 215 first test data, and 8828 additional new test data from 80 test images.The results are given in Table 3.3 and Table 3.4.

The hyperparameters of all four classifiers are selected using grid search and a 10 fold cross-validation. In GB classifier, an ensemble of weak learners of Decision Trees are considered and Logistic function is taken as the loss function; while, hyperparameters like maximum depth of the estimator is taken to be 7 and minimum required samples for splitting at the inter nodes is taken to be 8. For ANN construction, features are standardized prior to the learning process, along with the input layer size of 41 nodes (with a bias), 1 hidden layer, and a learning rate of 0.001 being used. For RF, maximum depth of trees is taken as 18 and minimum samples for splitting at internal nodes is taken to be 8. The number of estimators with 300 showed convergence for it. Finally, L-SVM learner with a linear kernel having the regularization penalty parameter set to 0.01 has been used for comparison. Once we obtain the learned predictions, we generate two outputs for visualization of the results: an auto-annotated image showing location of detected cracks and defective areas, as shown in Figure 3.7, and percentage of superpixels detected as crack. This helps to rank road surfaces, thus helping to come up with maintenance strategies. Higher percentage indicates that the road has severe defects and needs attention.

Classifier	Accuracy (%)	P (%)	R (%)	F1 (%)	TP	FP	TN	FN
GB	**91.16**	92.38	**89.81**	**91.08**	**97**	8	99	**11**
ANN	90.24	93.94	86.11	89.86	93	6	101	15
RF	90.69	**94.85**	85.98	90.61	92	**5**	**103**	15
L-SVM	74.88	75.96	73.15	74.53	79	25	82	29

Table 3.3: Performance of the classifiers on 215 test data.

Classifier	Accuracy (%)	P (%)	R (%)	F1 (%)
GB	92.77	87.62	94.88	91.11
ANN	90.63	81.37	93.91	87.19
RF	91.82	88.81	93.02	90.87

Table 3.4: Performance of the classifiers on additional 8828 test data from various locations, surface conditions and crack-types.

3.7 Discussion and Future Work

Digitalization in today's time has given rise to unprecedented traces of data (Goes 2014). Leveraging the process of datafication, through which consumer devices are being turned into sources of big data (Galliers et al. 2015), one may derive significant value for society through ML techniques, using data generated by portable and connected devices during consumers' everyday activities (Günther et al. 2017). In this work, we provided evidence for the effectiveness of data analytics based on data gathered through commodity devices (i.e., electric bikes equipped with cameras) that can be operated by standard consumers. More specifically, we

multiple cracks over the region
no crack
single crack
network cracks clustered at locations

(A)

network cracks
single crack and patch

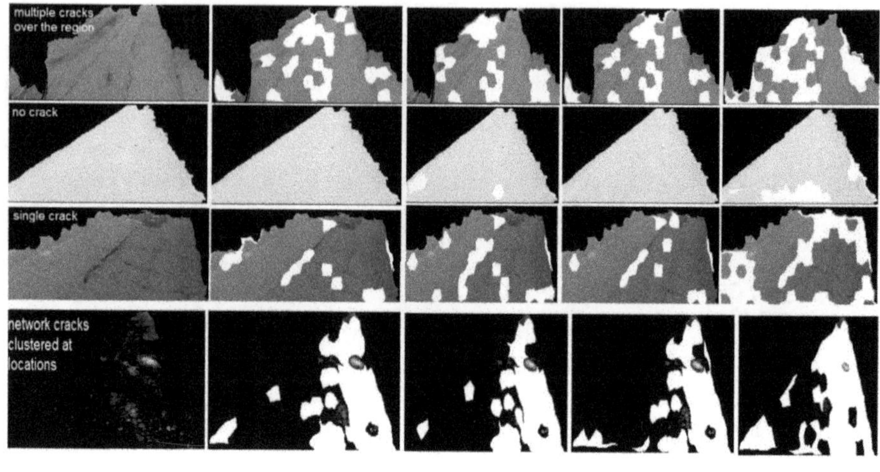

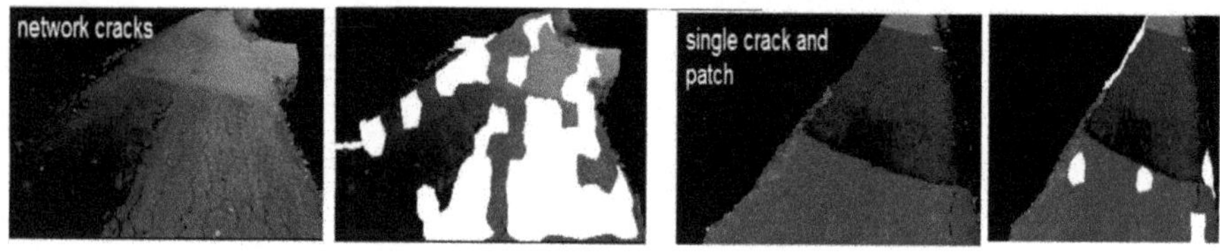

(B)

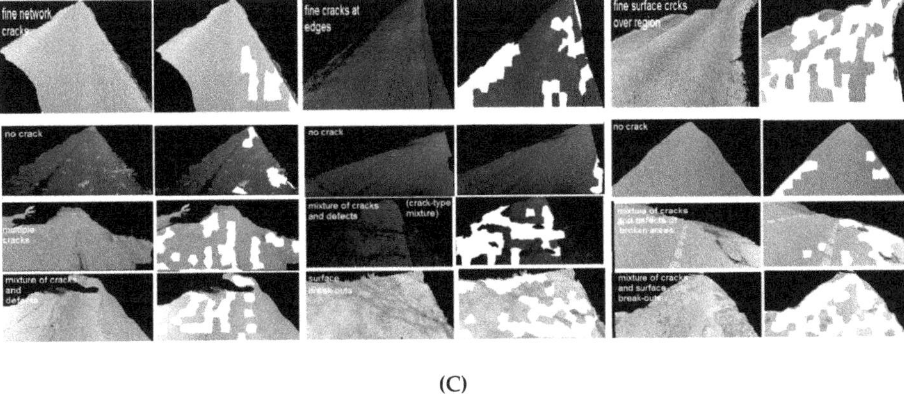

(C)

Figure 3.7: Detected crack areas on images marked in white. (A) First image is the original image, second image shows marked area (superpixels) detected to contain cracks using RF, third image using ANN, fourth using GB, fifth using L-SVM. (B - C) Crack detections with RF for given original images. Few crack-types and conditions are marked.

successfully developed a ML approach for detecting cracks and related defects in normal scene images to facilitate road maintenance process. We used state-of-the-art feature extraction algorithms and tuned their parameters using ML, along with incremental subset feature select ion method. Finally, we used ML to classify the image regions into crack and non-crack using tuned feature extraction algorithms and classifiers. Figure 3.7 shows different illumination, surface conditions, locations, crack-types (such as single, network, cracks at edges, etc.) and related surface defects or distresses that are handled by our approach for defective region detection.

This research contributes to research streams of decision support systems (Banker and Kaufmann 2004) by helping in intelligent decision making using automated tools for road maintenance and monitoring. The way front-view images are handled in this study for crack detection using the developed ML-based approach in Figure 3.2 shows the technical possibilities of a future modular and flexible decision support system, based on the algorithms developed in this work. This could help pavement management systems (BASt 2008; FHWA 2016) to come up with a pavement condition index (e.g. bad, medium, good, etc.) (BASt, 2008) in an automated manner and with reduced human interventions, for example using percentage of cracks detected.

Moreover, as we work with front-view images, image acquisition and analysis becomes cheaper and easier because simple everyday devices such as smartphones, car and traveler's cameras could be used, contributing toward a decentralized crowdsourcing based system for road condition assessment (Laubis et al. 2016). In this context, individual cars for example could be employed for crack detection and quick monitoring. GPS-based mapping systems may be used to combine different or same road segments that are analyzed separately in such cases.Additionally, autonomous vehicles can detect cracks and avoid such areas, thus incurring lower vehicle operating costs and select safer routes, consequently affecting road safety (Stilgoe 2017). Lately, using commodity devices, big data and crowdsourcing approaches for decision making in maintenance services is observed to be on a rise (Galliers et al. 2015; Nitsche, 2014). This helps in timely maintenance of roads to have less backlog and come up with strategies for efficient resource planning and monitoring (Laubis et al. 2017; Tang and Sun 2012). Additionally, citizens could be engaged in activities involving road monitoring such as voluntary data acquisition (e.g. from traveler's or cars).Intelligent decision making could also help in developing alert systems to notify citizens for surface defects and cracks so that they can select safer routes. Thus, it enhances collaboration between citizen and government for inclusive information technology-based societal development and smart services (Fink 2010). For such services one needs to develop approaches for analyzing road surface condition for defects automatically, timely, and quickly; motivating us to develop the ML-based approach in this work for intelligent decision making.

The ML approach for defect detection in this work shows robust behavior when first-order statistical features of variance and skewness are extensively used, along with GLCM second-order statistical features and Gabor filtering for feature extraction. While, first-order features showed variability over an image area or region, second-order features considered more local and neighborhood properties. Additionally, defining the new feature variant called Variance-of-Gabor (VoG) helped us to process crack and non-crack superpixels at different orientations. Table 3.2 gives the final set of features and their parameters. Here, we followed the incremental subset feature selection process and tuned feature extraction algorithm's parameters automatically using ML algorithm's performance metric; moving towards a systematic approach for feature mapping. Texture related features show more adaptability to various illumination conditions than edge-based features. To discuss their effectiveness, GLCM features alone, along with standard deviation or variance features, were found highly discriminative, while Gabor filters helped to make the system more generalized and adaptable by extracting interesting edges. Similarly, VoG features alone also show a high accuracy, as seen in Figure 3.6, whereas the best combination of identified features provided a higher accuracy of around 91.16%, as given in Table 3.3. However, only non-filtered texture features showed more sensitivity to lighting, roughness, or acquisition distance.

It is seen from the evaluations in Table 3.3 and Table 3.4 that RF and GB perform better following highest accuracy, good F1 and lowest false positives. L-SVM did not perform well. ANN's performance decreased for the dataset with varied conditions in Table 3.3, with a specific decrease in precision. This is because, it has been noticed that ANN gives more false positives for surfaces with very little crack area and single cracks (as in Figure 3.7 (C - first row, first image set)) or absolutely no crack (as in Figure 3.7 (A - second row, C - second row, second image set)). RF and GB can handle both single or network cracks and does not give many false positives even if crack does not exist. Overall performance shows better fit of ensemble ML techniques such as RF and GB for the task at hand, even when images from different location than those used for training were used. It is noted that lower false positives are an important criteria for defect detection, while not compromising the overall accuracy, and Random Forest shows highly consistent detection for all the datasets.The presented approach is applicable across different locations and crack-types.

In comparison to other related works for crack defect detection, we did not use downward-view images under controlled external conditions, thresholding or morphological approaches as a major detection step, or costly equipment systems with lasers or radars (MnDOT 2009;

Wu et al. 2016; Zalama et al. 2014). Moreover, we provide a systematic approach for ML based crack and related defect detection using feature selection and tuning feature extraction algorithm's parameters and a thorough comparison among different ML techniques. It is also seen that unlike this work, in most related works crack-type (e.g. linear, network) classification or recognition is done using ML using features such as crack angle, covered area, whereas the major crack detection or extraction step still uses noisy thresholding based approaches; making the overall approach sensitive toward cross-location application. Finally, as we used simple 2-D images which are easily acquirable, our approach is flexible, cost-efficient and scalable for either wider or narrower roads. The presented approach also makes data acquisition for such image-based maintenance easier as many service vehicles such as public transportation systems like buses and taxis, or patrolling cars could be fitted with front-view cameras to gather necessary images and data (Mertz 2011). This effects directly the increased automation for timely maintenance on local and urban roads which are seen to experience the highest safety issues (Gleave 2014). We can thus see that the immense use fullness of increased automation for infrastructure management using big data and ML can reduce human effort and increase the timeliness of maintenance. Moreover, as detection of defects is delayed, the defects (e.g. cracks) become worse and often need more time and money to rehabilitate and repair them. For example, if network cracks are not timely attended they could develop into potholes over time. This clearly shows the positive impacts of data-driven innovations (Abella et al. 2017) to create value using simple image data for continuous detection, monitoring and road maintenance. Thus, the approach for intelligent analysis of 2-D images in this study could bring about quicker monitoring of road maintenance, lower costs, provide safer routes and an enhanced traveling experience for the public.

Limitations and Future Work

One of the major limitations of the proposed approach is the lack of information on the depth of visual entities arising from the 2-D nature of the images. Nevertheless, detecting cracks and defects from these images and obtaining GPS locations of defective roads are major first steps towards automating road maintenance. Thereby, most of the road inspection tasks can be performed automatically and search spaces can be reduced drastically. Rather than using expensive sensors and 3-D analysis systems in general, images can be supplemented with 3-D information only at these specific defective search locations.The need to invest in costly equipment or systems at a larger scale can thereby be eliminated. Additionally, external elements such as drainage, manholes, as marked in Figure 3.7 (C- third row, first image set), could cause false detection. Another limitation is that the approach suffers if the surface contains weathering, swelling, or rough edges (as in Figure 3.7 (C- last row)), then the crack gets detected at the junctions although no explicit crack is visible. In future, we plan to handle these defects by incorporating pavement-type categorization technique, as defects or crack-types depend on pavement surface-type and material. Additionally, we aim to extend our approach for detecting other defects such as potholes, patches and classify cracks into types, e.g., linear or network category.

Finally, it can be stated that the approach developed in this paper constitutes a technology artifact (Lee et al. 2015) comprising ML models that process constant inputs of image and video data to automatically detect road surface defects. While we sketch the shape of the information flow and the social dynamics required to apply the system, we have not formally designed an information and social artifact that, along with the technology artifact, are necessary to form an information systems artifact (Lee et al. 2015). Therefore, we encourage researchers to further study the requirements for applying ML-based, crowdsourced surface defect detection in everyday life and – based on our technical contributions – develop a solution by considering the interaction of different actors, data sources and processes of data analysis.

3.8 Conclusion

In this work, we presented an ML-based approach for crack detection on road surfaces of natural 2-D scene images taken from a driver's viewpoint under normal daylight. We propose the usage of simple images with regard to the automation in defect detection, given their cost-efficiency, quickness and flexibility. In addition, this simplicity provides scalable solutions that could reduce manual efforts and long-term costs for maintenance, while increasing public safety. We used state-of-the-art feature extraction algorithms at the superpixel level, such as, GLCM, statistical measures of variance and skewness, and defined a new feature variant called Variance-of-Gabor using the Gabor filters. Tuning of important parameters of these feature extraction algorithms and incremental feature selection were automatically done in a systematic manner using ML algorithm's performance metric. It has been noticed that texture based features, after being filtered, are highly effective for the task of crack and defect detection in such images. We compared state-of-the-art classifiers like, Gradient Boosting, Artificial Neural Network, Random Forest and Linear Support Vector Machines, along with various feature extraction algorithms for the task at hand. Random Forest and Gradient Boosting show the best overall performance with the lowest false positives and high accuracy. As a result, crack regions belonging to different crack-types, such as single or network, and related defects are successfully detected on road images belonging to varied external conditions and locations. In this way, identified defects are located on road images, thereby helping in road surface condition evaluation by inspecting the defective area within an image.

Chapter 4: Defect Detection on Road Surfaces Using Fuzzy Image Descriptors and Keypoint Matching

Title	Defect Detection on Road Surfaces Using Fuzzy Image Descriptors and Keypoint Matching
Authors	Sromona Chatterjee[1], Mohit Kumar[2], Lutz M. Kolbe[1] [1] Chair of Information Management, University of Göttingen, Germany [2] Faculty of Computer Science and Electrical Engineering, University of Rostock, Germany and Software Competence Center, Hagenberg, Austria ∗ Corresponding author: sromona.chatterjee@wiwi.uni-goettingen.de
Outlet	Submitted at the Engineering Applications of Artificial Intelligence (as of July 2020)
Abstract	Traditionally, road maintenance has been a time consuming and manual process. Lately, using easily acquirable front-view scene images for road maintenance are seen to provide quicker and flexible solutions for infrastructure management. Here, we use simple front-view 2-D images for crack detection on road surfaces. In this work, we detect cracks at pixel level using a keypoint matching approach between a constant reference crack image and query images. To obtain the keypoints, we first convert the original intensity image to it's gradient image. In general, crack pixels are characterized better by higher gradient values. Consequently, Gamma Mixture Fuzzy Model (GMFM) based clustering has been used here to generate edge-based keypoints. After the keypoints are obtained, we encode the keypoints with fuzzy descriptors. Finally, we match the keypoints using KL-divergence between two Dirichlet distributions in order to find which keypoints in the query image match with that of the reference crack image. These matched keypoints are taken as crack pixels and are located in the query image. Evaluations on an experimentally collected image dataset comprising of varied road surfaces and conditions show promising results for crack detection using the developed approach in this work.
Keywords	Defect detection, crack detection, pavement management, gamma mixture model, fuzzy image descriptors, keypoint matching

Table 4.1: Fact sheet for chapter 4.

4.1 Introduction

Defects on road surfaces directly influence quality of the roads, economy and vehicle operating costs; requiring periodic checks and maintenance. Detecting defects such as cracks on road surfaces using images is an active research area for effective road management (Eisenbach et al. 2017; Gopalkrishnan 2018; Koch et al. 2015; PMIS 2011). However, roads are still predominantly monitored manually (Laubis et al. 2016, 2017; Radopoulou et al. 2016). Most images for road surface analysis are obtained using specialized vehicles which are highly costly, at times could be around $\$800,000$ (BASt 2008; Radopoulou et al. 2016); making them unaffordable for most road authorities or agencies, and being used infrequently. This results in major maintenance backlog (Gleave 2014). Further, due to their large sizes they may not be used on narrower roads or side walks. In today's time of digitalization, we are continuously surrounded by devices which could be easily used for obtaining large amount of data in affordable ways, such as by using smartphones, car cameras, etc. (Mertz 2011; Tedeschi and Benedetto 2016; Yoo 2010). For example, it can be seen in Mertz (2011) how simple service vehicles could be used within cities for acquiring images and defect detection on road surfaces. Thus, simple consumer devices could facilitate intelligent decision making for road management; thereby motivating us to use simple cameras to capture 2-D images of scenes around us and use them for defect detection in this work.

Most of the crack detection approaches that use camera images are seen to be more image-processing based using concepts related to thresholding, morphology, segmentation, edge detection (Chambon and Moliard 2011; Koch et al. 2015; Mohan and Poobal 2017). Lately, more works are seen using machine learning and computer vision in this domain (Gopalkrishnan 2018; Koch et al. 2015; Radopoulou et al. 2016). Generally, machine learning based systems for crack detection follow a classification based approach by extracting required features and classifying the pixels as crack or non-crack. Several methods related to texture/ color/ edge/ geometric features, along with supervised learning based classifiers are seen in the literature (Chatterjee et al. 2017; Prasanna et al. 2012; Tedeschi and Benedetto 2016; Varadharajan et al. 2014). Recently, more deep learning based approaches are also seen in the literature (Eisenbach et al. 2017). However, most of these works operate on 2-D images of the road surfaces acquired using cameras on specialized vehicles having focused or closer-view of the surfaces, or under controlled lighting (Eisenbach et al. 2017; Gavilan et al. 2011); making image acquisition costly and not flexible. Additionally, supervised approaches in general require large amount of labeled training images. They may also face challenges while handling thinner or lighter cracks, and for locating crack pixels precisely on images.

From this perspective and that defective crack pixels are in essence anomalies on road surfaces, we present an unsupervised approach in this work to handle the problem of crack and related defect detection and localization on road surfaces using an analytical model based approach. In our approach, we use mixture of Gamma distributions to cluster pixels for generating keypoints, followed by defining pixel-level fuzzy theoretic based feature descriptors at the keypoints, and finally a keypoint matching mechanism between a "reference" image's feature descriptors and the "query" image's feature descriptors.

Fuzzy descriptors are shown to provide distinctive characteristics for matching interesting points across image for various image matching applications (Kumar et al. 2016, 2019). As we are following a keypoint matching approach, we match fuzzy feature descriptors at the keypoints of a reference defective (containing cracks) image with that of a query image to see if both these images (images are defined as a collection of descriptors for all keypoints) are similar enough. Based on similarity, the query image can be nominated as a "defective" image i.e. the query image contains cracks and defective pixels. The reference image that we used and examples of query images are shown in Figure 4.1. An example of keypoint matching in this work is provided in Figure 4.2. Thus, in our approach, every new image in our database is considered as a query image that needs to be classified as a defective image or non-defective image. Further, in this work we use 2-D front-view scene images which are acquired from the driver's viewpoint under normal daylight. To the best of our knowledge no work until now uses an analytical model based on fuzzy image feature descriptors, coupled by a keypoint matching mechanism, for crack detection and localization on roads in front-view scene images. Hence, the research questions that we intend to attend here are the following:

> *RQ1: How can we generate keypoints, i.e. potential candidate crack pixels, in images for defect detection?*
> *RQ2: How can we model image features of such defective pixels using a fuzzy-theoretic based feature descriptors at the keypoints?*
> *RQ3: How can we detect and locate actual defective crack pixels in query images using a keypoint matching mechanism between the reference and the query images? By this we mean, a potential candidate defective pixel is finally detected as the real defective pixel in the query image if it's features are similar to that of reference image's pixels. The matching mechanism thus gives the "degree of belongingness" of query image's descriptors to that of the reference image.*

Figure 4.1: Reference image and examples of query images used in this work. (A) The constant reference crack image used in our work. (B - C) Examples of query images which are to be classified to contain cracks or not.

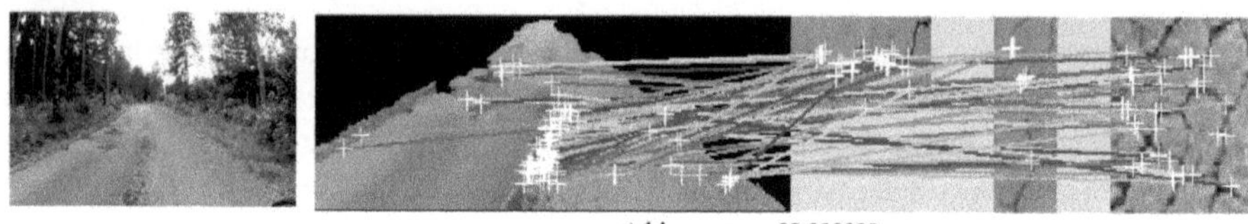

Figure 4.2: Example of a scene image (left most), corresponding query image containing only the road image (middle one), and matched keypoints between query and the reference image. Crack and defective pixels are localized on the query image post keypoint matching. High matching score of 83 shows that the query image definitely contains crack pixels.

4.2 The Framework

The framework that we follow in this work is shown in Figure 4.3. The steps are shown in the figure for both reference and query images. The major steps are the following:

1. A constant reference image is created (Figure 4.1, (A)).
2. Extract road area from the scene image using a road area detection approach, as discussed in the data preparation section below. Figure 4.2 (middle image) gives an example of a road image, which is then taken as the query image.
3. Keypoint generation using Gamma Mixture Fuzzy Model (GMFM) (Kumar et al. 2016) based clustering in the query image and in the reference image are performed separately using the following steps:
    - Image transformation: Transform the query and reference images into their corresponding gradient images.
    - Obtain potential candidate defective pixels on the transformed images, i.e. the keypoints, using GMFM-based clustering. Here, pixels with higher intensity gradients

are identified as edges using GMFM-based clustering and are taken as keypoints. GMFM has been adapted in this work for keypoint generation and shows stable, as well as, improved results in contrast to state-of-the-art algorithm like, Canny edge detection, as GMFM does not require threshold to identify the edges.

- After keypoints are obtained using GMFM (Figure 4.6), the orientations of these keypoints are obtained. For this, detected edge pixels are taken as keypoints, and we associate each of these edge-based keypoints to sift-based keypoints (Lowe 2004), such that these keypoints are centered at the edge pixel and has a scale of 2. Thus, orientations of these keypoints are then obtained using the sift-based approach in Lowe (2004).

4. An analytical model from Kumar et al. (2016) is used for defining fuzzy descriptors at the keypoints for both the reference and the query image using the orientation values of the keypoints.

5. A keypoint matching mechanism based on KL-divergence and Dirichlet distribution (see Figure 4.2) is developed to quantify the "degree of belongingness" of the query image's fuzzy feature descriptors to the reference image's fuzzy feature descriptors. The mechanism provides number of matched keypoints in the query image, as well as location of those keypoints.

6. The matched keypoints are marked on the query image as defective or crack pixels.

7. The number of matched keypoints in query images are then finally used to rank the query images. More matched keypoints implies more defective pixels; thereby implying that the road condition in the query image is bad.

The novelty of this work is that we developed an unsupervised approach using a combination of GMFM-based clustering for keypoint generation, fuzzy-theoretic based feature descriptor generation, and KL-divergence based keypoint matching for crack detection and localization in 2-D front-view images.

Our approach can be seen as an alternative to the traditional classifier based systems and we handle not only wider cracks, but also lighter cracks, for front-view scene images acquired under normal daylight and varied conditions. Additionally, unlike the classifier based systems, our approach do not require labeled training images; thus avoiding human bias, manual effort, and non-uniformity for labeling tasks. Moreover, considering that crack (defective) pixels are always less than non-crack (non-defective) pixels in images, here we propose that a mixture of Gamma distributions could better approximate such distribution of gradient values of the pixels than mostly followed Gaussian distribution. Hence, we develop a robust Gamma Mixture Fuzzy Model (GMFM) based clustering approach for keypoint generation that gives us potential candidate defective pixels. Furthermore, it has been previously seen that a combination of fuzzy membership function based feature descriptors and image matching shows more robustness and results in less number of wrong matches between images than traditional histogram based approaches such as SIFT (Kumar et al. 2016, 2019); thus motivating us to use the fuzzy descriptors in this work for crack and defect detection. The fuzzy-theoretic based approach also helps us to handle uncertainties and noise. This approach helps us to handle defect detection and localization for different crack-types (e.g. single, network (BASt 2008)), surface conditions under darker scenes, and lighter or thinner cracks in an unsupervised manner. Thus, the major contributions of this paper are as follows:

1. Presenting a novel Gamma Mixture Fuzzy Model based clustering technique for initial edge detection and localization of potential candidate crack pixels in images.These candidate pixels are taken as keypoints.

2. A combination of fuzzy image descriptors for keypoints and a KL-divergence based keypoint matching mechanism between images. KL-divergence between two Dirichlet distributions is considered to give the matching metric. This helps to measure the "degree of belongingness" of the query image's descriptors to the reference image's descriptor for detecting and locating actual crack and related defective pixels on the query image.

The rest of the paper is organized as follows: in the next section we state the related works, data preparation process, background concepts, and the methodology used for crack and related defect detection in this work. In the methodology section we briefly describe the Gamma distribution and GMFM-based clustering for keypoint generation and localization, followed by deriving fuzzy feature descriptors at the keypoints. After this, we present the last step of our system design, i.e. a KL-divergence and Dirichlet distribution based keypoint matching approach to detect defective pixels on road images. Finally, we present our evaluations on the collected image dataset and conclude our paper with a conclusion.

4.3 Related Work

Various methods such as vision-based techniques using 2-D images (Eisenbach et al. 2017; Varadharajan et al. 2014) or 3-D image analysis (Salari 2012; Staniek 2014) could be seen to be employed for road surface crack detection. In these publications the authors describe how pavement distresses could be detected using 3-D depth information and stereo images. 3-D

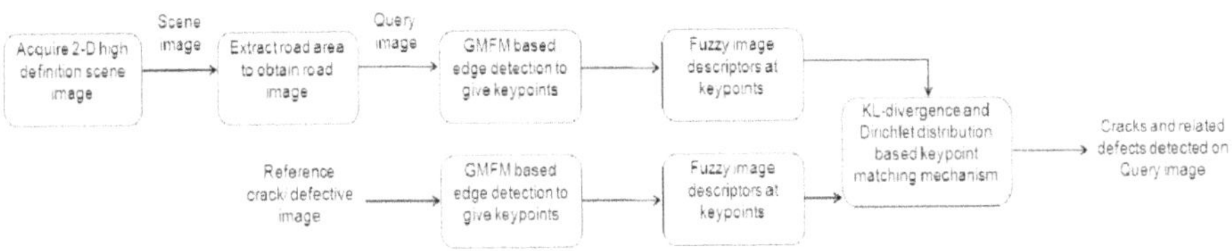

Figure 4.3: Framework for a fuzzy theoretic based feature descriptor and keypoint matching approach for detection and localization of crack and related defects in 2-D scene images.

approaches often include costly equipment such as laser scanners and computationally costly methods. In Staniek (2014), the author give how ANN and stereo images could be used for road surface evaluation.

Among all, 2-D image based ones require less equipment and computation. In this work, we aim to do crack detection using vision-based 2-D image analysis techniques. Some of the most common approaches for such images use image-processing based techniques such as thresholding, edge detection, binarization or histograms (Chambon and Moliard 2011; Mohan and Poobal 2017). Lately, machine learning is seen to be more used for crack detection (Li et al. 2014; Oliveira and Correia 2009, 2014; Varadharajan et al. 2014). Image features related to statistical measures, coupled with image-processing and decision logic, is also seen (Huidrom et al. 2013). Morphological dilation, morphological erosion, connected component and chain-coding techniques are also used here. In Kapela et al. (2015) a Histogram of Oriented Gradients (HoG) based crack detection approach is given for asphalt road surface types. Gabor filter based image features are also seen to be used in Salman (2013).

In Li et al. (2014), the authors classify different types of crack (transverse, longitudinal, linear, network) using bounded rectangle area around cracks and Artificial Neural Network (ANN), once crack pixels are detected using Otsu's thresholding approach. In Zhang et al. (2014), Support Vector Machine (SVM) and K-Nearest Neighbor are used for classifying cracks on subway tunnels, once cracks are segmented using morphology and thresholding techniques. In it, histogram shape descriptor that gives spatial shape difference between crack and non-crack objects is used as a feature, while, quantification of crack width and length are based on a skeleton graph. In Gavilan et al. (2011) Support Vector Machine (SVM) and histogram shape descriptor is used for detecting racks. In Nejad and Zakeri (2011) a Wavelet Transform and Neural Network based approach is used. Authors in Varadharajan et al. (2014) used SVM, along with Multiple Instance Learning and 138 hand crafted features, such as Local Binary Pattern (LBP), to identify cracks on front-view images. In Radopoulou et al. (2016) the authors also used front-view images, along with Wavelet Transform and Semantic Texton Forest, to identify cracks. While, Tedeschi and Benedetto (2016) gives a smartphone and cascade classifier based mobile system for automatic crack and pothole recognition. A segmentation and fuzzy c-means clustering based approach is also seen in the literature (Noh et al. 2017).

However, hand crafted features and image-processing based techniques suffer often from noise (Pauly et al. 2017). Recently, deep learning based approaches are seen for crack and defect detection. In Pauly et al. (2017) for example, the Convolutional Neural Network (CNN) based network has four convolutional layers and are used to classify image patches into crack or non-crack. Effect of depth of layers has been analyzed. Around 40,000 image patches of size 99×99 are extracted from original RGB images and are used for training. In Zhang et al. (2016) a deep CNN-based system for crack detection on asphalt road is given using 640,000 samples for training the network, while, the work Yokoyama and Matsuno (2017) gives a CNN based approach for crack detection on concrete roads. In Eisenbach et al. (2017) a good overview of deep learning approaches and a CNN with eight convolutional layers for detecting various defects is given. In Silvia and Lucena (2018) a CNN, along with transfer learning using VGG-16 network, have been used for crack detection on concrete surfaces. In Maeda et al. (2018) front-view scene images are processed for detecting five crack-types and also other defects like, rutting bump pothole separation, at bounding box level using DL-based object detection method like, single short multiple detector with Inception V2. In Li et al. (2018) a R-CNN based defect detection approach has been given for civil infrastructures. However, in most of these works road surface image patches are collected using downward-facing cameras or cameras having much closer view of the surface. Using unmanned aerial vehicles to collect images for concrete infrastructure surfaces, followed by a CNN based deep learning system for crack and spalling detection, can also be seen in the literature (Yang et al. 2018). Here, the authors also used pre-trained VGG-16 and then fine-tuned the network for final classification. Gopalkrishnan (2018) provides a good overview of deep learning based approaches for distress detection on pavement images.

As seen, machine learning is found to be used more, however, many approaches still rely on image-processing for crack detection or extraction; making them sensitive towards noise. Further, most of these approaches use road surface image patches collected using specialized vehicles having line scanner cameras and downward-facing cameras, or under controlled lighting (Chatterjee et al. 2018b; Eisenbach et al. 2017); making image acquisition costly and less flexible. Lately, few of the works are seen to use front-view images where either simple cameras are placed on car dashboard (Varadharajan et al. 2014), near the license plate (Radopoulou et al. 2016), or smartphone cameras have been used (Maeda et al. 2018; Tedeschi and Benedetto 2016).

However, simple front-view 2-D images suffer from challenges such as noise associated due to vibration, lighting, and presence of scene elements (such as buildings, vehicles, manholes, lane markings). Nevertheless, such simple images provide quicker and cheaper inspections, while reducing search area for more intensive and costly maintenance (Chatterjee et al. 2018a). In this work, we handle the problem of crack detection in 2-D front-view scene images without using noisy image-processing or ML approaches using lot of labeled training image data. Thus, we develop here a keypoint matching mechanism between a "reference" and "query" images.

4.4 Data Preparation

The images that we use in this work has been captured in Germany by mounting a high definition camera on a pedelec/ e-bike. We selected images that belong to varied scenes such as, rural and urban, and varied time such as, morning and afternoon; taken under normal daylight. Figure 4.4 (A) shows our data collection approach. We selected 20 images to develop our system and validate results. Finally, we used 140 out-of-sample test images for the purpose of evaluation. Here, we process scene images taken from front-view cameras, and so we have to first extract our region- of-interest in the scene image, i.e. road area is extracted, as shown in Figure 4.4 (B), for preparing the data for crack detection. In this work, we use "scene image" to refer the complete captured scene, while "road image" refers to the image with only extracted road area. Original scene images are 1242×720 and are obtained from video clips. Once road area is segmented, the road image is resized to smaller size of 360×140. Such images are then used as query images and the test dataset is formed.

A scene contains various elements like, cars, building, trees, etc. and needs to be removed before the road area could be extracted and used for surface defect evaluations. In this work, we used the approach in Chatterjee et al. (2017) to extract the road area region from the complete scene. Further, the approach in Chatterjee et al. (2017) is used to identify block shadows, to restrict interference in the later defect detection stages.

4.5 Background of the Concepts

4.5.1 Fuzzy Logic and Membership Functions

Here, we shortly describe the general approach of fuzzy-based analysis for images. Image processing has to deal with many uncertainties and noise, thus making fuzzy-based approaches

Figure 4.4: Data preparation for crack detection to obtain the road images. (A) Data acquisition method. (B) Original scene image, detected road area to give the road image, and the region-of-interest (within box). (C) Detected shadow area.

suitable. The core of fuzzy logic is a membership function that maps a given element (for images that could be pixel intensities, or some other image features) between the range of 0 and 1. A membership function μ_A on a fuzzy set A is thus defined as: $\mu_A : Z \rightarrow [0, 1]$, where, each element of Z is mapped to its degree of belongingness or membership to the fuzzy set A. Membership functions could be of various types such as triangular, trapezoidal or Gaussian. Here, in this study we use triangular shaped membership function and so we discuss it in more detail here.

Figure 4.5 shows a triangular membership function that has elements $z \in Z$ on the X-axis and degree of membership of these elements within the range $[0, 1]$ on the Y-axis. The function depends on a lower limit a, an upper limit c, and a value in-between $a < b < c$. Thus, the function is defined as:

$$\mu_A(z) = \begin{cases} 0, & \text{if } z \leq a \\ \frac{z-a}{b-a}, & \text{if } a < z \leq b \\ \frac{c-z}{c-b}, & \text{if } b < z < c \\ 0 & \text{if } z \geq c \end{cases} \tag{4.1}$$

4.5.2 Gamma Mixture Fuzzy Model

Here, we discuss the background of Gamma Mixture Fuzzy Model (GMFM) (Kumar et al. 2016) method. In GMFM it is assumed that the data (gradient values of pixels are modeled here) are generated from a mixture of finite number of Gamma distributions, and fuzzy-theoretic approach is used to estimate the parameters for the Gamma distributions. GMFM theory is based on the fact that the fuzzy mixing of Gamma distributions gives rise to a Dirichlet-type

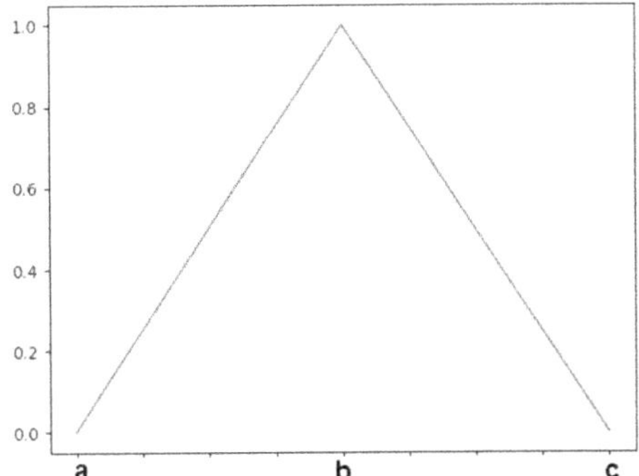

Figure 4.5: A triangular-shaped membership function.

mixing of distributions. Thus, the aim of using GMFM is to model the dataset $\{I(n)\}_{n=1}^{N}$ in an image by a fuzzy combination of N different Gamma distributions. In particular, the random variable I is modeled by the following type of fuzzy model: If I belongs to the ith cluster (with $\mu_i(I)$ as the membership value), then $I \sim Ga(I|r^i, r^i s^i)$ for all $i \in \{1, 2, \cdots, N\}$. Here, $Ga(I|r^i, r^i s^i)$ is the Gamma distribution and is defined as:

$$Ga(I|r^i, r^i s^i) = \frac{(r^i s^i) r^i}{G(r^i)} (I)^{r^i - 1} exp(-r^i s^i I) \tag{4.2}$$

with $r^i > 0$, $s^i > 0$, and $G(.)$ is the Gamma function in the integral form and is defined as:

$$G(x) = \int_0^\infty t^{x-1} exp(-t) dt. \tag{4.3}$$

Furthermore, variables r^i, s^i also follow Gamma distribution to further increase adaptability having prior distributions as follows:

$$r^i \sim Ga(r^i | {a_r}^i, {b_r}^i) = \frac{({b_r}^i)^{{a_r}^i}}{G({a_r}^i)} (r^i)^{{a_r}^i - 1} exp(-{b_r}^i r^i), \tag{4.4}$$

$$s^i \sim Ga(s^i | {a_s}^i, {b_s}^i) = \frac{({b_s}^i)^{{a_s}^i}}{G({a_s}^i)} (s^i)^{{a_s}^i - 1} exp(-{b_s}^i s^i). \tag{4.5}$$

Based on the above definitions, we define an objective function, as described in Kumar et al. (2016), to be $J(q(r^i), q(s^i), \mu_i(I(n)))$. This objective function is parameterized by $q(r^i)$, $q(s^i)$ and $\mu_i(I(n)))$. The goal of GMFM is to maximize J and infer the distributions $q(r^i)$ and $q(s^i)$, as well as the membership values $\mu_i(I)$ of the clusters. The maximization of J is performed under the following constraints: $\sum_{i=1}^{N} \mu_i(I(n)) = 1$, $\int dr^i q(r^i) = 1$, and $\int ds^i q(s^i) = 1$. Thus, for inferring and learning the parameters of r^i (i.e. $a_r{}^i$, $b_r{}^i$), s^i (i.e. $a_s{}^i$, $b_s{}^i$), and the membership values of the clusters i.e. $\mu_i(I(n))$ in order to maximize J, we use the GMFM method and the solution in Kumar et al. (2016), where, equations (56-60) give the GMFM solution and the update rules. These update rules are used to learn the parameters and update them in an iterative manner until a convergence criteria is reached. A convergence criteria is user-defined, for example, maximum number of iterations to be performed could be taken as the converging criteria and the learning (updating) of the parameters is stopped once this limit is reached. In this way, GMFM is used to learn the parameters of N Gamma distributions.

4.5.3 Image Feature Descriptors and Keypoint Matching

Visual features of images such as color, texture, gradient, shape characterize images or objects within the images uniquely. Features could be locally defined (such as for regions or objects within images), or globally defined (such as at the image level). Some of the most commonly used features are Scale-invariant Feature Transform (SIFT) (Lowe 2004), Speeded Up Robust Feature (SURF) (Bay et al. 2008), Haar-like features, edge and corner features, Histogram of Oriented Gradients (HoG), Local Binary Pattern (LBP), color histograms, different statistical measures, to name a few. Local features in images could be defined around interesting regions, called keypoints, such as corners, edges or blobs. Keypoints are usually matched using standard L1 or L2 distances.

As we are following keypoint generation and matching mechanism in this work, we will give a short overview of SIFT below, because we compare our approach on crack detection later with SIFT. Features with SIFT are locally defined and it uses interesting points (keypoints) to encode appearance of objects. These keypoints then can be matched across images for tasks such as, object recognition and detection, image matching, motion tracking, multi-view geometry. SIFT creates keypoints and after that they are encoded as 128-D feature descriptors consisting of histogram of orientations. These features are invariant to scale of an image, as well as if the images get rotated; giving them the property of being scale and rotation invariant.

4.6 Methodology

The methodological steps for crack and defective pixel detection on road surface images are described here. Once road surface images are obtained from the query images, as said in the data preparation section, further steps as per the framework in Figure 4.3 are performed.

4.6.1 Transforming the Intensity Image into Gradient Image

We describe here how we obtain the gradient image from the original image. Gradient image is subsequently used as an input to GMFM for edge-based keypoint generation, the very first step in our framework as shown in Figure 4.3. Let $I(x, y) \in [0, 1]$ is the pixel intensity at the (x, y)th pixel of the original intensity image I. This intensity image I is transformed into the gradient image I_G using the following filter:

$$I_G(x, y) = \sqrt{{F_x}^2 + {F_y}^2}, \tag{4.6}$$

where, $F_x = -I(x-1, y-1) + I(x-1, y+1) - 2\sqrt{2}I(x, y-1) + 2\sqrt{2}I(i, j+1) - I(x+1, y-1) + I(x+1, y+1)$. While, $F_y = -I(x-1, y-1) - 2\sqrt{2}I(x-1, y) - I(x-1, y+1) + I(x+1, y-1) + 2\sqrt{2}I(x+1, y) + I(x+1, y+1)$.

Here, F_x gives at any pixel the intensity change in the x-direction. For computation of F_x, the contribution of adjacent horizontal pixels is weighted by $2\sqrt{2}$, the contribution of adjacent diagonal pixels is weighted by 1, and the contribution of adjacent vertical pixels is weighted by 0. Similarly, F_y gives at any pixel the intensity change in the y-direction. For computation of F_y, the contribution of adjacent horizontal pixels is weighted by 0, the contribution of adjacent diagonal pixels is weighted by 1, and the contribution of adjacent vertical pixels is weighted by $2\sqrt{2}$. The rationale of taking the weighting of $2\sqrt{2}$ is motivated by the fact that the distance of adjacent diagonal pixel is $\sqrt{2}$ times the distance of adjacent horizontal pixel for F_x (and the adjacent diagonal pixel is $\sqrt{2}$ times the distance of adjacent vertical pixel for F_y). For more details, Kumar et al. (2016) can be referred.

4.6.2 Gamma Mixture Fuzzy Model Based Keypoint Generation

As crack pixels (in essence edges) are much less than non-crack (in essence non-edges) pixels in any image, we propose in the work that they could be represented as two Gamma distributions (each for crack and non-crack). Hence, we handle this problem of modeling such heavy-tailed distributions using GMFM and it is used to cluster the pixels into two groups- defective crack pixels and non-defective pixels. The cluster with higher magnitude of gradient is taken as the one containing crack pixels. It should be noted that in Kumar et al. (2016) the GMFM has been used to detect geometrically consistent matches between two images and it has been applied on orientation images. In this work, we extend GMFM to apply on gradient images and adapt it to find strong edges i.e. probable crack pixels, and these detected edge pixels are taken as keypoints of the image.

Firstly, a query image with the road area is transformed to its corresponding gradient image. This gradient image is then used by GMFM for detecting edges, which are taken as keypoints. In this work, we model I_G using a GMFM consisting of two fuzzy Gamma mixtures or clusters (crack/ defective pixels and non-crack/ non-defective pixels, or, more precisely edges and non-edges), thus giving $N = 2$ for the dataset of all pixel intensities $\{I_G(n)\}_{n=1}^{N}$. Here, I_G is the gradient image obtained using the image transformation method as described above. Thus, the main aim of GMFM here is to estimate the parameters and membership values of these two clusters (i.e. Gamma distributions), each modeled by equation 4.2, and number of clusters in equation 4.2 is given by $i \in \{1,2\}$. As a first step, we use fuzzy c-means clustering on $\{I_G(n)\}_{n=1}^{N}$ to guess the initial membership values for each of the two clusters, i.e., $\mu_1^o(I_G(n))$ and $\mu_2^o(I_G(n))$, such that, $\sum_{i=1}^{N} \mu_i^o(I_G(n)) = 1$. We perform the initial guess here to later estimate the final membership values of $\mu_1^*(I_G(n))$ and $\mu_2^*(I_G(n))$ that maximizes the objective function J, as defined in the previous theoretical background section. Following the solution for maximizing the objective function J in (Kumar et al. 2016), below mentioned steps are finally performed for detecting the edges on the images in our work:

- Step1: Transform the original road image into the corresponding gradient image, I_G, to create the dataset $\{I_G(n)\}_{n=1}^{N}$ providing $N = 2$ (denoting a mixture of two clusters are there).
- Step2: Use fuzzy c-means to estimate $\mu_1^o(I_G(n))$ and $\mu_2^o(I_G(n))$.
- Step3: Initialize the parameters $\hat{a_r}^i = {a_r}^i$, $\hat{b_r}^i = {b_r}^i$, $\hat{a_s}^i = {a_s}^i$ and $\hat{b_s}^i = {b_b}^i$ in equations (56-59) of Kumar et al. (2016). Initialize the prior distributions for equation 4.4 and equation 4.5 as: ${a_r}^i = {b_r}^i = {a_s}^i = {b_b}^i = 0.001$ for all $i \in \{1,2\}$ clusters. Initialize the final membership values $\mu_1^*(I_G(n)) = \mu_1^o(I_G(n))$ and $\mu_2^*(I_G(n)) = \mu_2^o(I_G(n))$
- Step4: Repeat until the convergence criteria is satisfied:
  Update the parameters following the rules in equations (56-60) of Kumar et al. (2016).
- Obtain the final learned parameters of the two Gamma distributions which gives the final $\mu_1^*(I_G)$ and $\mu_2^*(I_G)$ following equation (60) of Kumar et al. (2016). These final membership

values will define which pixels will be denoted as edges (i.e. potential cracks and defects) and non-edges (i.e. non-cracks and non-defects).

In the above Step4, we say here that convergence is achieved if number of iteration is 100 or the change in learned values is of very low order, i.e. < 0.0001. It should be noted that the number of iterations has been varied within the range of 50 and 100 without showing any significant changes in detecting edges using GMFM; thereby showing robustness of GMFM. In this way, we receive the final $\mu_1^*(I_G(n))$ and $\mu_2^*(I_G(n))$ to cluster the pixels as edges (probable cracks) and non-edges (non-cracks). When we have $\mu_1^*(I_G(n)) > \mu_2^*(I_G(n))$, then we denote $\mu_1(.)$ as the membership function for the edges (probable cracks) cluster and $\mu_2(.)$ as the membership function for the non-edges (non-cracks) cluster.The cluster with higher magnitude of gradient values are taken as probable cracks, so the pixels belonging to this cluster are taken as probable candidate crack pixels, called keypoints. In this way, we detect the edges and the initial probable crack and defective pixels on road surface images. The final obtained edge Image is dilated at the end.

Figure 4.6 shows an example of edge detection and keypoint generation with the GMFM based approach. The usefulness of using GMFM for initial edge detection, and thus guessing candidate crack pixels for keypoint localization, is that we do not use any threshold based approach for classifying the pixels as edge or non-edge. Figure 4.6 (B-C) show comparison between GMFM and Canny for edge detection. As Canny uses thresholding approach, it is seen that GMFM gives much stable results.

4.6.3 Obtaining Fuzzy Feature Descriptors at Keypoints

As seen in the framework of Figure 4.3, fuzzy image descriptors are obtained for both reference and query images, and then the images are matched using KL-divergence based approach to determine how many descriptors actually match. Depending on the number of matches, if it is above a threshold, the query image is classified to contain cracks/ defects and the crack/ defective pixels are marked on the query image. So, the reference image goes through the pipeline of GMFM based keypoint generation and fuzzy descriptor formation only once, after which the reference descriptors are stored and persisted. While, every time a new query image is given, query descriptors are obtained and matched against the persisted reference image descriptors. Now, we describe here how we obtain the fuzzy image descriptors (i.e. feature vectors) at the generated keypoints.

To obtain the fuzzy image descriptors at the keypoints, we follow the approach in Kumar et al. (2016) and the descriptors are 128 dimensional. So, for every keypoint 128-D local descrip-

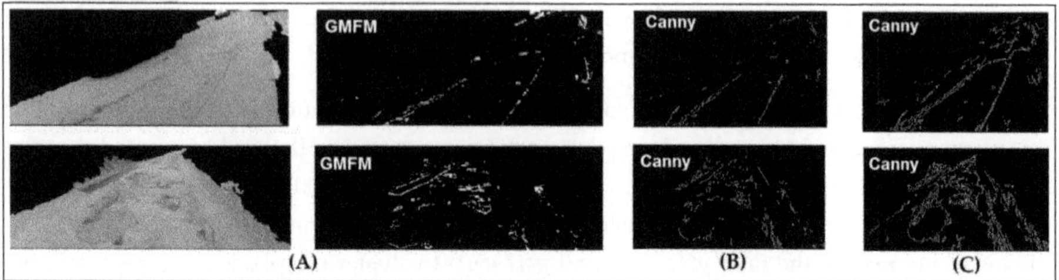

Figure 4.6: (A) Keypoint generation: Locating potential candidate crack or defective pixels on images, called keypoints. This is done using Gamma Mixture Fuzzy Model based approach for detecting edge-based keypoints. GMFM is applied on the gradient image in order to obtain the keypoints. (B-C) Give corresponding edge image of original images using Canny edge detection approach. In (B) Canny edge detection is performed between threshold values of (50, 100). These two thresholds of 50 and 100 signify the following: any intensity gradient below 50 is not considered as an edge, while, above 100 is surely considered as an edge. Similarly, in (C) Canny edge detection is performed between threshold values of (20, 60). GMFM is seen to give stable results and does not use thresholding approach. Edges at the juncture of foreground and background (black pixels) are omitted for all cases.

tors are obtained, and all such descriptors are taken together to give the global feature set of the whole image. We define the set of these keypoints as $\{x^*(k), y^*(k), s(k), \theta(k)\}_{k=1}^{K}$ with K = number of keypoints. Here, $\{x^*(k), y^*(k)\}$ are the x-coordinate and y-coordinate of the keypoint pixel location, $s(k)$ is the scale, and $\theta(k)$ is the orientation of the kth keypoint. $s(k)$ and $\theta(k)$ provide scale and rotational invariance to the feature descriptors obtained at the keypoints. Here, $s(k)$=2 is taken. To obtain $\theta(k)$ for every keypoint, the following method is followed, as done for SIFT detector (Lowe 2004). Around the keypoint, gradient magnitudes and gradient orientations are calculated. An histogram of gradient orientations is obtained having 36 bins. The bin counts are weighted by gradient magnitudes and a Gaussian weighting function. The dominant orientation from the histogram is assigned as $\theta(k)$, i.e. orientation of the keypoint.

To obtain the fuzzy image descriptors, a circular region of a radius equal to $6\sqrt{2}s(k)$ with $\{x^*(k), y^*(k)\}$ as the center is considered for every k^{th} key point. Let us take $W_k \in \mathbb{R}^{128}$ to be a feature descriptor at any given k^{th} keypoint for an image. The set of all such descriptors can be denoted as $\{W_k\}_{k=1}^{K}$, with K being the number of keypoints in the image. Thus, we can define $W_{r,k} \in \mathbb{R}^{128}$ to be a descriptor at any given k^{th} keypoint for the reference image r (see Figure 4.1 (A)). Similarly, we can define $W_{q,k} \in \mathbb{R}^{128}$ to be a descriptor at any given k^{th} keypoint for the query image q. Hence, the descriptor feature set for any query image is $\{W_{q,k}\}_{k=1}^{K_q}$ and that of the reference image is $\{W_{r,k}\}_{k=1}^{K_r}$, where, K_q is the number of keypoints in the query image q and K_r is the number of keypoints in the reference image r. To obtain such local descriptor W_k

for any keypoint, we do the following:

- We split the circular neighborhood of every keypoint $\{x^*(k), y^*(k)\}$ having a radius equal to $6\sqrt{2}s(k)$ into 16 (4×4 areas, see Fig a) circular subregions. Let these subregions be denoted as ${\Omega_k}^i$. It should be noted that the radius of each of these $({\Omega_k}^i)_{i=1}^{16}$ subregions is $1.5\sqrt{2}s(k)$. The center co-ordinates $({x_k}^i, {y_k}^i)_{i=1}^{16}$ of each of the $({\Omega_k}^i)_{i=1}^{16}$ subregions are obtained as follows:

$$\begin{aligned} {x_k}^i &= x^*(k) + 3s(k)C_x(i)cos(\theta(k)) - C_y(i)sin(\theta(k)), \\ {y_k}^i &= y^*(k) + 3s(k)C_x(i)cos(\theta(k)) - C_y(i)sin(\theta(k)), \end{aligned} \tag{4.7}$$

  where, $i = 1 \cdots 16$. The C_x and C_y are obtained as in Kumar et al. (2016). All the 16 center points are uniformly distributed.

- We define 8 uniformly distributed triangular-shaped membership functions for fuzzy sets $({A_k}^1, \cdots, {A_k}^8)$ (see Figure 4.5 as an example of a single triangular membership function) over the range of orientation values $[{O_k}^{min}, {O_k}^{max}]$ for each of the $({x_k}^i, {y_k}^i)_{i=1}^{16}$ subregions.

  The range of orientation values $[{O_k}^{min}, {O_k}^{max}]$ within a subregion ${\Omega_k}^i$ is obtained in the same way as $\theta(k)$ is obtained above, i.e. the histogram of gradient orientations (after weighting bin counts with gradient magnitudes and a Gaussian weighting function) is used to get the range of orientation values.

  So, as 8 knots (values) are required on the X-axis (see Figure 4.5 and equation (4.1)) for defining 8 membership functions, we get these knots as follows:

$$\begin{aligned} t_0 = {O_k}^{min}, t_1 = {O_k}^{min} + \delta_i, t_2 = {O_k}^{min} + 2\delta_i, \cdots, \\ t_6 = {O_k}^{min} + 6\delta_i, t_7 = {O_k}^{max}, \end{aligned} \tag{4.8}$$

  where,

$$\delta_i = \frac{{O_k}^{max} - {O_k}^{min}}{7}.$$

  With the above uniformly separated knots $(t_0, \cdots, t_7)$, the 8 membership functions are defined as follows:

$$\begin{aligned} \mu_{{A_k}^1(x)} &= max(0, min(1, \frac{t_1 - x}{t_1 - t_0})), \\ \mu_{{A_k}^j(x)} &= max(0, min(\frac{x - t_{j-2}}{t_{j-1} - t_{j-2}}, \frac{t_j - x}{t_j - t_{j-1}})), \\ \mu_{{A_k}^8(x)} &= max(0, min(\frac{x - t_6}{t_7 - t_6}, 1)). \end{aligned} \tag{4.9}$$

In equation (4.9), $j = 2, \cdots, 7$ and $\mu_{A_k{}^j(.)}$ is the membership value to the fuzzy set $A_k{}^j$. So, all the pixels within a subregion is assigned a membership value according to their "degree of belongingness" towards the membership functions.

- Finally, the membership values corresponding to each of the 8 membership functions are averaged within a subregion to give the averaged membership values $T_{\Omega_k{}^i, A_k{}^j}$ as follows:

$$T_{\Omega_k{}^i, A_k{}^j} = mean(\{\mu_{A_k{}^j}(I(y,x))\}_{(x,y)\in\Omega_k{}^i}). \tag{4.10}$$

Thus, for every subregion $\Omega_k{}^i$ we have a 8-D vector $[T_{\Omega_k{}^i, A_k{}^1} \cdots T_{\Omega_k{}^i, A_k{}^8}]$. Finally, for a single keypoint k, 16 subregion descriptors are all put together to give the 128-D feature descriptor of the keypoint as:

$$W_k = [T_{\Omega_k{}^1, A_k{}^1} \cdots T_{\Omega_k{}^1, A_k{}^8} \cdots T_{\Omega_k{}^{16}, A_k{}^1} \cdots T_{\Omega_k{}^{16}, A_k{}^8}]. \tag{4.11}$$

In this way, we obtain 128-D fuzzy feature descriptor for each of the keypoints in both the "reference" and the "query" image. As we have the feature descriptors, we will now discuss how we match the keypoints (i.e. the fuzzy feature descriptors) between the reference and query images to finally detect and localize cracks/ defects in the query image.

4.6.4 Keypoint Matching Between Images for Crack and Defect Detection

Once we obtain the feature descriptor sets $\{W_{r,k}\}_{k=1}^{K_r}$ and $\{W_{q,k}\}_{k=1}^{K_q}$ of both reference and the query image, we formulate the matching criteria between them.

Observing equations (4.10 - 4.11) that denote the 128-D feature descriptor of any k^{th} keypoint, we see that every subregion $\Omega_k{}^i$ has 8 membership values $T_{\Omega_k{}^i, A_k{}^1} \cdots T_{\Omega_k{}^i, A_k{}^8}$. These 8 membership values thus have a typical structure such that

$$\sum_{j=1}^{8} T_{\Omega_k{}^i, A_k{}^j} = 1. \tag{4.12}$$

Therefore, within W_k in equation (4.11) every 8 values sum to 1. Thus, every 8-D random vector in W_k (i.e. $T_{\Omega_k{}^1, A_k{}^1} \cdots T_{\Omega_k{}^1, A_k{}^8}, \cdots, T_{\Omega_k{}^{16}, A_k{}^1} \cdots T_{\Omega_k{}^{16}, A_k{}^8}$) sum to 1. This shows that W_k is composed of random variables $T_{\Omega_k{}^i, A_k{}^j} \in [0,1]$. This motivated the derivation of the following hypothesis, based on which distance between keypoints are obtained and matched.

Hypothesis for the underlying distributions of the descriptors

Let $L_{i,k} = [{L_{i,k}}^1 \cdots {L_{i,k}}^8]$ be a random vector such that $j \in 1, \cdots, 8$, ${L_{i,k}}^j \in [0,1]$, $\sum_{j=1}^{8} {L_{i,k}}^j = 1$, and $L_{i,k}$ follows a Dirichlet distribution:

$$p(L_{i,k};\alpha) = \frac{\Gamma(\sum_{j=1}^{8}\alpha_j)}{\prod_{j=1}^{8}\Gamma(\alpha_j)}\prod_{j=1}^{8}({L_{i,k}}^j)^{\alpha_j-1}. \tag{4.13}$$

Here, $\Gamma(x) = (x-1)!$ is the Gamma function in the factorial form. The Dirichlet distribution is characterized by $\alpha = [\alpha_1, \alpha_2, \cdots, \alpha_8]$ parameters. Further,

$$mode({L_{i,k}}^j) = \frac{\alpha_j - 1}{\sum_{j=1}^{8}(\alpha_j - 1)}, \tag{4.14}$$

where, $\alpha_j > 1$. Now, following equation 4.12, let,

$$T_{{\Omega_k}^i} = [T_{{\Omega_k}^i,{A_k}^1} \cdots T_{{\Omega_k}^i,{A_k}^8}] \tag{4.15}$$

denote an instance of such a 8-D random feature vector, where, $T_{{\Omega_k}^i,{A_k}^j} \in [0,1]$ and $\sum_{j=1}^{8} T_{{\Omega_k}^i,{A_k}^j} = 1$.

Here, we rely on the hypothesis that the calculated feature vector $T_{{\Omega_k}^i}$ of equation (4.15) is the mode value of the random vector $L_{i,k}$. So, from equations (4.12, 4.14, 4.15), we say that $T_{{\Omega_k}^i}$ is the most frequently observed value of $L_{i,k}$. Hence, we have

$$T_{{\Omega_k}^i,{A_k}^j} = \frac{\alpha_j - 1}{\sum_{j=1}^{8}\alpha_j - 1}. \tag{4.16}$$

Thus, a possible value of α_j satisfying equation (4.16) in view of equation (4.12) is given as:

$$\alpha_j = 1 + T_{{\Omega_k}^i,{A_k}^j}. \tag{4.17}$$

This property of equation (4.17) helps us to assume that the calculated 8-D fuzzy feature descriptors, after adding 1, can be interpreted as parameters of a Dirichlet distribution. Hence, we obtain D, the Kullback-Leibler Divergence, between two Dirichlet distributions, $q(L_1;\alpha)$ and $r(L_2;\beta)$. Here, $q(L_1;\alpha)$ signifies a Dirichlet distribution parameterized by α belonging to a query image keypoint descriptor, while, $\alpha \in W_{q,k}$, $W_{q,k} \in \mathbb{R}^{128}$ and $W_{q,k}$ follows equation (4.11). Similarly, $r(L_2;\beta)$ signifies a Dirichlet distribution parameterized by β belonging to a reference image keypoint descriptor, while, $\beta \in W_{r,k}$, $W_{r,k} \in \mathbb{R}^{128}$ and $W_{r,k}$ also follows equation (4.11).

Further, α and β are 8-D and are obtained following equation (4.17) for query and reference images, respectively. Finally, D is calculated as per equation (4.18).

$$D = log\Gamma(\alpha_0) - \sum_{d=1}^{8} log\Gamma(\alpha_d) - log\Gamma(\beta_0) + \sum_{d=1}^{8} log\Gamma(\beta_d) + \sum_{d=1}^{8}(\alpha_d - \beta_d)(F(\alpha_d) - F(\alpha_0)), \tag{4.18}$$

where, $\alpha_0 = \sum_{d=1}^{8} \alpha_d$, $\beta_0 = \sum_{d=1}^{8} \beta_d$, $\Gamma(x) = (x-1)!$ is the Gamma function in the factorial form and $F(x) = \frac{d}{dx}\ln(\Gamma(x))$ is the Digamma function. The difference in distributions of any two keypoint is calculated based on equation (4.18), giving the following similarity score S between two keypoints:

$$S = \exp(-\sum_{i=1}^{16} D_i), \tag{4.19}$$

where, i denotes the subregion ${\Omega_k}^i$ of the kth keypoint.

So, higher the value of S, higher is the matching between the keypoints. To finally nominate the matched keypoints between the query and the reference image, we see if the nearest query image keypoint's similarity score (from equation (4.19)) is greater than the similarity score between that keypoint in the query image and all other keypoints in the reference image. Such a keypoint in the query image is then nominated as the "matched keypoint". Finally, total number of such matched keypoints between the query and the reference image is taken as the matching score M.

4.7 Results and Evaluations

Here, we discuss our results. Total 140 images are used for testing. To prepare the dataset, the approach in the section on data preparation is followed. Figure 4.7 shows some of the road surface examples containing cracks. It also shows how crack pixels are detected and localized on the images. Number of matches (i.e. number of keypoints whose descriptors matched between the query and the reference image) give the required information on the extent of cracks present on the query images. Figure 4.8 shows performance of our approach on some examples of road surfaces which are free of cracks. Further, Figure 4.9 shows some scenarios where crack detection becomes challenging due to presence of some other defects such as large outer patches or potholes, external elements such as manholes, or very fine scattered shadows.

Additionally, in Table 4.2 we perform the evaluation on our test dataset of 140 images using precision, recall, F1 and accuracy metrics which are defined as:

$$Precision = \frac{TP}{TP+FP}, Recall = \frac{TP}{TP+FN}, F1 = 2\frac{Precision.Recall}{Precision+Recall}, Accuracy = \frac{TP+TN}{TP+TN+FP+FN},$$

where, TP denotes true positives (detecting defective and crack image as defective) and TN denotes true negatives (detecting non-defective image as non-defective). FP denotes false positive (detecting non-defective image as defective), FN denotes false negative (detecting defective image as non-defective). Here, we used experimentally verified threshold on M to classify query images into defective image and non-defective image. We used 20 images separately for developing the approach and ascertaining the required threshold. The threshold on matching score M is taken to be 70. So, with $M \leq 70$, the query image is classified as non-defective image, whereas, if $M > 70$ the query image is classified as defective image.

Finally, to compare our approach of Figure 4.3, Figure 4.10 shows comparison with state-of-the-art descriptor based keypoint matching approach SIFT.

Accuracy (%)	Precision (%)	Recall (%)	F1 (%)
91.16	92.19	91.17	91.88

Table 4.2: Evaluation of Road Surfaces on 140 test images. Images are classified into defective image and non-defective image based on number of matched keypoints.

4.8 Discussion

We see that GMFM-based clustering for keypoint generation can distinguish between crack and non-crack pixels on road surfaces (see Figure 4.6), although crack pixels are not very easily distinguishable in the front-view images. Thus, Gamma distribution shows better suitability for the task at hand. Additionally, GMFM does not use thresholding approach and shows stable results when compared to Canny for edge detection. So, by adapting and applying GMFM on gradient images for edge-based keypoint generation, non-distinguishable potential crack pixels could be located easily in this work.

Further, it is seen that SIFT-based features are not very suitable for the task at hand, as seen in Figure 4.10. Here, SIFT i selected as it is the one of the state-of-the-art approach for matching tasks. Most of the number of matched keypoints based on SIFT for all the test images were in the

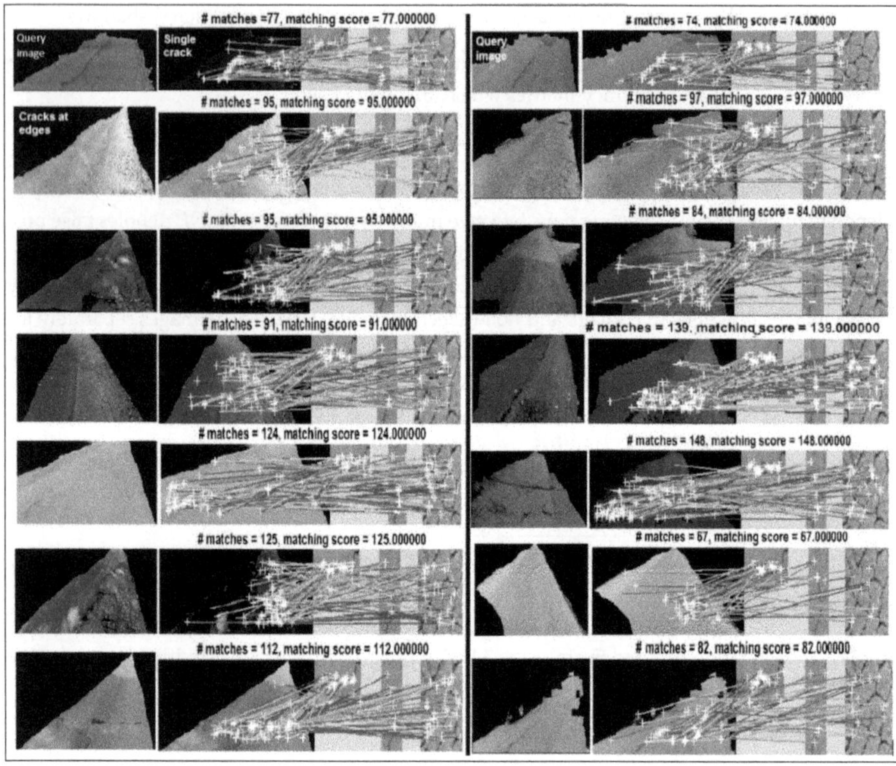

Figure 4.7: Crack detection and localization on front-view road surface images using our approach: Every image set shows the original query image and the matched keypoints between the reference and the query image. Query image contains only the road area. Cracks are successfully detected and localized on the query images containing single, network, or lighter cracks. Number of matches, M, indicate the number of matched keypoints between images. $M > 70$ is seen for all images containing cracks and are classified as defective images.

range of 8 to 20, showing that the keypoints are not distinctively identified in the images. This shows that the SIFT-based keypoint generation and matching approach is not highly suitable for the task at hand for crack and defect detection on front-view road surface images. Thus, it shows the usefulness of our approach that consists of GMFM-based keypoint generation, followed by fuzzy descriptors to encode the keypoints, and then finally matching the keypoints between the reference and test query images using KL-divergence and Dirichlet distribution based distance metric. Specifically, the developed keypoint matching criteria across images

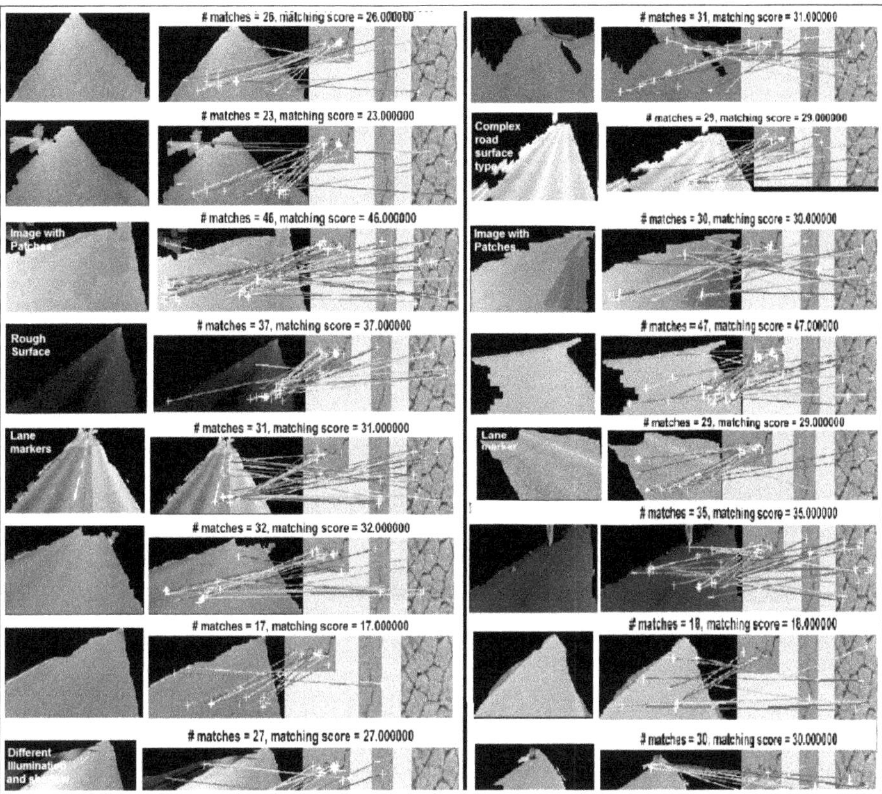

Figure 4.8: Performance of our approach on front-view road surface images containing no cracks: Number of matches, M, indicate the number of matched keypoints between images. $M \leq 70$ is seen for all images containing no cracks. Such images are classified as non-defective images.

using KL-divergence between two Dirichlet distributions showed high suitability for the task at hand.

Our approach shows adaptability to different road surface types and scene conditions. It can handle various crack-types such as lighter, wider, single, multiple distributed, or network cracks, under different illumination conditions, as seen in Figure 4.7 and Figure 4.9. Furthermore, the presented approach gives number of matched keypoints M which could be used for ranking the road surfaces according to the extent of defects. We further aim to improve the

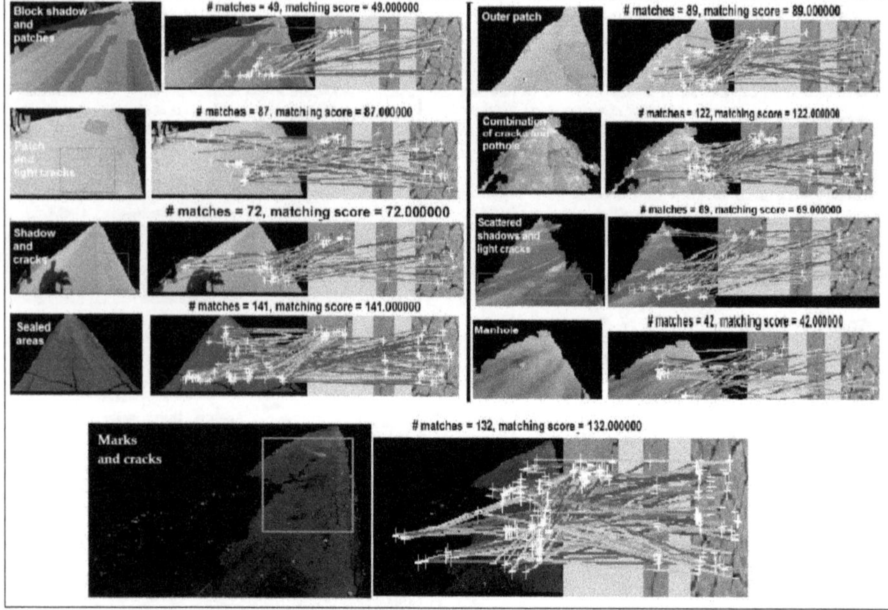

Figure 4.9: Crack detection in presence of many patches, other defects, some road elements, or shadows.

ranking system in future by integrating total M over a pre-defined kilometer of road length. It can also be seen that external elements like, lane markers (image sets in the fifth row of Figure 4.8), marks on roads (last row of Figure 4.9), also are handled and do not contribute to false detection in this work.

However, under certain situations the crack detection with our approach can generate false positives for crack pixels, as seen in Figure 4.9 (first row, second image set). Many times some of the edges of such patches are wrongly detected as crack pixels. In future, we aim to handle such cases by using an edge map and see if a shaped object (patch) is present or not on the road, thus we can ignore those keypoints at the patch edges; thereby filtering the matched keypoints. However, patches without very strong edges do not contribute to false detection (see Figure 4.8, second row of Figure 4.9). Moreover, additional objects on roads such as manhole's outer edges could also be falsely detected as cracks. Another challenging scenario is seen to be presence of very fine scattered shadows on road surfaces, as seen in Figure 4.9 (third row, second image set). Although solid block shadows could be handled using the approach in Chatterjee et al.

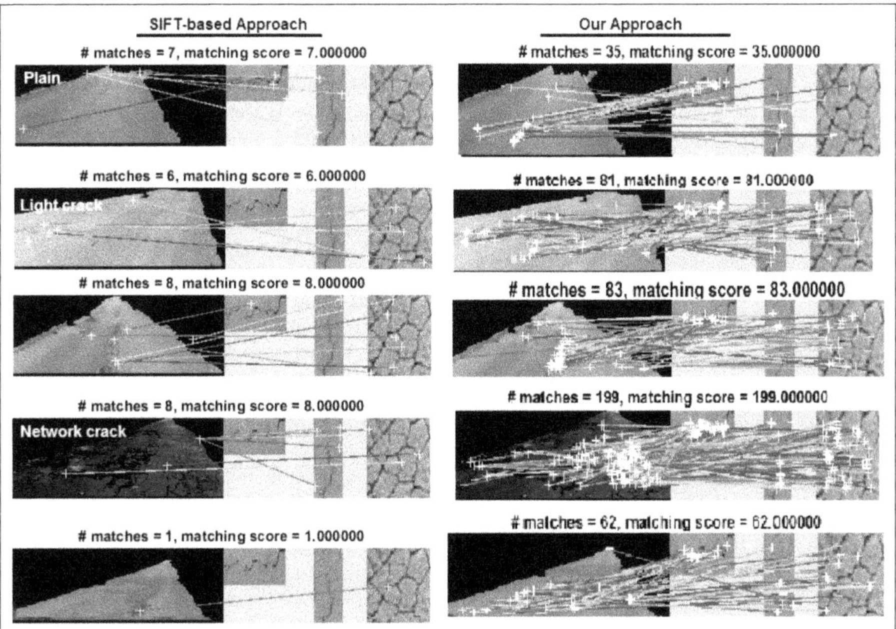

Figure 4.10: SIFT based keypoint generation and matching approach for crack detection on front-view road surface images: As cracks are not very distinguishable objects, keypoint generation and matching is seen to be challenging. In comparison, our approach comprising of GMFM based keypoint generation, fuzzy descriptors and KL-divergence between two Dirichlet distributions performs better.

(2017) (see Figure 4.4), but very fine scattered shadows are difficult to identify. In future, we aim to handle such shadows. However, block shadows do not interfere much with the crack detection step (Figure 4.8, last row; Figure 4.9, first and third rows).

4.9 Conclusion

In this work, we developed a keypoint matching based approach to detect crack pixels on road surfaces. We presented an edge-based keypoint generation mechanism using Gamma Mixture Fuzzy Model technique, along with 128-D fuzzy feature descriptors for these keypoints, to identify crack pixels on road surfaces. We used a KL-divergence between Dirichlet distributions for formulating a keypoint matching mechanism in order to match keypoints between a constant reference crack image and a given query image. We successfully classified query images into defective and non-defective images; along with localizing the defective crack pixels on query images. Further, we used number of matched keypoints, taken as the matching score, to rank query road images. The number of matches give a rough estimate of the condition of the road surface in the image. The presented approach shows promising results for crack and related defect detection and localization on road surfaces of 2-D front-view scene images having various road surface types, colors, crack-types, illumination conditions such as darker or normal daylight.

Chapter 5: Smart Infrastructure Monitoring: Development of a Decision Support System for Vision-Based Road Crack Detection

Title	Smart Infrastructure Monitoring: Development of a Decision Support System for Vision-Based Road Crack Detection
Authors	Sromona Chatterjee[1], Alfred Benedikt Brendel[1], Sascha Lichtenberg[1] [1] Chair of Information Management, University of Göttingen, Platz der Göttingen Sieben 5, 37073 Göttingen, Germany ∗ Corresponding author: sromona.chatterjee@wiwi.uni-goettingen.de
Outlet	Proceedings of the International Conference on Information Systems (ICIS), December 2018, San Francisco, USA
Abstract	Improvement of road conditions is a globally relevant topic, especially considering the astonishing rates of urbanization witnessed in recent decades. Given the large volumes of visual data that require rapid objective processing for timely infrastructure monitoring, processes such as detecting cracks on pavement surfaces are excellent candidates for automated information system-based solutions providing opportunities for improved sustainability and efficiency in road maintenance. In this work, we address the need for an easy-to-implement automated pavement crack detection approach by developing a machine learning based visual decision support system which processes 2D images acquired by front-facing cameras. The decision support system thus provides an improved alternative method for preventative and efficient infrastructure monitoring over traditional pavement management system approaches.
Keywords	Pavement management, crack detection, decision support system, road monitoring, machine learning, image processing

Table 5.1: Fact sheet for chapter 5.

5.1 Introduction

According to estimations from the United Nation's World Urbanization Prospects report, over 54% of the world's population lives in urban areas while projections of continued urbanization estimate that this number will reach 66% by the year 2050 (UN-DESA 2014, 2016). Mobility across the majority of global cities is primarily car-bound, causing strain on mobility infrastructures as urban populations continue to rise. With more cars driving on the same streets, increased road damage is inevitable. Public infrastructures such as roads and bridges represent a significant influential factor in societal transformation, connectivity, and growth. A recent policy report on European road surfaces provides insights on the consequences of poor road conditions including increased travel time, reduced economic development and trade, and higher vehicle operation costs (Gleave 2014). Degraded road conditions also lead to increased pollution and CO_2 emissions due to longer construction periods often required because of maintenance backlog. The policy report also points out huge backlog in major economies, demanding considerable investment of the GDP in road rehabilitation (Gleave 2014). Consequently, monitoring of road conditions is considered a crucial factor for sustainability across all social, economic, and environmental aspects (Kahn 1995), thereby classifying pavement monitoring and defect identification as essential components of urban sustainability.

The three major forms of pavement monitoring are: manual surveys by employees, automated utilization of specialized vehicles, and passive monitoring via reports from citizens. Currently, roads are predominantly surveyed through manual methods (Chambon and Moliard 2011; Gavilan et al. 2011; Radopoulou et al. 2016). Unsurprisingly, the time-consuming nature of manual pavement monitoring leads to inefficiencies in repair timeliness and cost-effectiveness, ultimately resulting in increased frequency of road accidents (Gleave 2014). Moreover, manual pavement monitoring leads to subjective and non-uniform results and sub-optimal maintenance. The alternative option to employ specialized vehicles equipped with multiple cameras, artificial lighting, friction sensors, laser profilers, radars, and other tools is drastically more expensive (Radopoulou et al. 2016). Furthermore, such large vehicles are not suitable for use on alleys, sidewalks, or any narrow passages. Consequently, most road authorities and agencies opt for manual monitoring(FHWA 2016), which makes intelligent automation a requirement.

One potential emerging solution is to embrace a data-driven approach, which is beginning to gain traction among more innovative economies. With the pervasiveness of economic digitalization, increased camera and video use means that images and videos are now more easily and affordably acquired (Yoo 2010). Ubiquitous car or travel cameras can now be used to capture precise scene images which can be used for infrastructure management. Images can be utilized by Decision Support System (DSS) to facilitate planning of road upgrades, to support maintenance decisions and quality checks, and to identify pavement defects (Dobson et al. 2014; Hosin and Suseon 2006); thus presenting an improved alternative to the traditional PMS (BASt 2008; FHWA 2016). Image data provides the opportunity to analyze many aspects of roads and their visual characteristics automatically such as visual defects (e.g. cracks, patches, potholes) or roadway marking conditions for effective region management in smarter and more affordable ways (Chatterjee et al. 2017). Such systems could be used for preventive maintenance, alert systems, and planning activities. In this way, automated methods can replace costly, inefficient, and subjective manual approaches covering larger areas over shorter periods. Smart road infrastructure monitoring can thereby contribute to social, economic, and environmental sustainability. In this context, vision-based (i.e. image-based) road crack or defect detection could cut down costs and increase the ability of cities to maintain roads. Thus, using 2-D digital images for the bulk of the first-hand automated infrastructure analysis is highly insightful and is a major ongoing research focus in infrastructure management (Koch et al. 2015).

However, the majority of algorithms regarding 2-D vision-based pavement monitoring are limited to analysis of images taken from a close distance facing directly downward toward the road, thus requiring specialized setup to gather the image data. These image-processing based methods are particularly sensitive to noise such as surface conditions and cannot be directly applied to different locations (Gavilan et al. 2011). However, the images from regular car cameras taken from the driver's front viewpoint are much easier and cheaper to acquire (e.g. by travelers or service vehicles of cities), although their true potential remains untapped (Mertz 2011).

Considering this, we utilize front-view images and state-of-the-art ML algorithms (e.g. Chatterjee et al. 2018a) in this study to provide automated solutions for pavement crack detection. Pavement cracks are one of the first defects that occur on road surfaces due to continuous wear and tear, and left unrepaired can lead to condition deterioration, reduced road lifecycle, and increased need for construction resulting in higher costs and traffic congestion (Gleave 2014; FHWA 2016). Thus, crack detection can serve as a preventative measure for identifying areas with poor road conditions before more expensive, inefficient, and invasive repairs are required.

Aside from the technicalities of vision-based crack detection, the requirements arising from the decision-making process must also be addressed. Thus, the design of DSS for road crack detection using 2-D images must be thoroughly investigated in order to avoid confusion or useless outputs in the context of road maintenance. Considering this context, this study aims to answer the following research questions:

RQ1: How can road cracks be detected automatically using 2-D digital front-view images?

RQ2: How should a DSS for road infrastructure analysis be designed?

5.2 Research Background

Using digital images for road crack detection in the context of infrastructure monitoring is a standard established approach. However, in order to realize the true potential of the available data, the following challenges must be addressed. Automated methods for image analysis must be developed, and the IS perspective to design such methods must be understood. We briefly describe related works and the literature background for these two research topics.

5.2.1 Vision–based Techniques for Road Surface Crack Detection

Automated inspection techniques for pavement evaluation commonly utilize radar, laser, accelerometer or vibration sensors, 3-D reconstruction, remote sensors and 2-D image-based techniques (BASt 2008; Koch et al. 2015). When comparing these approaches, image-based techniques are less expensive because other approaches demand more equipment and computation. However, image-based techniques face several challenges for increasing automation, primarily the challenge of coping with varying viewpoints, lighting, shadows, textures, surface-types and coverage areas.

Regarding automated image analysis methods, Gavilan et al. (2011) presented a comparative research report between several image-based analysis techniques developed by Transport Research Laboratory of UK. Two main findings were derived: 1) many false positives were obtained by detecting non-crack items, and 2) when analyzing road surfaces other than those inspected, lower accuracy was achieved. It was also observed that presence of shadows counted for many false positives and systems often required manual intervention. The most commonly utilized image-based techniques for crack detection on road surfaces are reviewed in Chatterjee et al. (2018a), Koch et al. (2015), and Mohan and Poobal (2017). We present a concise overview of these methods in Table 5.2 outlining two constructs: the techniques followed and the image acquisition viewpoint used (Chatterjee et al. 2018a). It becomes apparent that most of the methods use images taken from a downward-facing perspective (using specialized cameras or vehicles) rather than having a front-facing perspective. Moreover, most of the methods are seen to be more image-processing based with limited application of ML. Further, most methods use ML for crack recognition or crack-type (network, transverse, longitudinal (BaSt 2008)) classification, while most parts of crack extraction are still based on thresholding techniques, morphology, and such noisy approaches (Chatterjee et al. 2018a).

Articles	Techniques	Viewpoints	
		Downward View	*Front View*
Teomete et al. (2005)	Image processing	✔	
Oliveira and Correia (2009)	ML with limited feature set	✔	
Nejad and Zekeri (2011)	Image-processing, Dynamic NN	✔	
Prasanna et al. (2012)	Edge detection (image-processing), ML	✔	
Huidrom et al. (2013)	Image processing and heuristic decision logic	✔	
Zalama et al. (2014)	ML to classify crack type	✔	
Li et al. (2014)	ML for crack-type classification, crack extraction with image-processing	✔	
Varadharajan et al. (2014)	ML with Support Vector Machine		✔
Zhang et al. (2016) Eisenbach et al. (2017)	Deep Learning with Convolutional Neural Network	✔	
Wu et al. (2016)	ML for crack recognition, crack extraction with image-processing	✔	
Radopoulou et al. (2016)	Semantic Texton Forest-based ML		✔
Chatterjee et al. (2018a)	Supervised ML approach		✔

Table 5.2: Automatic vision-based road crack detection techniques for 2-D images.

5.2.2 Information Systems for Road Infrastructure Management

PMS and DSS have been recognized as a necessary step for infrastructure management, and their effective design is an ongoing process. Many areas of PMS (BASt 2008; FHWA 2016) are in development, such as, for example, pavement condition index (PCI) assessment (e.g. low, medium, high, or similar country-specific ranking of road health (PMIS 2011)) using traffic and surface characteristics (defects, smoothness, etc.), developing guidelines for making maintenance and management decisions, and creating relevant IS.

As previously described, the visual defect analysis is primarily carried out manually. Visual surface characteristics of distress mostly consist of different geometric variations of cracks, patches, potholes, ruts, ravels, breaks, and other characteristics. Loprencipe (2017) presented a PMS for mid-sized municipalities is developed using PCI assessment of visual data, followed by calculation of vehicle operating costs using traffic conditions such as smoothness. Next, life-cycle cost analysis is completed using a deterioration model for planning and maintenance strategies. Geographic IS (GIS) is used for maintaining road networks in the inventory. Authors in Chamorro et al. (2009) presented pavement distress detection guidelines based on data from Ontario, Canada. Multiple linear regression is used to understand the significance of each distress on overall pavement health. Prior to this, digital 2-D images were analyzed by service providers which consists of companies using partially-automatic techniques for assessment of the presence and extent of the defects. Moreover, the study also reported that not all companies followed the step of verifying whether the assessed defects could be replicated using similar techniques. In another publication (PMIS 2011), the study focused on deriving condition ratings for Texas roads where laser profilers were used to calculate smoothness, while visual analysis was carried out by contractors. Ongoing efforts to increase automation in PCI-based decision making using images are based on techniques related to morphology, histogram analysis, ML, filtering, shape analysis, segmentation, texture analysis, and video analytics for crack detection, as summarized in Table 5.2 (Chambon and Moliard 2011; Koch et al. 2015). To date, however, comprehensive PCI assessment still faces various challenges including lower degrees of automation, higher costs of specialized systems and sensors, avoidance of noisy thresholding techniques, unavailability of a diverse dataset for testing (Koch et al. 2015), lighting and shadow issues, road markings, false positives, and low adaptability of techniques across surface textures and locations (Gavilan et al 2011). More data management related systems are also seen for PMS. As an example, one study (Tang and Sun 2012) utilizes a database storage method to integrate digital image processing into the management aspects of PMS,provided by linking the image files, directory, and physical pavement segments that are inspected. In yet another study (Yang and Lin 2013), a cloud computing enabled platform is presented based on Google public cloud utilizing real-time data processing. An additional publication (Ong et al. 2014) utilizes a web and cloud computing-based system, which implements map-based data viewing and sharing, and stores terabytes of image data stressing the need for historical data.

When it comes to DSS, various tasks such as safety analysis and planning purposes are addressed. Gianfranco (2013) analyzes road safety using concordance analysis and objective functions belonging to the target area of traffic accidents, road geometry, and traffic flow. Although many DSS are developed for planning purposes, the initial steps of PCI that are the basis of subsequent decisions are not yet fully automated. One interesting DSS (Dobson et al. 2014) utilizes aerial helicopters to collect unpaved road image data and primarily uses remote sensing to process these images. Here, 3-D point cloud technology is used for the analysis of potholes and the DSS provides maintenance recommendations based on the gathered information. However, 3-D technology requires costly acquisition and computation techniques (Huidrom 2013). In (Laubis et al. 2016) the authors presented an interesting crowd based system to estimate roughness of the road, IRI, by integrating multiple sensor values such as GPS, accelerometer, gyroscope from multiple cars fitted with smartphones. Here, the authors used a self-calibration approach to handle heterogeneous sensor values from different vehicles by training models on ground truth data and used machine learning approaches like random forest regression and support vector regression. In spite of these varied existing approaches, a systematic implementation of a DSS for crack detection using easily acquirable front-view digital images is still missing.

In general, the state of current literature on automation in pavement management show varied directional focus related to methods of data collection and storage, data management, integrated data viewing, advanced use of technology for DSS-based planning activities, automated PCI generation using images, and derivation of guidelines for assessing pavement condition indicators. Some of the challenges in these areas include fusing multiple data sources, formats, and systems such as images and video, GIS, GPS data, data on cloud, sensor data, and system level construction of such IS tools. Developments across these domains need to be effectively integrated. Furthermore, the decision process of road maintenance decision makers is currently done manually or uses costly specialized vehicles(Laubis et al. 2016; Radopoulou et al. 2016); contributing towards a slow, costly and untimely decision making.

In sum, there is a need for more focus on design, development, use, and implementation of related IS, which can be achieved through increased understanding of the diversity of processes. Accordingly, in this paper we aim to contribute towards development of a flexible, inexpensive, modular, and extendable image data-based DSS for road surface monitoring and crack detection. In the next section we describe the research approach used to develop the DSS.

5.3 Research Approach

Developing novel IS-based solutions to address important and prevailing problems falls under the paradigm of DSR (Gregor and Hevner 2013). Hence, applying a DSR approach fits our research goal of developing a novel DSS for road crack detection. Our research follows the DSR framework (Arnott and Pervan 2012; Hevner 2007), adopting a research process as depicted in Figure 5.1. We completed all three cycles of DSR in an iterative fashion (Hevner 2007), including the relevance cycle, the rigor cycle, and the design cycle.

The relevance cycle inherits the interconnection of design activities and the application environment. This means that it enables an assimilation of requirements of real-world problems. Additionally, it enables the evaluation of newly designed artifacts in their fields of application. The rigor cycle connects the design activities and the existing research. Thus, theories and concepts can be integrated and extended. The design cycle is in the center of the DSR framework, consisting of the iterative construction and evaluation of the artifacts to be designed (Hevner 2007; Peters et al. 2015).

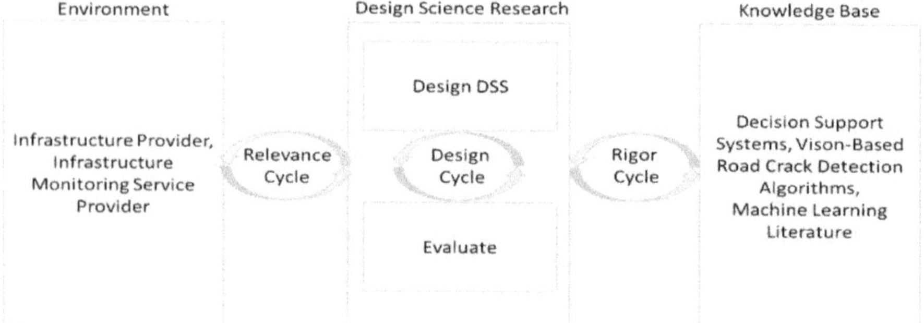

Figure 5.1: Design science research setting (adapted from Hevner 2007).

5.3.1 Iteration 1: Designing Framework for the DSS

The first iteration started with a relevance cycle, in which a literature review (see Research Background) revealed a lack of an inexpensive, flexible, and modular vision-based DSS for crack detection on road surfaces using easily acquirable 2-D front-view images. We identified initial requirements based on the previously identified publications. To verify the requirements, we discussed them with a field expert – in this case, a company based in Germany that provides road maintenance, smart monitoring services, and data analysis of road surface conditions to the government and municipalities. In combination with the literature review and expert interviews, we identified four requirements.

Next, we performed a rigor cycle to draw from existing knowledge in order to start the design cycle. While seeking an appropriate starting point for the design process, we identified available and promising ML approaches. In the following design cycle, we developed a framework for a vision-based crack detection DSS which uses low-cost, easily acquirable 2-D front-view images.

5.3.2 Iteration 2: Develop and Implement the DSS

In the second iteration, we start the relevance cycle by presenting the framework to the expert from the previous iteration for evaluation. The evaluation revealed that the framework sufficiently describes the DSS architecture. Nonetheless, two additional requirements for the implementation were gathered during the interview.

In the rigor cycle we review ways of implementing the requirements and the ML-algorithms that we used for crack detection in this work. We also followed best practices from current literature for reporting final data in a simple way for easy use for decision making. The requirement of crack percentage on road surfaces to ascertain the overall condition is in-line with the standard reporting format (Straube 2015).

Finally, in the design cycle we implemented the ML algorithms and superpixel based crack detection method in the backend and the interfaces at the frontend of the DSS. Here, model-view-controller based architecture is followed to develop the DSS. Figure 5.2 illustrates the different modules.

	Iteration 1		
	Relevance Cycle	*Rigor Cycle*	*Design Cycle*
Inputs	• PMS Literature • Road monitoring service providers	• Literature related to ML, crack detection on road surfaces, and DSS	• Requirements • Potential ML approaches for crack detection
Methods	• Literature review • Expert interview	• Literature review	• Framework development and prototyping
Steps	• Literature search • Analyze relevant publications • Formulate research gaps • Evaluate findings with the service provider • Elicit Requirements	• Gather literature • Analyze literature • Identify inputs for design cycle	• DSS framework design • Evaluate against requirements
Results	• Need of a vision-based DSS for detecting cracks using cheaply acquirable 2-D front-view images • Requirements	• Potential ML approaches for crack detection	• DSS framework

Table 5.3: Summary of iteration 1.

5.3.3 Iteration 3: Evaluation and Publication

For DSR, it is important to evaluate artifacts as closely as possible to their real-world environments and intended fields of application (Gregor and Hevner 2013; Hevner 2007). Therefore, we tested the implemented DSS in two ways.

Firstly, we gathered an extensive database of videos of roads in Germany and applied the implemented DSS to analyze the images. Here, we mounted an HD camera on an e-bike to take front-view images and videos that helped us to cover different road types such as rural, and urban roads, and narrower bikepaths. We used 50 diverse images from this dataset to test our

-	Iteration 2		
	Relevance Cycle	*Rigor Cycle*	*Design Cycle*
Inputs	• Road monitoring service provider	• Literature	• DSS Framework • Road detection approach • ML for detecting cracks • Format for DSS outputs
Methods	• Expert interview	• Literature review	• Prototyping • DSS development
Steps	• Formulate questionnaire about potential DSS framework • Hold expert interviews with service providers • Evaluate prototype • Gather requirements	• Analyze publications • Select ML algorithms • Identify DSS outputs • Identify technical inputs for implementation (programming language and libraries)	• DSS development • Implement the algorithms and interfaces
Results	• Verified framework • Additional requirements	• Road detection approach • ML for detecting cracks • Format for DSS outputs	• Vision-based crack detection DSS

Table 5.4: Summary of iteration 2.

selected ML-based crack detection approach to ascertain accuracy, precision, and recall of the algorithms.

Secondly, the DSS was presented to an expert in road maintenance and to monitoring service providers in Germany. This helped us to evaluate that the developed DSS fulfilled the previously gathered requirements.

To conclude the research process, we performed a final rigor cycle to add the artifact, its development process, and its implications to the existing body of knowledge. Then, we summarize and reflect on our results and add them to the knowledge base in form of a design theory (Gregor and Jones 2007) as well as the submission of this article for publication. However, there is no "universal" formula on how to develop a design theory. Furthermore, developing a design theory is often characterized as difficult and fuzzy (Gregory and Muntermann 2014, 2011; Mandviwalla 2015). Therefore, we adapted heuristic theorizing (Gregory and Muntermann 2014) and synthesized the artifact and its development process in the form of a design theory (Gregor and Jones 2007).

The approach emphasizes theory development based on iteration of problem structuring and artifact design. Thus, in order to develop a six component design theory (Gregor and Jones 2007), we performed the following steps after each research cycle: (1) We first review the current design theory and evaluate the need for refinement. (2) If refinement is needed, we iteratively add new components and/or adjust existing components until all new knowledge is incorporated.

-	Iteration 3		
	Relevance Cycle	*Rigor Cycle*	
Inputs	• Vision-based crack detection DSS on road surfaces • County Employee	• Development process • ML and vision-based crack detection • Literature	-
Methods	• Testing and evaluation with collected real image datasets • Expert interview	• Iterative theory building • Article and publication writing	
Steps	• Evaluate DSS performance • Expert DSS verification	• Summarize design theory • Document vision-based crack detection DSS and implementation details • Publication writing	
Results	• Evaluated vision-based crack detection DSS	• Evaluated vision-based crack detection DSS • Design theory • This article	

Table 5.5: Summary of iteration 3.

5.4 Results

In this section, we firstly present the requirements gathered during the DSR process which guided our development process. Secondly, the developed DSS and framework are presented and the individual modules and functions are described. Lastly, we present the results of our evaluation of the performance and the decision-support capabilities.

5.4.1 Requirements

In the first iteration, the following requirements were gathered based on the conducted literature review and the following expert interview:

R1 – Robustness: The DSS must be robust regarding the input images, e.g. able to analyze front-view images with a relatively high level of noise.
R2 – Automation: The DSS must be able to analyze the images automatically.
R3 – Performance: The DSS must provide a sufficient level of accuracy, e.g. identify cracks with a high certainty.
R4 – Adaptability: The DSS must be adaptable to different contexts, e.g. cities and road-types.

The evaluation of the developed DSS Framework in the second iteration provided two additional requirements:

R5 – Integrative: The DSS must be easy to integrate into existing processes and systems.
R6 – Understandable : The DSS must provide a high level of understandability regarding its outputs (e.g. visualization of defect rating).Providing information in an easy to understand way, enabling informed decision making, is the core object of DSS (Arnott and Pervan 2012). Hence, the DSS has to provide outputs that enable decision making in a way that it does not complicate the process. A too complicated process could lead to companies and decision makers opting for the common approach, rejecting the "convoluted" new approach (e.g. using the DSS).

R1 captures the main requirements for the functionality of the DSS. Current approaches and DSS require images with a very low level of noise (e.g. from a specific angle, close to the crack, etc.). Hence, the DSS to be developed must be more robust regarding the front-view input images which could originate from varied sources such as smartphones, travel cameras, car cameras, etc., and contain varied scene elements. To provide an improvement to the status-quo (e.g. manual surveys), the DSS must automate the crack detection process (R2). In addition to automation, the DSS must also provide a sufficient level of accuracy for crack detection (R3). Lastly, to ensure that the DSS can be applied by various practitioners and also to provide generalizable design knowledge, the DSS must be designed to be adaptable to different cities, road types (e.g. rural, urban, sidewalk, narrower, wider roads), and pavement surface textures.The DSS must function as a part of the overall system of pavement monitoring companies. Hence, it must be easy to integrate by using modular architecture, APIs, and specialized hardware (R5). Furthermore, the outputs of the DSS must be easy to understand for providing the necessary level of decision support (R6).

5.4.2 Vision-based Crack Detection Decision Support System

As discovered in the relevance cycle of the first iteration, it is evident that cheaper alternatives for automated road crack detection using simple 2-D front-view images are required, considering the ubiquitous nature of cameras in our modern economy. Hence, a vision-based crack detection DSS was developed. The DSS has two main parts: a front-end component and a back-end component. Via the front-end component, data can be input into the system and the parameters can be set. The back-end component consists of different modules for the different steps within a vision-based crack detection process, such as road-detection, crack detection, and visualization. The framework is presented in Figure 5.2 and the user interface is shown in

Figure 5.3. Different modules of the DSS are described below. For the implementation, we used Python as development environment.

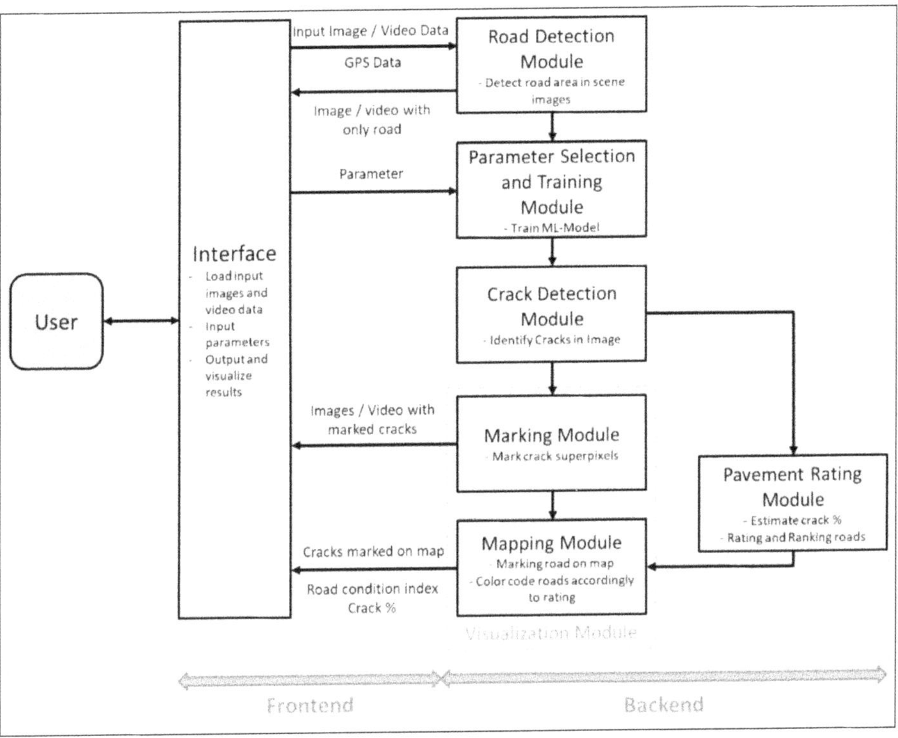

Figure 5.2: Framework of the vision-based DSS for crack detection.

Road Detection Module

In the first step, video or images are uploaded and the image is then divided into road and surroundings (Images are also extracted from videos at this step). This allows reduction of noise level and use of any front-facing images. We applied an approach developed by Chatterjee et al. (2017) to detect the road area in a complete scene image. Figure 3 shows an output of a road image containing only the detected road area (R6), created from a scene image containing all scene elements such as road, trees, buildings, sky, vehicles, etc. The algorithmic technique used is based on a graph-based hierarchical clustering approach where similar superpixels (groups of pixels) in an image are clustered so that at the end of the clustering, road area belongs to a cluster and is recognized as road in the image. In the approach, similarity between superpixels and image areas is obtained using a Gaussian kernel-based hybrid distance metric containing

Euclidean and Bhattacharyya distances. Such similarity measures are used to create a distance metric and group and merge the regions in an iterative manner using Hungarian algorithm as the optimization technique and pairwise assignment technique. The utilized approach helped us not only to detect the road area and eradicate complex scene elements, but also to detect shadows on road surfaces, thus decreasing false positives during crack detection in the later stages of the DSS. The road images are then forwarded to the next module.

Crack Detection Module

Cracks are then detected using the inputs from the previous module. For this step, the approach of Chatterjee et al. (2018a) was applied. At the beginning, every road image (i.e. the image with only road area where all other scene elements are removed) is converted from RGB color to grayscale. For this, every image pixel gets a weighted average of $0.29R + 0.56G + 0.11B$. The pixels in this grayscale image are then grouped into superpixels (groups of pixels) using a Simple Linear Iterative Clustering (SLIC) procedure (Achanta et al. 2012) to cluster the RGB color and (x, y) location values of the pixels. After superpixels are generated and contrast is balanced, following Chatterjee et al. (2018a) a set of 40 features is extracted for each of the superpixel.

These 40 features consist of the following: (1) first-order statistical measure of variance and skewness, (2) 6 features of Grey Level Co-occurrence Matrix(GLCM) (Haralick 1979) based second-order statistical features measuring homogeneity, angular second moment, energy, correlation, contrast and dissimilarity, and (4) 32 features from Variance-of-Gabor (VoG). GLCM properties or features have important parameters of (d_o, θ) i.e. angle θ (giving direction for the spatial relationship) and an offset do (neighbour pixels to be considered) and these are tuned for feature extraction. On the other hand, VoG is based on features extracted using Gabor filters (Gabor 1946). Edge and texture features are extracted by overlaying Gabor filters on images. For obtaining VoG fatures, Gabor filter parameters such as kernel size k, Gaussian function's scale parameter σ, wavelength of Gabor filter's sinusoid λ, and number of orientations α (taken as 32 here) are tuned. To obtain VoG features of a superpixel, a superpixel is Gabor filtered at different orientations and then variance is calculated for each of the orientation image.

We used the approach of feature mapping in Chatterjee et al. (2018a) to obtain tuned parameters for both GLCM and VoG feature extraction algorithms using classifier's performance and selected 40 feature-sets, giving the best performance. Once the 40 features are obtained for each of the superpixels, the test dataset (i.e. the set of superpixels) is fed to the classifiers for classifying these superpixels as crack or non-crack. The four classifiers that we use here, referring Chatterjee et al. (2018a), are Gradient Boosting (GB), Random Forest (RF), Linear Support Vector Machine (L-SVM) and Artificial Neural Network (ANN). In this way, we perform the ML-based crack detection for images in this work.

Parameter Selection and Training Module

Functionalities of the Parameter Selection and Training module are described here. These modules are developed to adapt and extend training of algorithms for the future. As mentioned in the ML-based Crack Detection module above, well-tuned default parameters and classifiers are available in our system following the approach in Chatterjee et al. (2018a). These two modules could be extended to try more feature extraction algorithms if needed, following the incremental feature selection process in Chatterjee et al. (2018a) so that varied data could be handled. Also, these modules give the opportunity to select the classifier and add or delete classifiers as required. The default classifier in our DSS is set as RF due to its improved performance over other alternatives. Default parameters of the 40 features include the variance and skew, as well as 32 VoG features with $\alpha = 32$, $k = 11$, $\sigma = 15$, $\lambda = 10$ for the Gabor filter, and 6 GLCM features with (d_o, θ) parameters set as the following: $d_o = 5, \theta = 45°$.

Pavement Rating Module

This module also increases flexibility of the DSS in adapting to different pavement condition index (PCI) assessment approaches (or similar country-specific ranking of roads). Here, we classify the roads based on deterioration of the pavement using % of superpixels in road images classified and marked as cracks based on the established criteria (Straube 2015). We estimate the crack percentage here using the ratio of superpixels detected as crack to all the non-black superpixels in the image. So,

$$Crack\% = \frac{Number\, of\, superpixels\, classified\, as\, crack\, in\, the\, image}{Total\, number\, of\, non-black\, road\, surface\, superpixels\, in\, the\, image} \times 100.$$

Thus, the crack % is also used to rank the road surfaces, so that road with more crack could be repaired and attended earlier. This allows for extension of the DSS to other monitoring services. Moreover, in future cracks could be classified into types such as network, transverse, longitudinal (BaSt 2008) and each of these separately could contribute toward PCI calculation according to given rules as seen in a prior study (Straube 2015). Thus, the PCI module could be adapted without interrupting other modules.

Visualization Module and Interface

The visualization module provides the outputs for the front end (e.g. interface). Hence we will describe its functionalities together with the user interface (see Figure 5.2 and Figure 5.3). Images of the individual steps, road detection, crack marking and road surface rating based on % of superpixels detected as cracks (taken as PCI and crack %) are shown in Figure 5.3. The crack % is used to rank the road surfaces, with higher percentage suggesting that the road needs immediate attention to repair and maintenance. When GPS coordinates are provided, the road condition is visualized on a map (see Figure 5.3). Roads are marked red if the crack percentage is over 15, yellow if the crack percentage is between 15 and 7, and green if the crack percentage is below 7.In this way, road conditions could be visualized. The percentage thresholds were selected experimentally.

5.5 Evaluation

In order to evaluate the developed DSS, we perform algorithm-level and functionality-level evaluations.

5.5.1 Performance

The developed DSS relies on the combination of established algorithms and approaches. Nonetheless, to ensure a sufficient level of accuracy (R3), crack detection performance was also evaluated. We performed the evaluation using precision (P), recall (R), F1-measure, and accuracy defined as: The developed DSS relies on the combination of established algorithms and approaches. Nonetheless, to ensure a sufficient level of accuracy (R3), crack detection performance was also evaluated. We performed the evaluation using precision (P), recall (R), F1-measure, and accuracy defined as: $P = \frac{TP}{TP+FP}, R = \frac{TP}{TP+FN}, F1 = 2\frac{P.R}{P+R}, Accuracy = \frac{TP+TN}{TP+TN+FP+FN}$. Here, TP denotes true positives (crack correctly detected as crack), TN denotes true negatives (non-crack correctly detected as non-crack), FP denotes false positive (incorrectly detecting non-crack area as crack), FN denotes false negative (incorrectly detecting crack as non-crack).

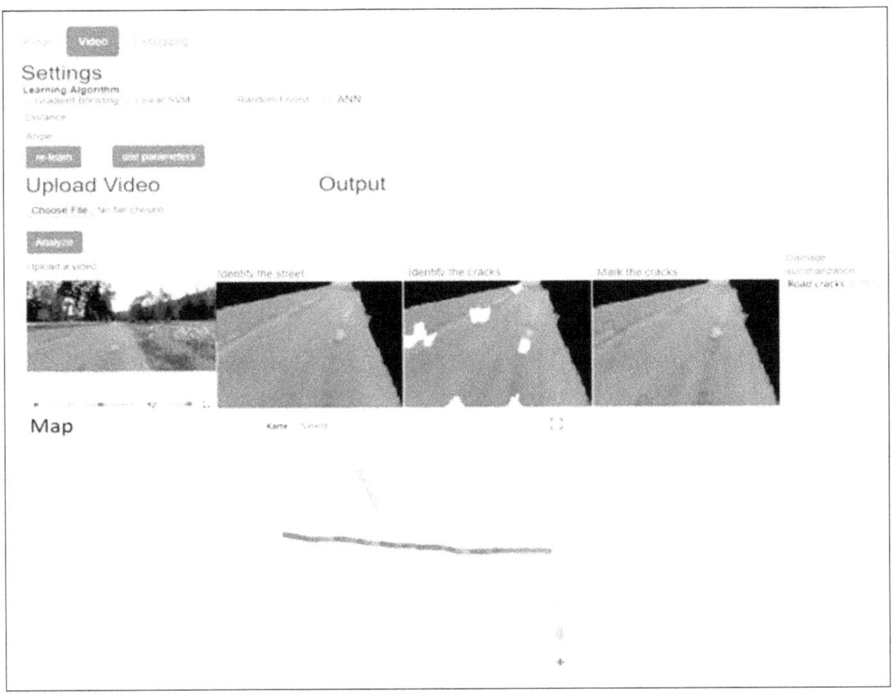

Figure 5.3: Prototype of the DSS interface.

F1 measures the harmonic mean of precision and recall. Figure 5.4 shows examples of detected cracks on images.

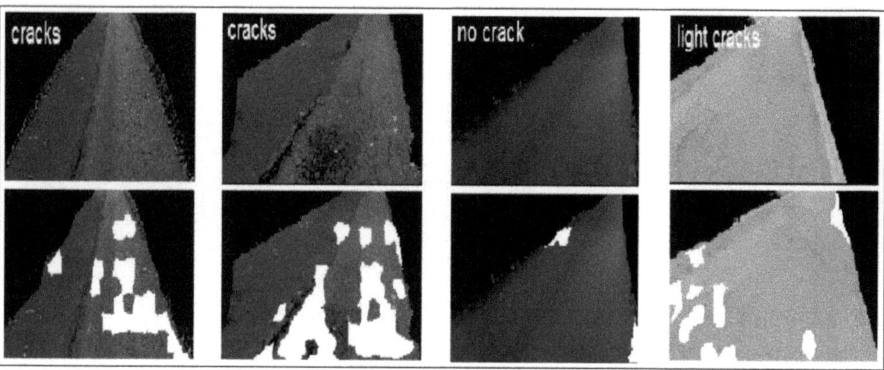

Figure 5.4: Detected cracks on front-view road images. Every image set shows an original image (upper row) and detected crack superpixels on it (in white) (bottom row) using Random Forest classifier.

The evaluation was performed at the superpixel level as in Chatterjee et al. (2018a). We used 50 test images containing both crack and non-crack areas to evaluate the pre-trained model from the authors. Because performance is ascertained at the superpixel level, 50 images have $50 \times 150 = 7500$ superpixels. Out of these, as marked in the road image of Figure 5.3 (2nd image named as "identify the street") and Figure 5.4, background black color pixels are also present. When road is extracted out of the scene image using the Road Generation module, non-road elements are blackened as the background. So, these black pixels with their RGB color of $(0,0,0)$ are not included in the test dataset. Hence, out of the 7,500 superpixels, our test dataset becomes 4,811 valid superpixels containing the road surface. Table 5.6 summarizes the evaluation on this dataset and shows that the RF is the best performing class of algorithm. Nonetheless, all four classifiers of RF, GB, ANN and L-SVM are implemented within the DSS.

Classifier	Accuracy (%)	P (%)	R (%)	F1 (%)
GB	92.93	84.80	91.53	88.04
RF	92.99	85.03	91.22	88.02
ANN	90.85	77.03	90.76	83.33

Table 5.6: Performance of the classifiers on 4811 test data from various locations.

5.5.2 Decision Support

We evaluated the DSS to see if it satisfies all the initial requirements. We tested the requirement R1 by giving noisy images of varied external conditions and surface conditions to the system and the DSS handled the images successfully to detect cracks and defects on it. R2 was evaluated successfully as the DSS automated the crack detection and showed the crack density at the end. R3 was satisfied as shown by the evaluations above, giving an accuracy of 92.93 percent when GB classifier was used. Requirement R4 was tested successfully as the DSS could handle images of various surroundings and road-types. To evaluate the use of the DSS, we held an expert interview with a German county employee, responsible for the county's biking paths. Therefore, the expert is familiar with the offerings for pavement monitoring in Germany as well as the process of pavement monitoring itself. For the expert interview, the DSS was presented and tested by the expert. The individual steps including data upload, algorithm selection, parameter setting,and output visualization were completed. During each step, the expert was requested to give positive as well as negative feedback. R5 and R6 requirements were specifically evaluated by the experts. Overall, the interview revealed that the system fulfills its task of providing automated crack detection based on 2-D front-view images. Nonetheless, the expert critiqued the usability of the DSS, requesting an advanced interface composition. Also, additional detection capabilities, e.g. for potholes, were requested. Hence, the DSS was evaluated as fulfilling all initial requirements, needing refinement regarding usability for productive usage and extension through further research.

5.6 Design Theory

Design theories offer prescriptions for constructing an artifact while meeting a set of defined requirements and solving a prevailing problem. The development of design theories has attained more attention because of the rising number and diversity of problems that require academically developed artifact-based solutions (Gregory and Muntermann 2014). Hence, we developed a design theory to formalize and summarize the knowledge gathered in the development process. Gregor and Jones (2007) defined the following six essential parts of a design theory: 1) Purpose and scope. 2) Constructs. 3) Principal of form and function. 4) Artifact mutability. 5) Testable proposition. 6) Justificatory knowledge. We illustrate the design theory of a vision-based road crack-detection DSS along these six components in Table 5.7 following Gregor and Jones (2007).

Component	Description
Purpose and Scope	The aim of the system is to detect defective areas containing cracks on road surface 2-D images taken from a front viewpoint. Meta-Requirements: Robustness (R1), Automation (R2), Performance (R3), Adaptability (R4), Integrative (R5), Understandable (R6)
Constructs	Crack, crack detection, 2-D images, front-view images, pavement, road, pavement management, pavement condition evaluation, pavement monitoring
Principle of Form and Function	• A vision-based crack detection DSS consist of 6 components: Road Detection Module, Parameter Selection and Training Module, Crack Detection Module, Pavement Condition Rating Module, Visualization Module, and Interface. (R2, R4, R5) • The inputs for the DSS are 2-D videos or images containing roads. (R1, R5) • To detect roads in images, hierarchical clustering can be applied. (R4) • ML should be applied for crack detection. (R1, R2, R3) • The rated pavement condition should be color coded and visualized on a map. (R6) • The individual outcomes of each step throughout the crack detection process (road identification, crack identification and crack rating) should be displayed. (R6)
Artifact Mutability	Using 2-D front-view images makes the system more adaptable to various image (data) input devices such as smartphones, car cameras, and other commodity cameras; and also to different road types (rural/ urban/ bike paths/ narrower/ wider). The modular architecture allows adding, extending, removing of modules in the backend.
Testable Propositions	The DSS is able to detect cracks using 2-D front-view images in an automated manner.
Justificatory Knowledge	Road maintenance and automated monitoring literature, DSS literature, machine learning literature.

Table 5.7: Design theory of vision-based crack detection DSS.

5.7 Discussion

The aim of this study was to answer two research questions. The first explores how road surface cracks can be automatically detected using 2-D front-view images. We address this by combining and applying ML-algorithms based on Chatterjee et al. (2017, 2018a). The second question regarding the design of a vision-based crack detection DSS has been answered by applying a DSR process in which the previously identified algorithms were combined to design such a DSS. This study holds contributions for the following research domains as discussed below.

The presented development process contributes to DSR through several means. Firstly, it provides an example for the application of DSR to solve the specific problem of vision-based crack detection. Secondly, when viewing the artifact within the DSR knowledge contribution formwork (Gregor and Hevner 2013), we argue that the problem of automating pavement monitoring is a rather new problem domain, constituted by the current state-of-the-art being manual or special vehicle supported pavement monitoring. Hence, the analysis of front-view images to identify road cracks remains a novel problem domain. Similarly, the application and combination of ML-algorithms to identify cracks in images can be seen as a novel approach. In sum, both the application domain maturity as well as solution maturity are considerably low. Subsequently, our developed model and its instantiation as a DSS can be seen as an improvement, as it provides an improved solution and also as an exaptation due to incorporation of established ML algorithms. Additionally, the contribution of this study is situated on two different levels of theoretical abstraction (Gregor and Hevner 2013). The developed and presented DSS framework and principals of form and function can be characterized as nascent design theory (level 2), while the implemented DSS provides a tangible instantiation (level 1).

This work further gives insights on how the big data could be leveraged to derive critical insights for automated decision support (Galliers 2015; Goes 2014). Specifically, we utilize ML for road area detection in scene images, followed by a superpixel and ML-based approach for crack detection in these images. The capability of our developed DSS for accepting 2-D front-facing images makes it valuable due to ease and low cost of data gathering with commonly available tools such as smartphone cameras and bypasses the need for specialized expensive equipment (Yoo 2010). Between the automated nature of machine learning methods used and the ubiquitous presence of common inexpensive tools for implementation, the developed DSS presents an affordable, scalable tool for an efficient and timely infrastructure monitoring. Thus, this research enables a wide variety of contributors across government agencies, service providers, and individual citizens to easily participate in road condition monitoring and opens opportunities for crowdsourcing and efficient management of mobility infrastructure maintenance (Laubis et al. 2016) and smart cities(Tilson et al. 2010; Khatoun and Zeadally 2016).The developed DSS and crowdsourcing could also be extended and integrated in the framework of a service map (Laubis et al. 2018) to provide various data, analysis, business, or smart services.Smart city service applications such as traffic alert or navigation apps can inform citizens of poor road conditions and could be developed.

Thus, the developed DSS addresses the important challenges of improving road maintenance capabilities, reducing time and resources needed, and making automated monitoring more affordable and accessible. Green IS research is a sub-domain of the IS discipline that investigates the design, implementation, and use of IS to positively impact the environment and support sustainability within organizations (Gholami et al. 2016; Malhotra et al. 2013). This fits the goal of the developed DSS as it enables better road maintenance and more efficient assessment of road conditions. For example, prolonged road maintenance works could be avoided by detecting defects at earlier stages and fuel consumption could be reduced by better road conditions, thus reducing emissions. Thus, developing this type of IS also adds to the research domain of Green IS (Watson et al. 2010). To be specific, vom Brocke et al. (2013) called upon the Green IS research community to provide tangible research outcomes in form of IS artifacts that enable more sustainable research practices. Further, delayed road maintenance contributes significantly to environment degradation (Gleave 2014). Hence, the developed DSS facilitates sustainable organizational actions (Melville 2010) in the context of road maintenance.

Besides contributing to IS research and decision support systems in the aforementioned ways, this study also provides important implications for practice. Firstly, this study systematically describes how vision-based crack detection DSS should be designed, enabling its implementation and adaptation for practice. Hence, practitioners can use the provided knowledge to enhance their pavement monitoring capabilities. Secondly, this study encourages cities to gather videos and images from their road networks. For example, public transportation vehicles (Mertz 2011) should be equipped with cameras to obtain the necessary image data. Eventually an IS similar to the presented one can be used to analyze the video and image data.

Limitations and Future Work

To understand the contributions of this study, its limitations must also be considered. Firstly, the artifacts were developed and evaluated in a German context, as the service provider of the first and second iteration is located in Germany and the employee of the last iteration is employed by a German county. Secondly, the evaluation within the DSR process was limited to two domain experts. Lastly, the timeliness constitutes a limitation for the relevance and rigor of the DSR approach. Only literature and algorithms which were known and accessible up to the time of submission is included.

DSR is an iterative search process for utility (Hevner 2007; Hevner et al. 2004). The aim is not to design the perfect artifact, but rather to provide an improvement over the status quo (Gregor and Hevner 2013; Mandviwalla 2015). Furthermore, our research provides two major directions for future research developments. Firstly, even though the application drastically improved the status-quo of pavement monitoring, future optimization (Rai 2017) of the applied algorithms optimization still constitutes an important research opportunity. For example, detected cracks could be classified into crack-types such as network, transverse, and longitudinal (BaSt 2008), while PCI and visualization modules aggregating crack-type information can be further improved upon. Also, information such as position of the crack (center, middle, edges) could be used for optimizing the PCI. In future, more additional features could be added, and certain road defects such as rut depth, for example, may need sensors. These sensor values could then be fed back to the PCI module to generate comprehensive road condition health index following specific rules. Furthermore, as cracks could be identified using the approach in this study by different vehicles independently in a crowdsourced manner, a GPS mapper module could be created in the DSS to ascertain the same inspected areas and update that information accordingly. Furthermore, the DSS could be extended to include estimates of repair costs and maintenance schedules. Secondly, the presented DSS should be applied in practice (Arnott and Pervan 2012; Hevner et al. 2004), e.g. to automate the pavement monitoring process of a county in a field-test. In this study the functionally and performance of the system was decisive. However, the application of the DSS might reveal important design implications in human-computer interaction design (Banker and Kauffman 2004).

5.8 Conclusion

This study presents a DSS for vision-based crack detection. The DSS was developed following the established DSR approach (Hevner 2007; Hevner et al. 2004). Overall, two interconnected artifacts were developed: a DSS framework and its instantiation. We evaluated the artifacts by conducting interviews with experts and practitioners as well as with common performance metrics. The evaluations revealed that the DSS is able to automate crack identification on pavements by analyzing front-facing images, which can be obtained with common car or travel cameras.Thus, this DSS supports informed and intelligent decision making. This study therefore contributes to IS research by exploring the capabilities of combining crowdsourcing and big data for gathering road images and analyzing them to support road management. Additionally, the IS provides valuable automation for the road maintenance decision process, facilitating faster response times, decreasing resource demand and generally increasing environmental sustainability.

Chapter 6: Contribution and Conclusion

6.1 Findings and Results

In this section the main findings of this dissertation is summarized with respect to the research questions.

6.1.1 Road Area Segmentation

> *$ResearchQuestion1$: How can the pavement(road) area be segmented within scene images for various scene settings such as rural, urban, unstructured, and road surface types, using a flexible approach?*

Chapter 2 of this dissertation answers $ResearchQuestion1$ and provides an adaptable algorithmic approach for the detection and segmentation of the road area within natural scene images. The approach removes external scene elements such as buildings, vehicles, people, vegetation, while detecting and extracting only the road area. Moreover, the approach also detects many types of shadows, thus helping in the crack detection phase as such areas could be avoided. To answer the subsequent research questions in this dissertation, crack and defect detection are performed on the extracted road area.

The developed algorithmic technique for clustering the road area, prior to its segmentation, is unsupervised in nature. It is based on hierarchical clustering and split-and-merge approaches where similar superpixels (Achanta et al. 2012) and regions in an image are clustered. A graph has been used as the underlying data structure having superpixels (later regions as merging and clustering continues) as nodes. This helps to preserve the regional adjacency of different regions, and in every iteration of clustering nodes are merged.

Color, texture, and histogram based feature descriptors are used. Features such as LBP, GLCM have been employed to provide texture features, while HoG provides edge features. Additionally, pixel locations have been used. Every superpixel or region is characterized by these features.

In the developed approach, similarity between superpixels (in progressive steps image regions) is obtained using a Gaussian kernel based hybrid distance metric containing Euclidean and Bhattacharyya distances. Such derived distance metric showed better adaptability for the task at hand than KL-divergence. Such similarity measures, along with the Hungarian algorithm and pairwise assignment, are used to group and merge the regions in an iterative manner; thus pointing toward hierarchical clustering. In every iteration of the merging and clustering procedure, scale parameter of the Gaussian kernel has been varied to effectively bring similar clusters closer. Number of clusters are automatically obtained in the process and the merging/ clustering procedure stops when number of formed clusters do not change. In this way, grouping of the pavement area is done.

Once the pavement area has been uniquely grouped and clustered, a simple approach combining Nearest Neighbor and ranking has been used to detect the group or cluster finally as the road. GLCM-based contrast measure has been utilized for the detection as roads/ pavements are generally one of the most homogeneous (least contrasted) region in an image. Other attributes such as geometric position of roads and color have also been used for the detection phase. In this way, once the clustering of the road area is done, the cluster depicting the road is finally detected and segmented in an image.

The developed approach has been successfully evaluated on the collected dataset of 300 diverse images (200 belonging to a mixture of rural and unstructured scene settings, 100 belonging to a mixture of rural and urban scene settings). It gives a F1 score of 91.14 % on the 200 image dataset, 87.13 % on the 100 image dataset. The approach is also tested on the KITTI (um-road) benchmark test dataset comprising of 96 images and gives a F1 score of 85.32 %.

The proposed approach has also been successfully compared with base classifiers such as SVM, Gaussian Naive Bayes, AdaBoost, and K-NN, with AdaBoost giving best result among all. AdaBoost gives a F1 score of 72.50 % on the 200 image dataset, 70.50 % on 100 image dataset within the collected dataset. It gives 73.13 % on the KITTI (um-road) test data. The detailed evaluations and results can be seen in Table 2.4 and Table 2.5 of Chapter 2.

Further, the approach does not use any image, scene, or camera specific characteristics such as vanishing point (Miksik 2012; Schreiber et al. 2014), road edges or markings (Beyeler et al. 2014), camera properties (Hoiem et al. 2005). This makes the developed approach adaptable to different scene types such as urban roads which have lane markers and are more structured, as well as rural roads which are less structured. At the same time, the approach does not use seed points or supervised approaches (Passani et al. 2014; Brust et al. 2015), making it less susceptible to training data. Finally, the developed road segmentation approach also do not require number of clusters to be provided in advance and is automatically obtained; thereby making it more adaptable, flexible, and scalable. Hence, it can handle various scene settings such as rural and urban, as well as different pavement surface types, such as paved and unpaved. While the approach is numerically simple, it shows promising ability to merge and group similar regions.

6.1.2 Classifier Based Defect Detection on Road Surfaces at the Superpixel Level

> $ResearchQuestion2$: *How can cracks and related defects on the road surfaces of front-view images be detected at the superpixel level using ML-based classifier techniques?*

As part of $ResearchQuestion2$, the sub-research questions within it are the following:

> $ResearchQuestion2.1$: *How state-of-the-art ML classifiers can be applied for crack and related defect detection?*
> $ResearchQuestion2.2$: *What are the most relevant image features for crack detection at the superpixel level, so as to make the cracks more distinguishable?*

Chapter 3 of this dissertation attends $ResearchQuestion2$ and the associated sub-research questions. It provides insights for analysis of front-view road surface images and crack detection at the superpixel level (i.e. region or area).

In the proposed ML-based approach, firstly an image is divided into coherent regions, called superpixels (Achanta et al. 2012), and these superpixels are encoded by feature descriptors. After this, the superpixels are classified into crack and no-crack classes using ML-based classifiers. The developed approach in chapter 3 also ensures that relevant image feature descriptors are identified using a systematic feature selection method. For this, various state-of-the-art feature extraction algorithms have been investigated in this dissertation. For optimal parameter selection of each of the feature extraction algorithm, as well as for obtaining the final feature set, step-wise incremental subset feature selection guided by the classifier's accuracy metric have been used. The feature subset and parameter set giving the highest accuracy has been selected as the final feature descriptor set to characterize the superpixels. A new feature variant, namely the Variance-of-Gabor (VoG), is formulated and used for the task at hand. Finally, 40 features containing statistical measures of variance, skewness, VoG features, and GLCM features have been used. The developed approach also provides a way of applying state-of-the-art ML classifiers such as Gradient Boosting, Random Forest, Artificial Neural Network, Support Vector Machine for crack and related defect detection at the superpixel level. Taken together, this methodological approach addresses $ResearchQuestion2.1$

The proposed technique has been tested on 215 test data (i.e. 215 test superpixels), as well as on an additional 8828 test data (i.e. 8828 test superpixels obtained from 80 images). These images are part of the collected dataset in this work and have been used for evaluation purposes. For both datasets, RF consistently gave good results with F1 score of 90.61% and 90.87%, respectively. Detailed evaluations could be seen in Table 3.3 and Table 3.4 of chapter 3.

Following observations are made about the developed ML classifier based crack detection approach in this dissertation:

1. First-order statistical properties, such as variance, and second-order GLCM statistical properties show high relevance and discriminative property for crack and related defect detection.
2. Gabor filter based VoG feature variant helped to obtain interesting edges and properties of the crack region at different orientations.
3. Texture related features, such as variance, GLCM, showed better suitability than edge related features, such as HoG.
4. Combination of first-order and second-order statistical features, along with VoG features, show better resilience to varied illumination and image acquisition distance.
5. Incremental subset feature selection, along with the guided parameter tuning of the feature extraction algorithms using classifier's performance metric, provided a systematic approach to feature selection and mapping for the task at hand.

These observations from (1) - (5) addresses $ResearchQuestion2.2$. Additionally, it is seen that ensemble ML methods like, Gradient Boosting (GB) and Random Forest (RF), are more suitable. RF gave less false positives which is an important criteria for defect detection. The proposed approach of chapter 3 does not use mostly followed noisy image-processing based methods, and shows promising crack detection results for various road surfaces belonging to different locations, illumination conditions, and crack-types (e.g. single, network).

6.1.3 Keypoint Matching Based Defect Detection on Road Surfaces at the Pixel Level

> *$ResearchQuestion3$: How can keypoint matching be formulated for crack detection at the pixel level on road surfaces of front-view images?*

The sub-research questions that are handled within $ResearchQuestion3$ are the following:

> *$ResearchQuestion3.1$: How can keypoints be generated in images for crack detection, considering density of defective crack pixels are much less in any image?*

ResearchQuestion3.2: How can keypoints be encoded with descriptors for crack detection, so as to make the descriptors more discriminative?
ResearchQuestion3.3: What is the matching criteria to ascertain matched keypoints across images for crack detection?

Chapter 4 of this dissertation addresses *ResearchQuestion3* and the associated sub-research questions. It provides insights into the modular approach for analysis of front-view road surface images and crack detection at the pixel level using a keypoint matching mechanism, inspired by image matching methods.

As discussed in the introduction of chapter 1, keypoints are important points or regions in images like corners, edges, blobs, which characterize local image regions or appearance of distinct objects in images (Kumar et al. 2016; Lowe 2014). The number of keypoints, encoded in feature descriptors, could be matched across images to identify the number of similar keypoints (or interesting points) in two images. This gives a direct estimation of how similar are two images. In this dissertation, keypoints between a constant reference crack image and query images (i.e. images with road surfaces on which cracks and defects are to be identified) are matched to ascertain their similarity. The developed algorithmic approach of chapter 4 primarily has three steps:

1. Firstly, the keypoints are generated using the statistical property that the density of defective and crack pixels (which are practically anomalies and edges in the image) in images are much less than non-defective ones (which are non-edges). Hence, this work proposes one Gamma distribution for defective pixels, and another Gamma distribution representing non-defective pixels. Thus, the pixels are clustered so as to belong to one of these distributions. Consequently, a fuzzy-theoretic approach called Gamma Mixture Fuzzy Model (GMFM) has been used to estimate the parameters of these two Gamma distributions. GMFM clusters the gradient values and the cluster with the higher gradient is taken as edges. Hence, GMFM clusters the pixels into edges (cracks or defects) and non-edges (non-cracks), while taking the edge pixels as keypoints i.e. probable crack and defective pixels. This methodology thus addresses *ResearchQuestion3.1*.

2. Secondly, after keypoints are generated, 128-D fuzzy descriptors are used to encode these keypoints. The descriptors are generated using triangular membership functions and orientations of keypoints. For every keypoint, a circular region is considered around it and this region is divided into 16 subregions. In every subregion, 8 membership functions are used. So, all the pixels within a subregion are assigned a membership value according to their "degree of belongingness" towards the membership functions, and all these val-

ues are averaged. So, every subregion is depicted with a 8-D vector. In this way, every keypoint is encoded with a 128-D (16×8) fuzzy image descriptor. Fuzzified descriptors provide strong discriminatory ability (Kumar et al. 2016). This methodology thus addresses $ResearchQuestion3.2$.

3. Thirdly, keypoints (encoded with fuzzy descriptors) between the reference crack image and the query image are matched to see which keypoints are similar and can be nominated as real crack pixels. The similarity metric has been developed using KL-divergence between two Dirichlet distributions. The number of matched (similar) keypoints, M, quantifies the extent of crack and defective pixels in query images. This methodology thus addresses $ResearchQuestion3.3$.

The developed approach is evaluated on the collected dataset of 140 images containing varied crack-types, illumination conditions, and road surfaces. Experimentally obtained threshold of 70 on number of matched keypoints M between the reference crack image and query image is used to classify query images into one of two classes. So, $M > 70$ makes the query images classified as defective image and with $M \leq 70$ the query image is classified as non-defective image. High F1 score of 91.88% has been observed for classifying road surface images into defective or non-defective classes. Table 4.2 and Figure 4.7 - Figure 4.9 of chapter 4 show detailed evaluations. The approach has been further successfully compared with state-of-the-art histogram feature descriptor based matching algorithm SIFT, and shows better results than SIFT for keypoint detection. The results in chapter 4 also shows that the method for crack detection adapts well to complex scenarios like in presence of lane markers, oil marks, varied illumination and road surface textures. Following observations about the developed keypoint based crack detection approach have been made:

1. Classifier based approaches to detect cracks at the superpixel or region level may suffer from handling lighter or thinner cracks, cracks formed at edges, shaded road surface texture, and require a lot of labeled training data. This prompted development of approaches in order to have more precise crack detection on varied road surface textures in an unsupervised manner.

   Thus, this dissertation provides a keypoint matching based crack and related defect detection methodology, which can be seen as an alternative to the mostly followed image-processing and classifier based approaches. In order to compare the two approaches developed for crack detection in this dissertation, i.e. ML-based classifier and keypoint matching techniques, Figure 6.2 can be referred.

2. As crack pixels are not easily distinguishable against the background, the fuzzy-theoretic

and keypoint matching approach in this dissertation helped to better handle the associated uncertainties.

3. It is seen that the number of defective pixels are always much less than non-defective pixels in any image. So, this dissertation proposes that a mixture of Gamma distributions could better model such a mixture of gradient values than mostly followed Gaussian distribution.

   Thus, in this work the data (gradient values of the pixels) is assumed to be generated from a mixture of finite number of Gamma distributions (one representing defective, another non-defective). Accordingly, GMFM is used to estimate the parameters of these Gamma distributions and cluster pixels into defective and non-defective groups.

4. As an additional result of this dissertation, it is important to mention that GMFM, when applied on gradient images, shows better robustness for edge detection in images, as seen in Figure 4.6 of chapter 4. The results show better stability of the GMFM-based edge detection than traditional methods such as Canny edge detection. This further shows usefulness of the method to generate edges in images using a mixture of Gamma distributions.

5. It is also seen that due to using membership value based fuzzy descriptors, properties of these descriptors lead to make these descriptors follow a mixture of Dirichlet distributions. This made KL-divergence between two Dirichlet distributions highly suitable for finding the similarity between two descriptors.

6. SIFT-based features are not very suitable for the task of keypoint matching based crack detection, as the number of generated keypoints are always between 8 and 20, regardless of the complexity or presence of cracks on road surface images. Thus, a fuzzy-theoretic and keypoint matching based approach of this dissertation shows better suitability in this regard.

6.1.4 A Vision-based Decision Support System for Road Surface Defect Detection

ResearchQuestion4: How can a modular and flexible DSS be designed for crack and defect detection on the road surfaces of front-view images?

Chapter 5 of this dissertation addresses *ResearchQuestion4*. The chapter provides how the DSS has been designed by incorporating developed algorithmic approaches and the DSR approach, followed by how the DSS has been evaluated.

Following the iterations as per the DSR approach, literature review, and expert interview, the meta-requirements for a DSS to monitor road surfaces and cracks were identified as follows:

1. Robustness
2. Automation
3. Performance
4. Adaptability

The evaluation of the DSS further pointed out the following two additional requirements:

5. Integrative
6. Understandable

In this dissertation, the DSS has been designed with a modular structure to satisfy the above requirements. It takes 2-D natural scene images/ videos and GPS as inputs. The ML-classifier based methodological approach for crack detection of chapter 3 has been used to develop the DSS in this work. Different components of the DSS, as shown in Figure 5.2 of chapter 5, are as follows:

1. *User Interface:* This module is responsible for showing results and taking inputs from users such as, service agencies, municipalities, and similar road maintenance organizations.
2. *Road Detection Module:* In this module, the approach of chapter 2, as discussed in chapter 5, is used to detect the road area within a scene image. This new image is referred as "road image" and has only the road area. It can be used for multi-various purposes such as crack detection and other defect detection, like potholes. Road image could also used for lane marker analysis, parking place analysis using the road markers, etc.
3. *Parameter Selection and Training Module:* As mentioned above, ML-classifier based approach of chapter 3 and chapter 5 has been used to develop the DSS here and consequently, this module. In this module, various supervised learning approaches can be used for re-training, if required, or for selection of specific algorithmic approaches from the repository.

   In this dissertation Random Forest, Gradient Boosting, L-SVM, and ANN are trained and persisted so that users can select one of them based on different cases, if required. Similarly, different feature extraction algorithms can be included in this module. Accordingly, Random Forest is selected as the default classifier for the developed DSS due to its good performance for detecting different crack-types present on various road surface conditions. Default feature extraction algorithms, like GLCM, statistical measures, VoG, along with their default parameters, as in chapter 5, are set in this module. However, according to the incremental subset feature selection method of chapter 3, this module can be extended to train and included other feature extraction algorithms. This is described in chapter 5.

4. *Crack Detection Module:* In this module the ML classifier based crack detection at the superpixel level, as seen in chapter 5, has been incorporated. In short, firstly the road image obtained from "Road Detection" module is divided into superpixels using SLIC. Followed by this, the tuned set of 40 features consisting of variance, skewness, 6 GLCM fetaures, 32 VoG features is extracted for each of the superpixel and classified using the Random Forest classifier. Other classifiers and settings can be selected from the "Parameter Selection and Training" module, if required.

5. *Pavement Rating Module:* This module is responsible for rating the road surfaces based on detected cracks. Cracks are detected using the "Crack Detection" module and using the output of this module the road surfaces are ranked. This module helps to incorporate different PCI approaches for ratings about the pavement condition index, so that the DSS can be flexible and extended in the future. In this work, following standard criteria, crack % is used to rank the road surfaces. Here, crack % is calculated using number of defective superpixels detected to contain cracks.

6. *Visualization Module:* This module helps to map the road surface images to their corresponding physical location and visualize the ranked road surfaces. GPS coordinates are used for the mapping. Here, thresholds on crack % (output from the "Pavement Rating" module) are used to color code them into the following: Red (crack % > 15), yellow ($7 \leq$ crack % ≤ 15), green (crack % <7).

The developed DSS in this work has been evaluated by an expert interview with a professional German county employee. The employee was responsible for the monitoring of biking paths, as mentioned in the results section of chapter 5. All the functionalities of the DSS, like uploading data, selecting parameters and classifiers, visualizations and outputs, were tested and feedbacks were taken. It showed that the meta-requirements of the DSS have been satisfied. However, better visualization, further extension of the system, other defect detection functionality such as for potholes, were requested for future developments of the DSS in order to enhance their effectivity. Further, evaluations containing the performance of the DSS at the crack detection level showed 92.00% accuracy, as shown in Table 5.6. Finally, a design theory

(Gregory and Muntermann 2014), as given in Table 5.7, has been developed.

6.1.5 Comparison Between Different Approaches for Crack Detection

To provide a comparison between the developed approaches in this work and various constructs that can guide selection of different approaches, Figure 6.2 has been provided below. This can help practitioners to select a suitable approach. Apart from the developed methodologies in chapter 3 and chapter 4 for crack detection, a state-of-the-art architecture called U-Net (Iglovikov and Shvets 2017) has been also included here for comparative purposes. Before going into the detailed constructs that can guide the selection of different approaches, the adapted transfer learning approach using U-Net is described shortly here.

Transfer learning can be described as the algorithmic approach of improving or applying prelearned algorithmic knowledge to new or related tasks. It typically contains a pre-trained deep learning model on a large training data, which can then be fine-tuned or extracted features could be re-trained using new comparatively smaller datasets. Thus, transfer learning helps in reducing the amount of training data for new tasks, in contrast to traditional deep learning approaches that require a huge amounts of data in thousands to be labeled and used for training. As examples, in Pauly et al. (2017) a CNN-based network classified image patches into crack or non-crack. Around 40,000 image patches of size 99×99 are extracted from original RGB images and are used for training. In Zhang et al. (2016) a deep CNN-based system for crack detection on asphalt road is given that uses 640,000 samples for training. In the ML community transfer learning lately is seen to gain a lot of traction, especially for tasks dealing with image data. Nevertheless, labeling a considerable amount of data for training is still required in most of the cases.

U-Net is a Fully Convolutional Network (FCN) based deep learning architecture composed of encoders and decoders. It is a state-of-the-art approach and often used for semantic segmentation in images, like medical images and satellite images. Semantic segmentation deals with segmenting at a pixel level to classify it to given classes. U-Net is used in this study for applying the transfer learning based crack detection on road surfaces of front-view images. It has been selected as the architecture showed promising results with less amount of training data, thus requiring less labeled data than other architectures. As described in Iglovikov and Shvets (2017), U-Net has two paths- encoder and decoder. Encoder downsamples feature maps, while, the decoder unsamples them and is used for localization. In this work, the encoder is built with ResNet-50 architecture. ResNet-50 is originally built using CNN and is pre-trained on the ImageNet dataset. For re-training, 40 crack images were labeled as shown in Figure 6.1, and the developed model is thereafter tested on test images. Further, the following parameters have been used for training the model: learning rate of 0.0001, the number of epochs is taken as 60, and the input images were resized to 512×512. Here, U-Net is used to provide visual comparisons on a limited dataset, as in Figure 6.2.

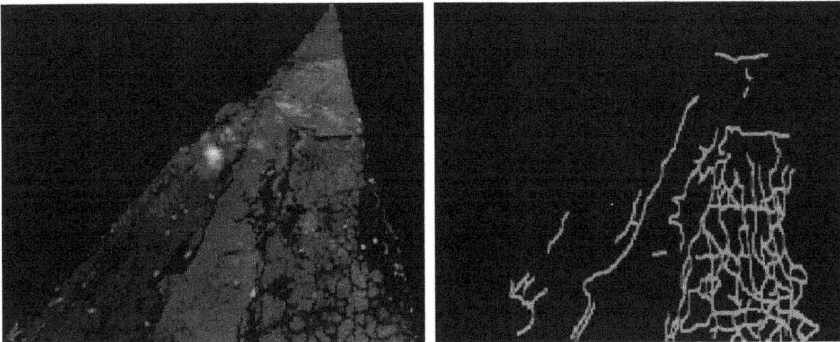

Figure 6.1: Data labeling approach followed for training the U-Net. It shows the original image and the corresponding labeled crack area.

It can be seen from Figure 6.2 that crack detection is a challenging task and many external conditions, road surface texture types, presence of non-crack elements or defects, scattered shadows, illumination conditions, could arise and need to be handled for precise detection and localization of cracks. To summarize how algorithmic approaches could be selected for crack detection on different road surface images, the following observations are detailed below:

1. *Classifier Based Defect Detection on Road Surfaces at the Superpixel Level:*
   - The developed supervised ML approach of chapter 3 using state-of-the-art hand crafted features, mostly being texture based, along with a systematic feature selection method and ensemble classifiers, like Random Forest, shows promising results for detecting cracks at the superpixel (region) level.
   - The systematic approach of selecting features by tuning parameters of state-of-the-art feature extraction algorithms helped to identify most suitable features in an automatic manner.
   - Superpixels are classified as crack and non-crack for every image, and the cracks ones are marked on images.

No crack
Multiple cracks
Network crack
no crack
Single crack
network crack
matches = 32, matching score = 32.000000
matches = 105, matching score = 105.000000
matches = 72, matching score = 72.000000
matches = 32, matching score = 32.000000
matches = 74, matching score = 74.000000
matches = 139, matching score = 139.000000

(A)

Outer patch
Complex road surface type
Markes and cracks
matches = 89, matching score = 89.000000
matches = 29, matching score = 29.000000
matches = 132, matching score = 132.000000

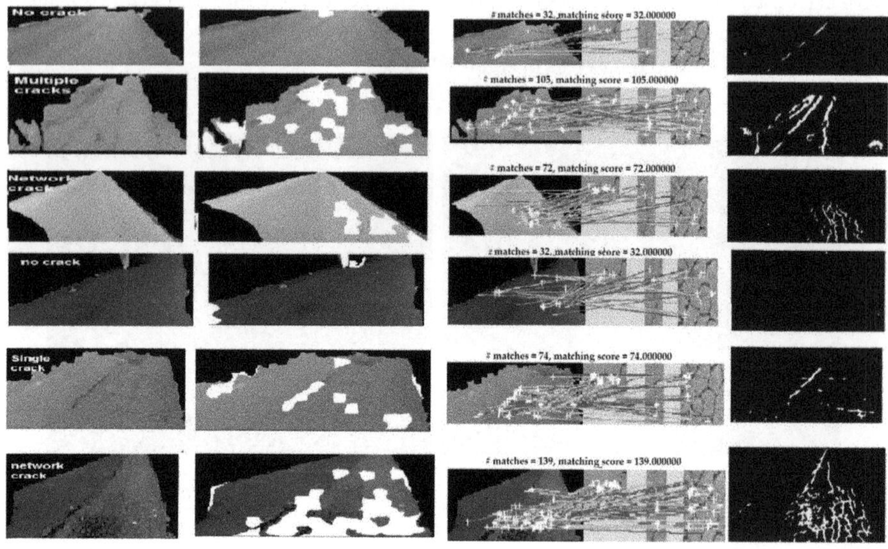

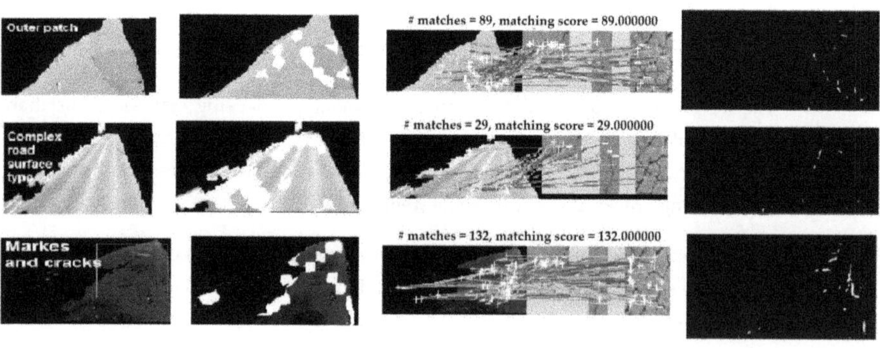

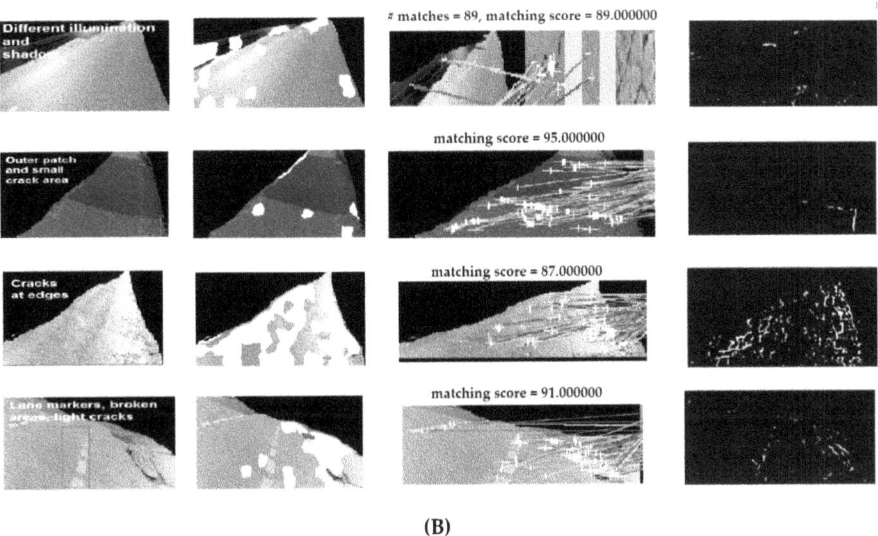

(B)

Figure 6.2: (A) In every image set, the first image is the original road surface image, the second image is the result for crack detection at the superpixel level using the developed approach of chapter 3, the third image gives the results for detecting cracks at the pixel level using the developed keypoint matching approach of chapter 4, and the fourth image gives the results for detecting cracks using U-Net based transfer learning. It can be seen that comparable results are shown for different crack-types and road surface conditions. (B) gives the images where crack detection becomes challenging due to various external objects on road surfaces, illumination conditions, presence of other surface distress like, patches, lane markers, oil marks, etc.

- Number of defective superpixels in an image gives a measure of the road condition and can be used to rank road surfaces for devising maintenance strategies.
- The approach requires labeled image patches (superpixel regions are extracted as image patches) for training, as the approach follows supervised ML. Here, 1000 training image patches have been used.
- The results show that cracks can be successfully detected for varied road surfaces, crack-types, and locations.
- The approach mostly suffers when road surface types are highly complex (see second and fourth rows of Figure 6.2 (B)), or if very thin and indistinguishable cracks are there.
- Also, crack detection is not precisely done at the pixel level, thereby restricting understanding cracks at a more detailed level like, deriving important characteristics of the cracks.
- Sometimes edges of patches, manholes are falsely detected as cracks (Figure 3.7 (C), third row, leftmost image set).

2. *Supervised ML approach of transfer learning using state-of-the-art encode-decoder architecture like, U-Net, helps in crack detection on the road surfaces of front-view scene images:*

   - U-Net is selected in order to compare the developed approaches of chapter 3 and chapter 4 in this work as it showed promising results with less number of training images than other architectures for transfer learning, yet has a complex architecture for image understanding tasks.
   - Transfer learning helps to harness the power of pre-trained deep learning models with millions of labeled training images. However, labeled data is still required for new tasks in order to fine-tune or re-train the network. Supervised deep learning based approaches still require a lot of labeled training data. With more labeled data, the results become better, while requiring more manual effort.
   - Semantic segmentation using deep learning based methods thus helps to detect and localize crack pixels using complete labeled images for training, unlike image patches.
   - Different road surface types or illumination could be handled for crack detection.
   - As lot of training data and pixel wise labeling are required, covering many cases for data preparation is a difficult task. Moreover, precise pixel level labeling for more

robust results is more time consuming.

- Detection of cracks suffer if complete scene images are used, whereas images containing only the segmented road area, as used in this work, give better results.
- While cracks are detected, quantifying them to rank the road surfaces based on a simple threshold could be challenging.
- However, Figure 6.2 shows that problems like detecting edges of patches or manholes (Figure 6.2 (B), leftmost image set on first row), or falsely detecting road joints (Figure 6.2 (A), first row, leftmost image set) still remain.

3. *Keypoint Matching Based Defect Detection on Road Surfaces at the Pixel Level:*

- The developed fuzzy-theoretic, unsupervised ML, and keypoint matching based approach of chapter 4 gives an effective alternative to mostly followed classifier, supervised ML, or image-processing based approaches.
- GMFM-based edge detection method of chapter 4 shows stable results. This helps not only in clustering pixels into edges and non-edges, but the edge image can also be used for detecting object structures, like potholes or patches on roads in future. Improved results are seen in comparison to state-of-the-art Canny edge detector.
- Clustering using a mixture of Gamma distributions shows better modeling capabilities for edge detection than Gaussian distribution.
- 128-D Fuzzy descriptors for encoding the keypoints, along with a Dirichlet distribution and KL-divergence based mechanism to match the keypoints, helped to ascertain final crack pixels from nominated ones. The method showed much better performance than keypoint descriptor based state-of-the-art SIFT for the task at hand.
- A simple threshold on the number of matched keypoints, i.e. crack pixels, is used to classify images into defective (images containing cracks) and non-defective (images free of cracks). Thus, number of matched keypoints is also used to rank the road surfaces for devising maintenance strategies. A higher number indicates that the road condition is very bad.
- The keypoint matching mechanism for crack detection gives an unsupervised approach to crack detection. This is in contrast to mostly followed noisy image-processing based approaches that are mostly used for detecting cracks in unsupervised ways.

- The approach requires only one reference image to be created for detection of cracks in road surface images (query images).
- No training labeled data is required, unlike supervised ML approaches.
- Varied complex road surface types and crack-types from different locations can be handled by this approach. Comparison with state-of-the-art U-Net architecture in Figure 6.2 shows its robust performance.
- As seen in Figure 4.7, Figure 4.8, Figure 4.9, keypoint matching based approach can handle varied marks on road surfaces, lane markers, solid shadow areas.
- False detection at very strong edges of patches present on road surfaces are observed with this approach.

Therefore, it is seen from above comparisons that the selection of algorithmic approaches in practice is motivated by various factors such as:

1. *Image acquisition method:* Downward-view image patches having focused and closer view of the road surface contain less external objects than front-view images. Similarly, images acquired under controlled lighting have less illumination variation and shadows than the front-view images that are acquired under normal daylight. Traditionally, most methods in the literature are seen to use downward-view images, with recent efforts been noticed to use front-view images. Front-view images can be easily acquired using cheaper methods, as done in this work, by mounting simple commodity cameras on vehicles or smartphones. Algorithms that can handle such front-view images under normal daylight, like the ones developed and used in this work, can be selected.
2. *Standardizing a distance from where image acquisition can be done for all images/ videos:* This will help to process data in an easier way. For example, all front-view images or videos can be captured by keeping simple commodity cameras at a distance of car dashboards.
3. If images are obtained in a standardized manner, the developed approach of chapter 3 gives good prediction for detecting cracks. To handle more complex road surface texture or illumination glares, the approach of chapter 4 shows better robustness. For example, the developed algorithm of chapter 4 or complex architecture based approach like, U-Net, can be used if the road surface has complex texture (see Figure 6.2 (B), second row).
4. Algorithms that can detect and localize cracks on different pavement surface material (e.g. concrete, asphalt) or texture types, like the ones developed on this work, are required for more generalization and need to be developed further.

5. Algorithms that can handle various crack-types on road surfaces belonging to different location should be selected. Thus, noisy image-processing based approaches are challenging to use, while end-to-end ML-based approaches are more resilient in nature.

6. Algorithms can be selected depending on the requirement of detecting cracks at the superpixel, region, or pixel level.

7. Algorithms can be selected depending on the availability of training resources and the possibilities of creating training data. Supervised ML approaches require lot of labeled data, which in turn require manual effort. On the other hand, an unsupervised and keypoint matching approach, like in chapter 4, requires no training data. Moreover, it is not an easy task to prepare data for different conditions.

8. As front-view images are complex, algorithms that can handle external road surface elements like, oil marks, lane markers, are required.

9. While solid shadows are handled in this work, fine edges of scattered shadows still gets detected wrongly as cracks (see Figure 4.9). Thus, pre-processing of images using shadow removal algorithms prior to crack detection can be done for more robust results.

10. In most algorithmic approaches patch, pothole, or manhole edges can sometimes be detected as cracks. To minimize this, potholes and patches can be additionally segmented; thereby reducing false detection further.

Hence, with the above findings and results, implications of this work from theoretical and practical viewpoints are given in the next section.

6.2 Implications for Theory and Practice

6.2.1 Implications for Theory

IS research has been categorized into different streams by Banker and Kauffman (2004). This dissertation is part of the Design Science and Decision Support System research streams. As stated in the introduction, this dissertation contributes toward the following research areas:

- Developing automated approaches for crack and related defect detection on road surfaces of front-view scene images

    1. Developing an unsupervised ML approach for detecting road areas within scene images for various scene types, such as rural, urban, and surface types, such as paved or unpaved.

2. Developing a supervised ML-based classifier approach and identifying relevant image features for crack detection at the superpixel level.
3. Developing an unsupervised ML and keypoint matching based approach, motivated by image matching applications, for crack detection at the pixel level.

- Designing a DSS for crack detection in front-view images, consequently leading to the development of a design theory for it.

To start describing the above contributions, a numerically simple clustering approach for grouping of road area in scene images has been designed as part of this dissertation. Chapter 2 contains details of this approach. The developed approach contributes toward a clustering method for road area grouping and does not require a pre-defined number of clusters, in contrast to the likes of k-means or spectral clustering (Chatterjee et al. 2017). The approach can work with high dimensional data, while the data consists of the feature set that helps in merging of the road area into a group. The varied scale of the Gaussian kernel based similarity metric in this approach, along with Hungarian method based optimization and pairwise assignment, helps in developing a graph-based hierarchical clustering technique. Thus, the technique can be used to group road area in an unsupervised manner and contributes toward a split and merge based algorithmic technique for road area grouping.

The developed approach for road area grouping, when combined with simple Nearest Neighbor and ranking approach for the final road area detection, showed promising results for road detection when compared to other approaches like AdaBoost, SVM, K-NN. The approach does not use any camera specific (Schreiber et al. 2014), scene specific characteristics such as lane markers or separators (Beyeler et al. 2014), or other supervised learning approaches for road detection, like using lot of training data or seed points. As a result, the technique can be used for road/ pavement area grouping under various scene settings like rural, urban, or unstructured, in an adaptable and flexible manner.

While chapter 2 helps in road area grouping and detection, chapter 3 contributes toward finding out the most relevant features and how ML can be applied using such features for a classification based crack detection on road surfaces. Here, a systematic feature selection methodology comprising of an incremental and subset approaches for feature selection has been devised to select suitable features and the parameters of different feature extraction algorithms. A new feature variant using Gabor filters, namely VoG, has been obtained and used in this work. Other interesting feature descriptors, like statistical measures and GLCM, have also been noticed to give promising results than edge-based feature descriptors such as HoG. These feature descriptors are then used for encoding the superpixels, which are then classified into defective and non-defective classes using state-of-the-art ML classifiers. As a result of this approach, the community can benefit from the findings that in general texture-based features, along with ensemble ML techniques, like Random Forest and Gradient Boosting, have been seen to be more informative and discriminating for crack detection. Furthermore, the systematic approach for feature selection and parameter tuning of feature extraction algorithms by using ML classifier's accuracy metric helps to identify suitable features for crack detection. Hence, further development can be done based on such conclusions.

One of the major theoretical contribution of this dissertation is also to provide an approach that addresses detecting cracks using an unsupervised ML and keypoint matching approaches. Accordingly, an analytical fuzzy-theoretic based approach and a keypoint matching mechanism is used for the first time in this work for crack detection on road surfaces. In this dissertation, a novel GMFM method has been adapted for clustering the gradient values and has been developed for edge detection, leading to the generation of keypoints. Keypoints are generated in both reference (a constant image containing cracks) and query (the image on which cracks are to be detected) images. These keypoints are then encoded with fuzzy image descriptors which are obtained using orientations of the keypoints. The keypoints are then matched across the reference and the query image to see how many keypoints are similar between them, giving an estimate on how similar is the query image to the reference image. Regarding the matching mechanism to calculate the similarity between any two keypoints (encoded with fuzzy descriptors), a novel method has been developed in this work by which a fuzzy descriptor (whose all elements sum to 1) has been interpreted and justified as parameters of a Dirichlet distribution. This led to the usage of KL-divergence between two Dirichlet distributions to calculate the similarity between any two keypoints. Such a developed approach showed better suitability than keypoint generation and feature descriptor matching approach, like SIFT (Lowe 2004), for the task of crack detection on front-view road surface images.

Hence, the keypoint matching approach for crack detection of chapter 4 gives the community an alternative to the mostly followed classification or supervised learning based approaches, as seen in the literature (Eisenbach et al. 2017; Koch et al. 2015; Mohan and Poobal 2017), thus requiring less labeled training data, manual labor, and limiting human bias while labeling. It provides an approach to detect different types of cracks and related defects under various external conditions like, illumination variation, darkness, different road surface textures and types, or in the presence of lane markers or oil marks. In this approach, a given reference image is the only single image which can be customized or adapted, if required, to adapt crack detection for different cases. Further, it also shows that fuzzy image feature descriptors have higher discriminatory power for crack detection at the pixel level, given that cracks are not easily distinguishable objects against the background.

Additionally, it has been proposed in this work that a mixture of two Gamma distributions, one modeling cracks (taken as edges) and another modeling non-cracks (taken as non-edges), can better cluster the pixels into cracks and non-cracks than Gaussian distributions. This is due to the fact that cracks are always sparse in any image which makes the distribution of gradient values highly heavy tailed. Hence, this helps in the usage of a mixture of Gamma distributions as a potential contributor to clustering techniques. Consequently, a novel method called GMFM has been adapted in this dissertation to cluster the pixels, so as to belong to one of the Gamma distributions, in an unsupervised manner. The cluster with higher magnitude of gradient is taken as cracks, i.e., edges. GMFM uses an analytical fuzzy-theoretic approach to estimate the parameters of the Gamma distributions and does not use any explicitly given strong threshold for clustering. As a result, the adapted GMFM in this work has been used for edge detection in images and shows robust behavior than threshold based state-of-the-art edge detection method like, Canny (Gonzales and Woods 2002). Researchers can use this algorithmic approach developed in chapter 4 for edge detection in images.

In sum, three ML-based approaches have been developed in this work to process front-view images and analyze them for detecting cracks and related defects on the road surfaces:

1. Road area grouping and detection in images: Here, an unsupervised hierarchical clustering approach has been developed to group image regions and cluster them. Once clustering and grouping is done, Nearest Neighbor and a ranking based approach have been used for the final detection phase where the cluster containing the road area is detected and segmented in an image.

2. Superpixel level crack detection using state-of-the-art ML classifiers, along with a systematic feature selection process to integrate feature extraction algorithms and tune their parameters.

3. Pixel level crack detection consisting of GMFM based clustering to generate the keypoints, fuzzy descriptors to encode the keypoints, and a novel keypoint matching mechanism using KL-divergence between Dirichlet distributions.

As crack detection on front-view images is challenging in contrast to mostly used downward-view images due to the lack of focused view, varied illumination conditions, varied road surface types, and other road surface elements (Chatterjee et al. 2018a; Varadharajan et al. 2014), developed algorithmic approaches in this work contribute to make such analysis more effective and flexible. The approaches in this work help to detect cracks and related defects at both superpixel and pixel levels in a front-view scene image. Pixel level crack detection offers the possibility to classify different crack-types or to ascertain various characteristics of cracks in the future. The developed crack detection approaches in this work do not depend on mostly followed noisy image-processing based approaches such as thresholding, morphology, edge detection or segmentation, to name a few, as seen in the literature (Chatterjee et al. 2018b). This dissertation also offers two ML-based perspectives for crack detection on the road surfaces:

1. A supervised learning approach using labeled training images and systematic application of ML-based classifiers and feature extraction algorithms. Crack detection is done at the superpixel (region) level.

2. An unsupervised learning and keypoint matching based approach consisting of a Gamma mixture based clustering technique using GMFM, fuzzy image descriptors, and a keypoint matching mechanism using a single reference image. Crack detection is done at the pixel level.

Finally, all the above algorithmic contributions helped to enrich the knowledge base for designing a DSS following the DSR approach (Henver 2007). In the end, a design theory for a vision-based crack detection DSS which uses front-view scene images/ videos has been derived in this dissertation, as shown in Table 5.7 of chapter 5. Different components of the design theory, namely purpose and scope, constructs, the principle of form and function, artifact mutability, testable propositions, and justificatory knowledge have been designed for the DSS. This included identifying the meta-requirements for the scope of the DSS, modules and data usage within the DSS to attend the requirements for the functionalities of the DSS, as well as to make the DSS more adaptable, explainable, and extendable. The developed design theory can be used by the researchers to further enhance the capabilities of such DSSs for devising an effective road monitoring strategy.

6.2.2 Implications for Practice

It is seen in practice that many types of IS are used for road asset maintenance. Some related developments are shortly discussed here. As an example, a PMS is designed for small and medium-sized municipalities compromising of functionalities such as PCI generation using visual surveys, vehicle operating cost assessment based on traffic distribution, GIS-based road network inventory management for devising maintenance strategies and budgeting (Loprencipe 2017). Many such PMS and DSS are seen regarding road maintenance or planing acclivities, cost analysis, automated PCI generation, road surface condition analysis, road surface roughness analysis using sensor data, data storage and viewing, data integration, to name a few (Laubis et al. 2016; PMIS 2011; Tang and Sun 2012; Yang and Lin 2013).

PCI is one of the most important indicators for road condition evaluation and assigns an index to roads (e.g. a number indicating health of the road asset), following which roads can be ranked to see which ones need immediate attention, thereby directly influencing road maintenance strategy and resource allocation. Calculating PCI is quite country specific and is commonly done by considering various factors, like percentage of cracks for different crack types and road surface material, edge breaks, roughness of the road surface, skid resistance of the road (Straube 2015). As cracks form one of the major surface distresses for roads, identifying such distresses is a necessary step for road surface condition analysis and PCI calculation (BaSt 2008; Gleave 2014; Eisenbach et al. 2017). Cheaper and quicker ways are highly required in today's time, especially for small and medium-sized municipalities and towns which account for maintaining most of the urban roads in any country (Gleave 2014; Loprencipe 2017). Moreover, automated approaches using advanced data analytics for crack and distress detection is an essential step in this process to reduce human bias, subjective analysis, and time requirement, while increasing the speed of monitoring for devising effective road maintenance strategies (Eisenbach et al. 2017; Gopalkrishnan et al. 2018; Varadharajan et al. 2014).

This dissertation contributes toward the design of a DSS and required algorithmic approaches for road crack detection and monitoring which uses easily acquirable front-view images/ videos. The images can easily be acquired by mounting cameras on vehicles (Chatterjee et al. 2017; Radopoulou et al. 2016; Varadharajan et al. 2014) or smartphone cameras (Maeda et al. 2018); thereby drastically reducing the cost of data gathering and sensor usage. Thus, practitioners can benefit from the low-cost solutions offered in this work. This work provides a cost-effective practical solution in contrast to the status-quo of manual surveys and usage of costly vehicles which take images for crack evaluation using specialized cameras directly viewing downward to the road surface under specific settings and lighting conditions. In this work, the front-view scene images are acquired by mounting a high definition commodity camera on a pedelec/ e-bike. The images are taken from the driver's viewpoint. This makes the image acquisition not dependent on controlled environment or specific setups, showing promising possibilities to crowdsource data and image gathering. Front-view images could also be easily gathered using public or service vehicles, like garbage collector, buses, shared cars, and citizens (Mertz 2011). Specifically, road maintenance administrators of municipalities can avail such setups to gather data in flexible and cheaper ways and use the algorithmic approaches, along with the DSS, developed in this work to analyze the image data automatically.

Thus, the developed DSS and the algorithmic approaches in this work using front-view images help the practitioners such as infrastructure maintenance providers, city maintenance service providers, or road monitoring administrators in the following ways:

1. *Detecting different crack-types on varied road surfaces:* The solutions in this works helps to detect different crack-types, like single cracks, network cracks, cracks formed at edges or in blocks. Here, cracks can be detected on diverse road surface types under various illumination conditions like, darkness, normal sunlight etc. Figure 3.7, Figure 4.7, Figure 4.8 and Figure 4.9 show some examples. Cracks are one of first and major surface distress found on roads and lead to severe damages when left unattended.

2. *Increasing coverage area and resource utilization by using front-view images:* Detecting cracks at different parts within the front-view image, thereby offering more coverage of the road area. Whole roads can be imaged by passing less number of times over it, in contrast to taking downward-view images which is more time and resource consuming.

3. *Detecting cracks using easily acquirable image data:* In this work, simple setup using commodity cameras have been used for acquiring easily available front-view images, in contrast to specific and costly setups, like usage of specialized vehicles, for acquiring downward-view images, thus increasing flexibility and cost-effectiveness of the system.

4. *Provides a practical way of data-driven planning, road monitoring, and maintenance strategies:* Detected cracks are quantified in percentage, giving a direct estimate of road deterioration. Here, number of superpixels detected to contain cracks (or number of pixels which are detected as cracks) are counted and the percentage of cracks is obtained. The roads are then easily ranked according to the percentage of cracks. Higher the percentage, more severe is the road condition; thus requiring immediate attention and greater investment of resources for maintenance and rehabilitation. Thus, this work also contributes toward generating PCI automatically using advanced ML-based approaches.

5. *Reduces subjective analysis, delays, and human bias, while causing timely maintenance:* Here, simpler ways of data acquisition and automated ways of analyzing the image data using advanced ML approaches have been used. Thus, this dissertation provides practical low-cost solutions for automated crack detection that reduce delays caused by manual surveys or back-office analysis using humans, thereby helping to achieve timely maintenance and cover many road areas for inspection in limited time period.

6. *The comparative approach of this work provides a way to select suitable algorithms for crack detection:* Practitioners can refer the insights given under the section 6.1.5 above to select suitable algorithmic approaches for the task at hand.

7. *The designed DSS can be used for road monitoring and crack detection:* The final deigned DSS

in this work uses simple images and ML-based algorithms for crack detection. It has been designed by taking feedback from professional road monitoring administrators, so as to increase the effectivity of the DSS in real world. Thus, it provides a cost-effective and an intelligent way to detect cracks on road surfaces for the practitioners.

8. *Modular structure of the DSS gives more control to the administrators for enhancements:* Due to the modular design of the DSS, as seen in chapter 5, additional functionalities could be easily integrated into the existing DSS. As examples, more classifiers using the "Parameter Selection and Training" module could be added, while new crack detection approaches could be integrating using the "Crack Detection" module. Further, extending the "Pavement Rating" module to include advanced PCI calculation methods could also be easily done.

9. *Data gathering for further processes:* Due to integration of GPS data and corresponding scene images in this work, gathered data can be persisted and mapped for future purposes. For example, how a road infrastructure deteriorates over a time period or performs after rehabilitation can be viewed using historical and new data belonging to similar GPS coordinates.

10. *Road images, once detected and segmented from the scene images, could be used for many purposes:* The "Road Detection" module of the DSS, based on the developed approach in chapter 2, gives the road images from the scene images. Such scene images could be used not only for crack detection, but also for various other purposes, like road surface sign analysis, evaluating other road surface defects such as patches or potholes. Moreover, the segmented road area can also be used for other tasks, such as analyzing parking places.

In summary, this dissertation provides a cheaper, intelligent, and automated way of detecting cracks on road surfaces for road maintenance administrators and agencies using simple front-view scene images. This results in cost-effective and timely monitoring of roads, thereby also increasing their lifecycle. Further, timely pavement management also impacts the environment positively, as good quality of roads lessens fuel consumption and rehabilitation woks (Gholami et al. 2016; Gleave 2014; Louhghalam et al. 2017). Moreover, various other social impacts of such low-cost and data-driven automated solutions, as provided in this work, also can be realized, such as a potential decrease in vehicle operating costs as road quality improves due to timely maintenance, better connectivity and trade opportunities, reduction in number of accidents, reduction in traffic congestion and delays, satisfaction of commuters due to better health of the road.

6.3 Limitations and Future Research

In this work, front-view scene images are analyzed using ML-based methods for detecting the presence and location of cracks and related defects on road surfaces. Some of the associated limitations of this work and how that can be attended in the future are discussed here.

Here, 2-D images are used for crack detection, so 3-D information is missing. Hence, in this work, precise information such as crack depth could not be obtained. Here, cracks are detected and localized at the region (superpixel level or region level) and pixel level. While just for the purpose of detection, detecting cracks at the region level is enough, pixel level identification could be used to detect cracks more precisely and quantify their characteristics. From this perspective, once the pixels are detected as cracks, as done in this work using the unsupervised ML and keypoint matching mechanism, count or shape of the connected pixels could be used in various ways. In future the study can be extended to ascertain the types of cracks like, single line crack of longitudinal or transverse nature, network or alligator crack, block crack, edge crack, etc. (BaSt 2008). Classifying such crack-types could also help in a more precise calculation of PCI, giving the road condition index, as can be seen in Straube (2015). This would also help to locate the position of cracks like, edge cracks can cause more wear and tear in the long run than a single crack. Similarly, network cracks are more severe than single cracks, and if left unattended, could give rise to sever defects, like potholes. Thus, in the future one can classify different types of cracks for devising more advanced road maintenance strategies.

Further, it is seen that sometimes strong edges of other defects on the road surface such as patches or potholes could be falsely detected as cracks. Such false detection could be minimized by identifying patches and potholes using object detection or semantic segmentation methods as such surface defects are in a closed form, unlike cracks. In this way, not only crack detection at such spurious edges could be minimized, but the detection of patches and potholes would also lead to an integrated surface level defect detection on a single platform. This would not only further impact advanced PCI generation, but also detection of severe defects, like potholes. So in the future, patches and potholes could also be detected and integrated, in addition to cracks. Furthermore, if the road surface has too much of scattered shadows (see Figure 4.9), then sometimes certain edges could be detected falsely as cracks. To avoid this in the future, pre-processing by using shadow removal algorithms could be done prior to defect detection. However, solid shadows (see first image in the first row, first image in the third row of Figure 4.9) can be handled by the approach in chapter 2, and do not interfere with crack detection at the later stages. Moreover, from the algorithmic perspective, in the future it will be interesting to integrate various algorithms for crack and defect detection in a need-based manner depending on different constructs like, type of data available, training data creation and resource capabilities, processing time and speed requirements, in-time processing or retrospective processing of the data.

Finally, the DSS can be extended in the future by adding superpixel, region, and pixel level detection approaches, as well as modules for detecting other defects, like patches and potholes. The DSS could also have inputs, following the comparison in section 6.1.5, to help the administrators select a suitable type of algorithmic approach for the task at hand. In this work, the condition of the road in an image is devised based on the number of defective superpixels or pixels that get detected to contain cracks. Hence, once cracks are detected and localized, they can be summed over a pre-defined length of the road, like 100 m (Al-Mistarehi 2017), for a more holistic deduction of the road condition. Additionally, a crowdsourcing approach could be employed to gather data, while, GPS, historic road images, data, and analysis could be used together to see how the rehabilitation works improve future road conditions. However, it should be noted that while crowdsourcing data, image elements such as human faces, license plates, should be blurred to maintain privacy.

6.4 Conclusion

This dissertation proposes a low-cost solution based on ML approaches for crack and related defect detection on road surfaces of front-view 2-D natural scene images acquired using simple commodity cameras. Scene images are captured here from a driver's viewpoint under normal daylight by mounting a simple HD commodity camera on a pedelec/ e-bike. In this work, various algorithmic approaches have been developed, along with a Decision Support System, for the task of an end-to-end design of an adaptable and flexible system for crack and related defect detection. The end-to-end design for crack detection uses the following steps: To start with, firstly scene images are captured and the road area within the images are detected. Once the road area is detected and segmented in an image, cracks and related surface defects are detected on it. Secondly, cracks are detected at the superpixel level using a developed approach based on ML classifiers. Thirdly, cracks are detected at the pixel level using a developed approach based on ML and keypoint matching. Finally, to demonstrate the practical integration of the above said developed approaches, a Decision Support System has been designed in this work. The Decision Support System used the developed road detected algorithm, crack detection algorithm at the superpixel level, and Design Science Research approaches. Its demonstration in practice, the developed prototype, and feedback from professional road administrators in a German county showed promising results for vision-based crack detection on road surfaces using front-view scene images. In this work, the number of superpixels detected to contain cracks (for the superpixel based method) and the number of keypoints detected as crack pixels (for the keypoint matching based method) help to quantify the road condition and have been used to rank the roads. Three algorithmic approaches have been developed in this work for the purpose of crack detection at both the superpixel and the pixel level.

Firstly, a region grouping approach for clustering road area in images have been proposed. It helps to detect the road area within a scene image. The approach uses a graph-based hierarchical clustering technique using Gaussian kernel based region similarity measure. The kernel uses a mixture of Bhattacharyya and Euclidean distance metrics. The process initially starts with a split and merge approach where superpixels are formed, thereafter, they are initially merged using a simple signal-to-noise ratio based criteria. After this, in successive steps, the Gaussian kernel based similarity measure is used, along with a varying scale parameter, for the merging process. Hungarian algorithm is used for the optimization and pairwise assignment process in this hierarchical clustering approach and the iterative merging. The developed approach is numerically simple and shows promising result on collected datasets for grouping larger homogeneous regions like, roads, in an unsupervised manner. The developed road area detection approach thus does not require external information like shape, pavement lane markers, camera characteristics; making it more flexible and adaptable. As a result, road area within scene images belonging to different scene types, such as rural, urban, unstructured, as well as different pavement surface types like, paved and unpaved, could be grouped and detected.

Secondly, a superpixel level crack detection approach on the road surfaces has been developed in this work using state-of-the-art feature extraction algorithms and ML classifiers, like Gradient Boosting, Random Forest, Support Vector Machine, Artificial Neural Network. Here, features like, GLCM, statistical measures such as variance, and a new feature variant called VoG using Gabor filters, were extracted for every superpixel. Thereafter the superpixels, encoded with feature descriptors, were classified into two classes, crack and no-crack, using ML-based classifiers. In general, it has been experimentally observed that texture-based features were found to be more suitable for the task of crack detection. Further, contrast enhancement and filtering of the images improves the results, while ensemble classifiers like, Random Forest, showed better performance. The approach also provides a systematic feature selection process using ML-based classifier's accuracy metric to integrate and tune parameters of feature extraction algorithms.

Thirdly, an unsupervised learning and keypoint matching based approach for crack detection has been developed in this work. In this approach, a mixture of two Gamma distributions has been used to model the gradient values of road surface images. Consequently, GMFM has been adapted in this work to estimate parameters of the distributions and cluster the pixels into the edge and non-edge groups. Thus, GMFM has been adapted in this work for edge detection and shows promising results in comparison to a state-of-the-art threshold based edge detection method, like Canny edge detector. Once edges are detected in an unsupervised manner, it led to the generation of edge-based keypoints. A constant reference image has been used here, against which query images containing road surfaces are matched to see the similarity between keypoints of the images. Once keypoints are generated in both reference and query images, they are encoded using fuzzy descriptors and are matched using a methodology comprising of KL-divergence between two Dirichlet distributions. Similar keypoints are finally nominated as crack pixels in the query images and are marked on them. The number of matched keypoints gives an estimate on the extent of road deterioration. The developed edge-based keypoint generation, keypoint matching, and fuzzy-theoretic based approach show much better results than the state-of-the-art SIFT approach for the task of crack detection. In this way, cracks and related defects are detected and localized on road surface images in this work at both superpixel and pixel level.

Comparison between the developed methodologies gives insights not only between the two perspectives of crack detection- supervised ML-classifier and keypoint matching, but also provides conditions that can influence the choice of algorithm and data-driven road maintenance strategies. This, in turn, will help to monitor roads in a cost-effective and timely manner. Hence, the developed algorithms in this work helped to successfully detect cracks and related defects using easily available front-view scene images under different situations, like varied illumination conditions and road surfaces, darker lighting conditions, presence of varied types of cracks, presence of lane markers and oil marks. Thus, the developed crack detection approaches in this work using the easily available front-view scene image and advanced data analytics could help to devise effective strategies for different areas, such as road maintenance procedures, urban planning and route planning.

References

Abbasi, A., Sarker, S., and Chiang, R. H. 2016. "Big Data Research in Information Systems: Toward an Inclusive Research Agenda," *Journal of the Association for Information Systems* (17:2).

Abella, A., Ortiz-de-Urbina-Criado, M., and De-Pablos-Heredero, Carmen. 2017. "A model for the analysis of data-driven innovation and value generation in smart citie's ecosystems," *Cities* (64), pp. 47-53.

Achanta, R., Shaji, A., Smith, K., Lucchi, A., Fua, P., and Susstrunk, S. 2012. "Slic Superpixels Compared to State-Of-The-Art Superpixel Methods," *IEEE Transactions on Pattern Analysis and Machine Intelligence* (34:11), pp. 2274–2282.

Agarwal, R., and Dhar, V. 2014. "Editorial—Big Data, Data Science, and Analytics: The Opportunity and Challenge for IS Research," *Information Systems Research* (25:3), pp. 443–448.

Al-Mistarehi, B. 2017. "An Approach for Automated Detection and Classification of Pavement Cracks," Doctoral Thesis, Institute of Engineering Geodesy (IIGS), University of Stuttgart, Germany.

Alvarez, J. M., Gevers, T., and Lopez, A. M. 2014. "Road Detection by One-Class Color Classification: Dataset and Experiments," *CoRR (abs/1412.3506)*, pp. 1-10.

Alvarez, J. M., LeCun, Y., Gevers, T., and Lopez, A. M. 2012. "Semantic Road Segmentation via Multi-Scale Ensembles of Learned Features," in *Proceedings of the 12th International Conference on Computer Vision* (2), Springer-Verlag, Florence, Italy, pp. 586-595.

Arnott, D., and Pervan, G. 2012. "Design Science in Decision Support Systems Research: An Assessment using the Hevner, March, Park, and Ram Guidelines," *Journal of the Association for Information Systems* (13:11), pp. 923–949.

Banker, R. D., and Kauffman, R. J. 2004. "50th Anniversary Article: The Evolution of Research on Information Systems: A Fiftieth-Year Survey of the Literature in Management Science," *Management Science* (50:3), pp. 281–298.

BASt. 2008. "Road Monitoring and Assessment (ZEB - Verfahrensbeschreibung)," Federal Highway Research Institute (Bundesanstalt für Straßenwesen - BASt), http://www.bast.de.

Bay, H., Tuytelaars, S., and Gool, L. 2008. "Surf: Speeded up robust features," *Computer Vision and Image 320 Understanding (CVIU)* (110:3), pp. 346-359.

Beyeler, M., Mirus, F., and Verl, A. 2014. "Vision-based robust road lane detection in urban environments," in *Proceeding of the IEEE International Conference on Robotics and Automation (ICRA)*, Hong Kong, pp. 4920-4925.

Breiman, L. 2001. "Random Forests," *Machine Learning* (5:1), pp. 5-32.

Brust, C., Sickert, S., Simon, M., Rodner, E., and Denzler, J. 2015. "Convolutional Patch Networks With Spatial Prior for Road Detection And Urban Scene Understanding," in *Proceedings of the 10th International Conference on Computer Vision Theory and Applications*, Berlin, Germany, pp. 1-9.

Burt, P. 1981. "Fast Filter Transforms for Image Processing," *Computer Graphics and Image Processing* (16), pp. 20-51.

Canny, J. A. 1986."Computational Approach to Edge Detection," *IEEE Trans. Pattern Analysis and Machine Intelligence* (8:6), pp. 679–698.

Chambon, S., and Moliard, J. 2011. "Automatic Road Pavement Assessment with Image Processing: Review and Comparison," *International Journal of Geophysics*, pp. 1-20.

Chamorro, A., Tighe, S., Li, N., and Kazmierowski, T. 2009. "Development of Distress Guidelines and Condition Rating to Improve Network Management in Ontario, Canada," Transp. Res. Rec., 2093, pp. 128-135.

Chatterjee, S., Brendel, A.B., and Lichtenberg, S. 2018b. "Smart Infrastructure Monitoring: Development of a Decision Support System for Vision-Based Road Crack Detection," in *Int. Conf. Information Systems (ICIS)*, San Francisco, USA, pp. 1-19.

Chatterjee, S., Hildebrandt, B., and Kolbe, L.M. 2017. "Understanding the Scene Data – Pavement Area Grouping in Images." in *Int. Conf. Information Systems (ICIS)*, Seoul, South Korea, pp. 1-20.

Chatterjee, S., Saeedfar, P., Tofangchi, S., and Kolbe, L.M. 2018a. "Intelligent Road Maintenance: A Machine Learning Approach for Surface Defect Detection." in *European Conf. Information Systems (ECIS)*, UK, pp. 1-16.

Cherian, A., Morellas, V., and Papanikolopoulos, N. 2009. "Accurate 3d Ground Plane Estimation from a Single Image," in *Proceedings of the IEEE International Conference Robotics and Automation (ICRA)*, Kobe, Japan, pp. 2243-2249.

Conners, R.W., M. T., and Harlow, C. 1984. "Segmentation of a High-Resolution Urban Scene Using Texture Operators," *Computer Vision, Graphics, and Image Processing* (25:3), pp. 273-310.

Cortes, C., and Vapnik V. 1995. "Support-vector Networks," *Machine learning* (20:3), pp. 273-297.

Dalal, N., and Triggs, B. 2005. "Histograms of Oriented Gradients for Human Detection," in *Proceedings of the 2005 IEEE Computer Society Conference on Computer Vision and Pattern Recognition (CVPR'05)*, Volume 1, Washington, DC, USA, pp. 886-893.

Daugman, J.G. 1985."Uncertainty Relation for Resolution in Space, Spatial Frequency, and Orientation Optimized by Two-dimensional Visual Cortical Filters," *JOSAA* (2:7), pp. 1160-1169.

Day, D., McGath, A. and Natarajan, B. 2012. "Image Based Detection of D-cracking In Pavements," in *Proceedings of the International Conference on Image Processing, Computer Vision, and Pattern Recognition. The Steering Committee of The World Congress in Computer Science, Computer Engineering and Applied Computing (WorldComp).*

Dobson, R., Colling, T., Brooks. C., Roussi, C., Watkins, M., and Dean, D. 2014. "Collecting Decision Support System Data Through Remote Sensing of Unpaved Roads," *Transportation Research Record: Journal of the Transportation Research Board* (2433), pp. 108-115.

Dobson, R., J., Brooks. C., Roussi, C., and Colling, T. 2013. "Developing an Unpaved Road Assessment System for Practical Deployment with High-Resolution Optical Data Collection using a Helicopter UAV," in *Proceedings of the International Conference on Unmanned Aircraft Systems (ICUAS)*, Atlanta, pp. 235-243.

Eisenbach, M., Stricker, R., Seichter, D., Amende, K., Debes, K., Sesselmann, M., Ebersbach, D., Stoeckert, U., and Gross, H. 2017. "How to Get Pavement Distress Detection Ready for Deep Learning? A Systematic Approach," in *Int. Joint Conf. on Neural Networks*, USA, pp. 2039-2047.

FHWA. 2016. "Long-Term Pavement Performance Program - Pavement Performance Measures and Forecasting and the Effects of Maintenance and Rehabilitation Strategy on Treatment Effectiveness," Report No: FHWA-HRT-16-046.

Fink, D. 2010. "Road Safety 2.0: Insights and Implications for Government," in *23rd Bled eConference eTrust: Implications for the Individual, Enterprises and Society*, Slovenia.

Friedman, J. 1999. "Greedy Function Approximation: A Gradient Boosting Machine," IMS 1999 Reitz Lecture.

Fritsch, J., Kuehnl, T., and Geiger, A. 2013. "A New Performance measure and evaluation benchmark for road detection algorithms," in *Proceedings of the 16th IEEE International Conference on Intelligent Transportation Systems (ITSC)*, Hague, Netherlands, pp. 1-8.

Fritsch,J., Kühnl, T., and Kummert. F. 2014. "Monocular Road Terrain Detection by Combining Visual and Spatial Information," *IEEE Transactions on Intelligent Transportation Systems* (15:4), pp. 1586-1596.

Gabor, D. 1946. "Theory of communication. Part 1: The analysis of information," *Journal of the Institution of Electrical Engineers-Part III: Radio and Communication Engineering* (9:26), pp 429-441.

Galliers, R., Newell, S., Shanks, G., and Topi, H. 2015. "Call for papers for the special issue: The Challenges and Opportunities of 'Datification'; Strategic Impacts of 'Big'(and 'Small') and Real Time Data–for Society and for Organizational Decision Makers," *Journal of Strategic Information Systems* (24:3).

Gavilán, M., Balcones, D., Marcos, O., Llorca, D.F., Sotelo, M.A., Parra, I., Ocana, M., Aliseda, P., Yarza, P., and Amirola, A. 2011. "Adaptive Road Crack Detection System by Pavement Classification," *Sensors* (11:10), pp. 9628–9657.

Gholami, R., Watson, R. T., Hasan, H., Molla, A., and Bjorn-andersen, N. 2016. "Information Systems Solutions for Environmental Sustainability: How Can We Do More?," *Journal of the Association for Information Systems* (17:8), pp. 521–516.

Gianfranco, F., Carta, M., and Fadda, P. 2013. "A Decision Support System for Road Safety Analysis," *Transportation Research Procedia* (5), pp. 201-210.

Gleave, S. D. 2014. "EU Road Surfaces: Economic and Safety Impact of the lack of Regular Road Maintenance–Study," Policy Department Structural and Cohesion Policies, European Parliament, pp. 1-223.

Goes, P.B. 2014. "Big Data and IS Research," *MIS Quarterly* (38:3), pp. 3-8.

Goldberger, J. and Tassa, T. 2008. "A Hierarchical Clustering Algorithm Based on the Hungarian Method," *Pattern Recognition Letters* (29:11), pp. 1632 – 1638.

Gonzales, R. C. and Woods, R. E. 2002. "Digital Image Processing," 2nd. Edition, New Jersey, Pearson Education.

Gopalkrishnan, K. 2018. "Deep learning in data-driven pavement image analysis and automated distress detection: A review," *Data* (28:3).

Gregor, S., and Hevner, A. R. 2013. "Positioning and Presenting Design Science - Types of Knowledge in Design Science Research," *MISQ* (37:2), pp. 337–355.

Gregor, S., and Jones, D. 2007. "The anatomy of a design theory," *Journal of the Association for*

Information Systems (8:5), pp. 312–334.

Gregory, R. W., and Muntermann, J. 2011. "Theorizing in Design Science Research: Inductive versus Deductive Approaches," *Int. Conf. Information Systems (ICIS)* (2), pp. 1–16.

Gregory, R. W., and Muntermann, J. 2014. "Heuristic theorizing: Proactively generating design theories," *Information Systems Research* (25:3), pp. 639–653.

Günther, W. A., Mehrizi, M. H. R., Huysman, M., and F. Feldberg. 2017. "Debating Big Data: A Literature Review on Realizing Value from Big Data," *The Journal of Strategic Information Systems*.

Guo, R., Dai, Q., and Hoiem, D. 2013. "Paired Regions for Shadow Detection and Removal," *IEEE Transactions on Pattern Analysis and Machine Intelligence* (35:12), pp. 2956–2967.

Haralick, R.M. 1979. "Statistical and Structural Approaches to Textures," in *Proceedings of the IEEE* (67:5), pp. 786–804.

Hassani, M. El., Jehan-Besson,S., Brun,L., Rebevu,M., Duranton, M., Tschumperle,D., and Rivasseau, D. 2008. "A Time-consistent Video Segmentation Algorithm Designed for Real-time Implementation," *VLSI Design*, pp. 1-11.

Hastie, T., Tibshirani, R., and Friedman, J. 2009. "Boosting and additive trees," The Elements of Statistical Learning, pp. 337-387.

Henfridsson, O., and Lindgren, R. 2005. "Multi-contextuality in Ubiquitous Computing: Investigating the Car Case through Action Research," *Information and Organization* (15: 2), 95-124.

Hevner, A. R. 2007. "A Three Cycle View of Design Science Research," *Scandinavian Journal of Information Systems* (19:2), pp. 87–92.

Hevner, A. R., March, S. T., Park, J., and Ram, S. 2004. "Design Science in Information Systems Research," *MISQ* (28:1), pp. 75–105.

Hillel, A.B., Lerner, R., Levi, D., and Raz, G. 2014. "Recent Progress in Road and Lane Detection: A Survey," *Machine Vision and Applications* (25:3), pp. 727-745.

Hoeller, S. 2012. "Concrete pavement in Germany – construction, surface layer, interlayer, drainage and base course," *ICPPA*, Argetina.

Hoiem, D., Efros, A. A., and Hebert, M. 2005. "Geometric Context from a Single Image," in *10th IEEE International Conference on Computer Vision (ICCV)*, pp. 654–661.

Hosin, L., and Suseon, Y. 2006. "Enhancing Pavement Management Information System by

Integrating Digital Image Processing and Management Features," Transportation Research Board 85th Annual Meeting, pp. 1-14.

Huidrom, L., Das, L.K., and Sud, S.K. 2013. "Method for Automated Assessment of Potholes, Cracks and Patches from Road Video Clips," *Procedia- Social and Behavioral Sciences* (104), pp. 312-321.

Iglovikov, V., and Shvets, A. 2017. "TernausNet: U-Net with VGG11 Encoder Pre-Trained on ImageNet for Image Segmentation," https://arxiv.org/pdf/1801.05746.pdf.

Jouili, S., Mili, I., and Tabbone, S. 2009. "Attributed Graph Matching Using Local Descriptions," in *Proceedings of the 11th International Conference on Advanced Concepts for Intelligent Vision Systems (ACIVS)*, Blanc-J. Talon, W. Philips, D. Popescu, P. Scheunders (eds), Bordeaux, France, pp. 89-99.

Kahn, M. 1995. "Concepts, definitions, and key issues in sustainable development: the outlook for the future," in *Proceedings of the Int. Sustainable Development Research Conference*, Manchester.

Kapela, R., Sniatala, P., Turkot, A., Rybarczyk, A., Pozarycki, A., Rydzewski, P., Wyczalek, M., and Bloch, A. 2015. "Asphalt surfaced pavement cracks detection based on histograms of oriented gradient," in *22nd Int. Conf. on Mixed Design of Integrated Circuits and Systems*, Torun, Poland, pp. 579-584.

Khatoun, R., and Zeadally, S. 2016. "Smart Cities: Concepts, Architectures, Research Opportunities," *Communications of the ACM* (59:8), pp. 46-57.

Kitchin, R. 2014a. "Big Data, New Epistemologies and Paradigm Shifts," *Big Data and Society* (1:1).

Kitchin, R. 2014b. "The real-time city? Big data and smart urbanism," *GeoJournal* (79), pp. 1-14.

Kitchin, R. 2016. "Big Data," in *International Encyclopedia of Geography: People, the Earth, Environment and Technology*, D. Richardson, N. Castree, M. F. Goodchild, A. Kobayashi, W. Liu and R. A. Marston (eds).

Koch, C., Georgieva, K., Kasireddy, V., Akinci, B., and Fieguth, P. 2015. "A Review on Computer Vision Based Defect Detection and Condition Assessment of Concrete and Asphalt Civil Infrastructure," *Advanced Engineering Informatics* (29), pp. 196-210.

Kong, H., Audibert, J., and Ponce, J. 2010. "General Road Detection from a Single Image," *Transactions of Image Processing* (19:8), pp. 2211-2220.

Kuhn, H. 1955. "The Hungarian Method for the Assignment Problem," *Naval Research Logistic Quarterly* (2), pp. 83-97.

Kumar, M., Chatterjee, S., Zhang, W., J. Yang, and Kolbe, L.M. 2019. "Fuzzy theoretic model based analysis of image features," *Information Sciences* (480), pp. 34-54.

Kumar, M., Stoll, N., Thurow, K., and Stoll, R. 2016. "Fuzzy membership descriptors for images," *IEEE Transactions on Fuzzy Systems* (24:1), pp. 1-13.

Laubis, K., Konstantinov, M., Simko, V., Gröschel, A., and Weinhardt, C. 2018. "Enabling Crowd-sourcing Based Road Condition Monitoring Service by Intermediary," *Electronic Markets*, pp. 1-16.

Laubis, K., Simko, V., and Schuller, A. 2016. "Road Condition Measurement and Assessment: A Crowd Based Sensing Approach," in *Int. Conf. Information Systems (ICIS)*, Dublin, pp. 1-10.

Laubis, K., Simko, V., Schuller, A., and Wienhardt, C. 2017. "Road Condition Estimation Based on Heterogeneous Extended Floating Car Data," in *Proceedings of the 50th Hawaii International Conference on System Sciences (HICSS)*, Hawaii.

Lee, A., Thomas, M., and Baskerville, R. 2015. "Going Back to Basics in Design Science: From the Information Technology Artifact to the Information Systems Artifact," *Information Systems Journal* (25), pp. 5-21.

Li, J., Hu, Q., and Li, M. Ai. 2016. "Joint Model and Observation Cues for Single-Image Shadow Detection," *Remote Sensing* (8), pp.1-18.

Li, L., Sun, L., Ning, G., and Tan, S. 2014. "Automatic Pavement Crack Recognition Based on BP Neural Network," *Swarm Intelligence in Transportation Engineering, PROMET - Traffic and Transportation* (26:1), pp. 11-22.

Li, R., Yuan, Y., Zhang, W., and Yuan, Y. 2018. "Unified Vision-Based Methodology for Simultaneous Concrete Defect Detection and Geolocalization," *Computer-Aided Civil and Infrastructure Engineering*.

Liu, X., Lin, L., and Yuille, A. L. 2013. "Robust Region Grouping via Internal Patch Statistics," in *Proceedings of the IEEE Conference of Computer Vision and Pattern Recognition (CVPR)*, Portland, Oregon, USA, pp. 1931-1938.

Loprencipe, G., Pantuso, A., and Di Mascio, P. 2017. "Sustainable Pavement Management System in Urban Areas Considering the Vehicle Operating Costs," *Sustainability* (9:3), 453.

Louhghalam, A., Akbarian, M., and Ulm, F. 2017. "Carbon management of infrastructure performance: Integrated big data analytics and pavement-vehicle-interactions," *Journal of Cleaner Production (Special Volume on Improving natural resource management and human health to ensure sustainable societal development based upon insights gained from working within 'Big Data Environments)* (142), pp. 956–964.

Lowe, D. 2004. "Distinctive image features from scale-invariant keypoints," *International Journal of Computer Vision* (60:2), pp. 91- 110.

Maeda, H., Sekimoto, Y., Toshikazu, S., Kashiyama, T., and Omata, H. 2018. "Road Damage Detection and Classification Using Deep Neural Networks with Smartphone Images," *Computer-Aided Civil and Infrastructure Engineering*, pp. 1-15.

Mandviwalla, M. 2015. "Generating and justifying design theory," *Journal of the Association for Information Systems* (16:5), pp. 314–344.

Melville, N. P. 2010. "Information Systems Innovation for Environmental Sustainability," *MISQ* (34:1), pp. 1–21.

Menychtas, A., Kranas, P., Donovang-Kulisch, M., Heindrichs-Krusch, M., Coote, R., Schade, U., Osman, K., Kallipolitis, L., Van Der Graf, S., Brebels, W., Coenen, T., Rana, P., and Perennez, P. 2011." European Platform for Intelligent Cities (EPIC) Consortium," European Commission, ICT Policy Support Programme (2011), Online service delivery baseline and technical requirements report (D2.3 B).

Mertz, C. 2011. "Continuous Road Damage Detection Using Regular Service Vehicles," in *Proceedings of the ITS World Congress*.

Miksik, O. 2012. "Rapid Vanishing Point Estimation for General Road Detection," in *Proceedings of the IEEE International Conference Robotics and Automation (ICRA)*, St. Paul, Minnesota, USA, pp. 4844-4849.

Miller, J.S. 1993. "Long term pavement performance management," in US Department of Transport.

MnDOT. 2009. "Pavement Condition Executive Summary," Minnesota Department of Transportation, Report No. MnDOT/OMRR-PM–2009-01.

Moghadam, P., Starzyk, J.A, and Wijesoma, W.S. 2012. "Fast Vanishing-Point Detection in Unstructured Environments," *IEEE Transactions of Image Processing* (21:1), pp. 425-430.

Mohan, A., and Poobal, S. 2017. "Crack Detection Using Image Processing: A critical Review and Analysis," *Alexandria Engineering Journal*.

Moon, H., and Kim, J. 2011. "Intelligent Crack Detecting Algorithm on the Concrete Crack Image Using Neural network," in *Proceedings of the 28th Int. Symposium on Automation and Robotics in Construction*, Seoul, South Korea, pp.1461-1467.

Nejad, F.M., and Zakeri, H. 2011. "An Expert System Based on Wavelet Transform and Radon Neural Network for Pavement Distress Classification," *Expert Systems with Applications* (38:6), pp.9442–9460.

Nitsche, P., Van Geem, C., Stüt, R.., Mocanu, I., and Sjögren, L. 2014. "Monitoring Ride Quality on Roads with Existing Sensors in Passenger Cars," in *Proceedings of the 26th ARRB Conference*, Sydney.

Noh, Y., Koo, D., Kang, Y., Park, D., and Lee, D. 2017. "Automatic crack detection on concrete images using segmentation via fuzzy C-means clustering," *International Conference on Applied System Innovation (ICASI)*, Sapporo, pp. 877-880.

Ojala, T., and Pietikainen, M. 1996. "Unsupervised Texture Segmentation Using Feature Distributions," *Pattern Recognition*, pp. 477–486.

Oliveira, H., and Correia, L. 2014. "Crackit an image processing toolbox for crack detection and characterization," in *IEEE International Conference on Image Processing (ICIP)*, Paris, France.

Oliveira, H., and Correia, L. 2009. "Supervised Crack Detection and Classification in Images of Road Pavement Flexible Surfaces," *Recent Advances in Signal Processing*, pp. 159-184.

Ong, B., Wade, J., Howard, A., and Swan, D.J. 2014. "Using Cloud-Computing to Promote Asset Management Practices – A Ministry of Transportation Ontario Case Study," in *Proceedings of Conference of the Transportation Association of Canada*, Montreal, Cubed, Canada, pp. 1-11.

Passani, M., Yebes, J. J., and Bergasa, L. M. 2014. "CRF-based Semantic Labeling in Miniaturized Road Scenes," in *Proceedings of the 17th International IEEE Conference on Intelligent Transportation Systems (ITSC)*,Qingdao, China, pp. 1902–1903.

Pauly, L., Peel, H., Luo, S., Hogg, D., and Fuentess, R. 2017. "Deeper Networks for Pavement Crack Detection," in *Proceeding of 34th Int. Symposium on Automation and Robotics in Construction*, Taepei, pp. 479-485.

Peters, C., Blohm, I., and Leimeister, J. M. 2015. "Anatomy of Successful Business Models for Complex Services: Insights from the Telemedicine Field," *Journal of Management Information Systems* (32:3), pp. 75–104.

PMIS. 2011. "Condition of Texas Pavements- Pavement Management Information Systems," Texas Department of Transportation, PMIS Annual Report FY 2008-2011.

Prasanna, P., Dana, K., Gucunski, N., and Basily, B. 2012. "Computer-vision Based Crack Detection and Analysis," in *Proceedings of SPIE Smart Structures and Materials, Nondestructive Evaluation and Health Monitoring, International Society for Optics and Photonics*, pp.834.

Qin, H., Zain, J., Ma, X., and Hai, T. 2010. "Scene Segmentation Based on Seeded Region Growing for Foreground Detection," in *Proceedings of the 6th International Conference on Natural Computation* (8), IEEE, Yantai, China, pp. 3619-3623.

Rababahh, H., Vrajitoru, D., and Wolfer, J. 2005. "Asphalt Pavement Crack Classification: A comparison of GA, MLP, and SOM," in *Proceedings of Genetic and Evolutionary Computation Conference*.

Rabari, C., and Storper, M. 2014. "The digital Skin of Cities: Urban Theory and Research in the Agè of the Sensored and Metered City, Ubiquitous Computing and Big Data," *Cambridge Journal of Regions, Economy and Society* (8), pp. 27–42.

Radopouluo, S., Brilakis, I., Doycheva, K., and Koch, C. 2016. "A Framework for Automated Condition Monitoring," in *Proceedings of Construction Research Progress*, Puerto Rico.

Rai, A. 2017. "Diversity of Design Science Research," *MISQ* (41:1), pp. 3–18.

Rojas, R. 1996. "Neural Networks," Springer-Verlag, Berlin.

Salari, E. 2012. "Pavement Distress Evaluation Using 3d Depth Information from Stereo Vision. Report No: MIOH UTC TS43 2012-Final," Michigan Ohio University Transportation Center.

Schreiber, M., Poggenhans. F., and Stiller, C. 2014. "Detecting Symbols on Road Surface for Mapping and Localization using OCR," in *Proceedings of the IEEE International Conference Intelligent Transportation Systems*, Atlanta, pp. 1-6.

Shmueli, G., and Koppius, O. R. 2011. "Predictive analytics in information systems research," *MIS Quarterly*, pp. 553–572.

Silva, C., Bouwmans, T., and Frelicot, C. 2015. "An Extended Center-symmetric Local Binary Pattern for Background Modeling and Subtraction in Videos," in *Proceedings of the 10th International Joint Conference on Computer Vision, Imaging and Computer Graphics Theory and Applications*, Berlin, Germany, pp. 1-9.

Silvia, W., and Lucena, D. 2018. "Concrete cracks detection based on deep learning image classification," in *18th International Conference on Experimental Mechanics (ICEM18)*, Brussels, Belgium.

Sinha, S., and Fieguth, P. 2006. "Automated Detection of Cracks in Buried Concrete Pipe Images," *Automation in Construction* (1), pp. 58–72.

Soukup, D. and Huber-Mörk, R. 2014. "Convolutional neural networks for steel surface defect detection from photometric stereo images," *Advances in Visual Computing*, Springer International Publishing (8887), pp. 668–677.

Staniek, M. 2014. "Neural Networks in Stereo Vision Techniques of Road Pavement Evaluation," in *Proceedings of the International Symposium- Non Destructive Testing in Civil Engineering*, Germany: Berlin.

Stilgoe, J. 2017. "Machine Learning, Social Learning and the Governance of Self-Driving Cars," *Social Studies of Science* (48:1).

Straube, E. 2015. "Erhaltung von Strasse, " University of Duisburg Essen, http://duepublico.uniduisburg-essen.de/servlets/DerivateServlet/Derivate-17018/Erhaltung%20-%20Pr%C3%A4sentation.pdf

Su, T., and Yang, M. 2014. "Application of morphological segmentation to leaking defect detection in sewer pipes," *Sensors* (14), pp. 8686–8704.

Tang, J., and Sun, B. 2012. "An Integrated Digital Image Processing Pavement Management Information System," *ICLEM 2012: Logistics for Sustained Economic Development—Technology and Management for Efficiency*.

Tedeschi, A., and Benedetto, F. 2016. "A real-time automatic pavement crack and pothole recognition system for mobile android-based devices," *Advanced Engineering Informatics* (32 :2), pp. 11- 25.

Teomete, E., Amin, V., Ceylan, H., and Smadi, O. 2005. "Digital Image Processing for Pavement Distress Analyses," in *Mid-continent Transportation Research Symposium*, Iowa.

Tilson, D., Lyytinen, K., and Sørensen, C. 2010. "Research Commentary —Digital Infrastructures: The Missing IS Research Agenda," *Information Systems Research* (21:4), pp. 748-759.

UN-DESA. 2014. "2014 revision of the World Urbanization Prospects," in World Urbanization Prospects, pp. 1–493.

UN-DESA. 2016. "The World's Cities in 2016," in World Urbanization Prospects, pp. 1-26.

Varadharajan, S., Jose, S., Sharma, K., Wander, L., and Mertz, C. 2014. "Vision for Road Inspection," in *Proceedings of the IEEE Winter Conference on Application of Computer Vision (WACV)*, Colorado, USA, pp.115-122.

Venter, F., and Stein, A. 2012. "Images andVideos: Really Big Data," *Analytics*, pp. 1-12.

Vitor, G., Lima, D., Victorino, A., and Ferreira, J. 2013. "A 2D/3D Vision Based Approach Applied to Road Detection in Urban Environments," in *Proceedings of the IEEE Intelligent Vehicles Symposium*, pp. 952-957.

vom Brocke, J., Watson, R. T., Dwyer, C., Elliot, S., and Melville, N. 2013. "Green information systems: Directives for the IS discipline," *Communications of the Association for Information Systems* (33:1), pp. 509–520.

Watson, R. T., Boudreau, M.-C., and Chen, A. J. 2010. "Information systems and environmentally sustainable development: energy informatics and new directions for the IS community," *MISQ* (34:1), pp. 23–38.

Wu, L., Mokhtari, S., Nazef, A., and Nam, B. 2016. "Improvement of Crack Detection Accuracy with Novel Crack Defragmentation Technique in Image-based Road Assessment," *Journal of Computing in Civil Engineering* (30:1).

Yang, C.C., and Lin, J.D. 2013. "Establishment of Pavement Information Decision Management Platform via Cloud Computing Technology," *Advanced Materials Research* (723), pp. 829-837.

Yang, L., Li, B., Li, W., Liu, Z., Yang, G., and Xiao, J. 2017. "Deep concrete inspection using unmanned aerial vehicle towards cssc database," in *International Conference on Intelligent Robots and Systems (IROS)*, 2017 IEEE/RSJ, Vancouver, Canada.

Yokoyama, S., and Matsumoto, T. 2017. "Development of an automatic detector of cracks in concrete using machine learning," *Procedia Engineering*, pp. 1250-1255.

Yoo, Y. J. 2010. "Computing in Everyday Life: A Call for Research on Experiential Computing," *MIS Quarterly* (34:2), pp. 213-231.

Yoo, Y. J., Boland, R. J., Lyytinen, K., and Majchrzak, A. 2012. "Organizing for Innovation in the Digitized World," *Organization Science* (23:5), pp. 1398-1408.

Zakeri, H., Nejad, F. M., and Fahimifar., A. 2016. "Image Based Techniques for Crack Detection, Classification and Quantification in Asphalt Pavement: A Review," *Archives of Computational Methods in Engineering* (24;4), pp. 935-977.

Zalama, E., Gómez-García-Bermejo, J., Medina, R., and Llamas, J. 2013. "Road Crack Detection Using Visual Features Extracted By Gabor Filters," *Computer-Aided Civil and Infrastructure Engineering* (29:5), pp. 342-358.

Zhang, C. 2009. "Monitoring the condition of unpaved roads with remote sensing and other technologies," South Dakota State University, Brookings.

Zhang, L., Yang, F., Zhang, Y.D., and Zhu, Y.J. 2016. "Road Crack Detection Using Deep Convolutional Neural Network," in *Proceedings of IEEE Int. Conf. on Image Processing (ICIP)*, pp. 3708-3712.

Zhang, W., Zhang, Z., Qi, D., and Liu, Y. 2014. "Automatic crack detection and classification method for subway tunnel safety monitoring," *Sensors* (14), pp. 19307-19328.

Zhou, S., and Iagnemma, K. 2010. "Self-supervised Learning Method for Unstructured Road Detection using Fuzzy Support Vector Machines," in *Proceedings of the IEEE/RSJ International Conference on Intelligent Robots and Systems (IROS)*, Taipei, pp. 1183-1189.

Zhou, S.J., Gong, G., Xiong, H. C., and Iagnemma, K. 2010. "Road Detection Using Support Vector Machine Based on Online Learning and Evaluation," in *Proceedings of the IEEE Intelligent Vehicles Symposium*, CA, USA, pp. 256–261.

Zuiderveld, K. 1994. "Contrast limited adaptive histogram equalization," Graphics gems IV. USA: Academic Press Professional, Inc. pp. 474-485.

Appendix

Appendix A: Overview of the author's contribution in the publications included in this dissertation.

Chapter Number	Title	Outlet	Rating	Author's Contribution
2	Understanding the Scene Data: Pavement Area Grouping in Images	Proceedings of the International Conference on Information Systems (ICIS) 2017, Seoul, South Korea	VHB Rating A	**Sromona Chatterjee 90 %** Björn Hildebrandt 5 % Lutz M. Kolbe 5 %
3	Intelligent Road Maintenance: A Machine Learning Approach for Surface Defect Detection	Proceedings of the European Conference on Information Systems (ECIS) 2018, Portsmouth, UK	VHB Rating B	**Sromona Chatterjee 85 %** Pouya Saeedfar 5 % Schahin Tofangchi 5 % Lutz M. Kolbe 5 %
4	Defect Detection on Road Surfaces Using Fuzzy Image Descriptors and Keypoint Matching	Engineering Applications of Artificial Intelligence	Impact Factor 4.2	**Sromona Chatterjee 85 %** Mohit Kumar 10 % Lutz M. Kolbe 5 %
5	Smart Infrastructure Monitoring: Development of a Decision Support System for Vision-Based Road Crack Detection	Proceedings of the International Conference on Information Systems (ICIS) 2018, San Francisco, USA	VHB Rating A	**Sromona Chatterjee 70 %** Alfred Benedikt Brendel 20 % Sascha Lichtenberg 10%

Appendix B: Overview of the published and submitted publications of the author till date.

Chatterjee, S., Kumar, M., and Kolbe, L. M. 2020. "Defect Detection on Road Surfaces Using Fuzzy Image Descriptors and Keypoint Matching." *Engineering Applications of Artificial Intelligence.* (Submitted)

Kumar, M., **Chatterjee, S.**, Zhang, W., Yang, J., and Kolbe, L. M. 2019. "Fuzzy Theoretic Model Based Analysis of Image Features." *Information Sciences.*

Chatterjee, S., Brendel, A.B., and Lichtenberg, S. 2018. "Smart Infrastructure Monitoring: Development of a Decision Support System for Vision-Based Road Crack Detection," in *Int. Conf. Information Systems (ICIS)*, San Francisco, USA, pp. 1-19.

Chatterjee, S., Saeedfar, P., Tofangchi, S., and Kolbe, L.M. 2018. "Intelligent Road Maintenance: A Machine Learning Approach for Surface Defect Detection." in *European Conf. Information Systems (ECIS)*, UK, pp. 1-16.

Chatterjee, S., Hildebrandt, B., and Kolbe, L.M. 2017. "Understanding the Scene Data – Pavement Area Grouping in Images." in *Int. Conf. Information Systems (ICIS)*, Seoul, South Korea, pp. 1-20.

Ebermann, C., Piccinini, E., **Chatterjee, S.**, and Kolbe, L.M. 2016. "What are the Behavioral Characteristics of Heavy Users of Pedelecs? A Longitudinal Field Study of the Use of Sustainable Mobility Concepts." in *31st International Congress of Psychology (ICP)*, Yokohama, Japan.

Ebermann, C., Piccinini, E., **Chatterjee, S.**, and Kolbe, L.M. 2016. "The Adoption of Pedelecs ? A Longitudinal Field Study About Psychological Factors Influencing the Use of Sustainable Mobility Concepts." in *The Int. Conf. on Traffic and Transportation Psychology*, Brisbane, Australia.

Chatterjee, S., Nachstedt, T., Tamosiunaite, M., Wörgötter, F., Enomoto, Y., Ariizumi, R., Matsuno, F. and Manoonpong, P. 2015. "Learning and Chaining of Motor Primitives for Goal-directed Locomotion of a Snake-like Robot with Screw-drive Units." *International Journal of Advanced Robotic Systems* (12:176).

Chatterjee, S., Nachstedt, T., Wörgötter, F., Tamosiunaite, M., Manoonpong, P., Enomoto, Y., Ariizumi, R. and Matsuno, F. 2014. "Reinforcement Learning Approach to Generate Goal-directed Locomotion of a Snake-like Robot with Screw-drive Units." in *23rd IEEE Int. Conf. on Robotics in Alpe-Adria-Danube Region (RAAD)*, Smolenice, Slovakia, pp. 1-7.

Göttinger Wirtschaftsinformatik

Herausgeber: Prof. Dr. J. Biethahn† • Prof. Dr. L. M. Kolbe • Prof. Dr. M. Schumann

Band 31: Christian Stummeyer
Integration von Simulationsmethoden und hochintegrierter betriebswirtschaftlicher PPS-Standardsoftware im Rahmen eines ganzheitlichen Entwicklungsansatzes
ISBN 3-89712-874-8

Band 32: Stefan Wegert
Gestaltungsansätze zur IV-Integration von elektronischen und konventionellen Vertriebsstrukturen bei Kreditinstituten
ISBN 3-89712-924-8

Band 33: Ernst von Stegmann und Stein
Ansätze zur Risikosteuerung einer Kreditversicherung unter Berücksichtigung von Unternehmensverflechtungen
ISBN 3-89873-003-4

Band 34: Gerald Wissel
Konzeption eines Managementsystems für die Nutzung von internen sowie externen Wissen zur Generierung von Innovationen
ISBN 3-89873-194-4

Band 35: Wolfgang Greve-Kramer
Konzeption internetbasierter Informationssysteme in Konzernen
Inhaltliche, organisatorische und technische Überlegungen zur internetbasierten Informationsverarbeitung in Konzernen
ISBN 3-89873-207-X

Band 36: Tim Veil
Internes Rechnungswesen zur Unterstützung der Führung in Unternehmensnetzwerken
ISBN 3-89873-237-1

Band 37: Mark Althans
Konzeption eines Vertriebscontrolling-Informationssystems für Unternehmen der liberalisierten Elektrizitätswirtschaft
ISBN 3-89873-326-2

Band 38: Jörn Propach
Methoden zur Spielplangestaltung öffentlicher Theater
Konzeption eines Entscheidungsunterstützungssystems auf der Basis Evolutionärer Algorithmen
ISBN 3-89873-496-X

Cuvillier Verlag Göttingen
Nonnenstieg 8 • 37075 Göttingen

Göttinger Wirtschaftsinformatik

Herausgeber: Prof. Dr. J. Biethahn† • Prof. Dr. L. M. Kolbe • Prof. Dr. M. Schumann

Band 39: Jochen Heimann
DV-gestützte Jahresabschlußanalyse
Möglichkeiten und Grenzen beim Einsatz computergeschützter Verfahren zur Analyse und Bewertung von Jahresabschlüssen
ISBN 3-89873-499-4

Band 40: Patricia Böning Spohr
Controlling für Medienunternehmen im Online-Markt
Gestaltung ausgewählter Controllinginstrumente
ISBN 3-89873-677-6

Band 41: Jörg Koschate
Methoden und Vorgehensmodelle zur strategischen Planung von Electronic-Business-Anwendungen
ISBN 3-89873-808-6

Band 42: Yang Liu
A theoretical and empirical study on the data mining process for credit scoring
ISBN 3-89873-823-X

Band 43: Antonios Tzouvaras
Referenzmodellierung für Buchverlage
Prozess- und Klassenmodelle für den Leistungsprozess
ISBN 3-89873-844-2

Band 44: Marina Nomikos
Hemmnisse der Nutzung Elektronischer Marktplätze aus der Sicht von kleinen und mittleren Unternehmen eine theoriegeleitete Untersuchung
ISBN 3-89873-847-7

Band 45: Boris Fredrich
Wissensmanagement und Weiterbildungsmanagement
Gestaltungs- und Kombinationsansätze im Rahmen einer lernenden Organisation
ISBN 3-89873-870-1

Band 46: Thomas Arens
Methodische Auswahl von CRM Software
Ein Referenz-Vorgehensmodell zur methodengestützten Beurteilung und Auswahl von Customer Relationship Management Informationssystemen
ISBN 3-86537-054-3

Cuvillier Verlag Göttingen

Nonnenstieg 8 • 37075 Göttingen

Göttinger Wirtschaftsinformatik

Herausgeber: Prof. Dr. J. Biethahn† • Prof. Dr. L. M. Kolbe • Prof. Dr. M. Schumann

Band 47: Andreas Lackner
Dynamische Tourenplanung mit ausgewählten Mataheuristiken
Eine Untersuchung am Beispiel des kapazitätsrestriktiven dynamischen Tourenplanungsproblems mit Zeitfenstern
ISBN 3-86537-084-5

Band 48: Tobias Behrensdorf
Service Engineering in Versicherungsunternehmen
unter besonderer Berücksichtigung eines Vorgehensmodells zur Unterstützung durch Informations- und Kommunikationstechnologien
ISBN 3-86537-110-8

Band 49: Michael Range
Aufbau und Betrieb konsumentenorientierter Websites im Internet
Vorgehen und Methoden unter besonderer Berücksichtigung der Anforderungen von kleinen und mittleren Online-Angeboten
ISBN 3-86537-490-5

Band 50: Gerit Grübler
Ganzheitliches Multiprojektmanagement
Mit einer Fallstudie in einem Konzern der Automobilzulieferindustrie
ISBN 3-86537-544-8

Band 51: Birte Pochert
Konzeption einer unscharfen Balanced Scorecard
Möglichkeiten der Fuzzyfizierung einer Balanced Scorecard zur Unterstützung des Strategischen Managements
ISBN 3-86537-671-1

Band 52: Manfred Peter Zilling
Effizienztreiber innovativer Prozesse für den Automotive Aftermarket
Implikationen aus der Anwendung von kollaborativen und integrativen Methoden des Supply Chain Managements
ISBN 3-86537-790-4

Band 53: Mike Hieronimus
Strategisches Controlling von Supply Chains
Entwicklung eines ganzheitlichen Ansatzes unter Einbeziehung der Wertschöpfungspartner
ISBN 3-86537-799-8

Band 54: Dijana Bergmann
Datenschutz und Datensicherheit unter besonderer Berücksichtigung des elektronischen Geschäftsverkehrs zwischen öffentlicher Verwaltung und privaten Unternehmen
ISBN 3-86537-894-3

Cuvillier Verlag Göttingen
Nonnenstieg 8 • 37075 Göttingen

Göttinger Wirtschaftsinformatik

Herausgeber: Prof. Dr. J. Biethahn† • Prof. Dr. L. M. Kolbe • Prof. Dr. M. Schumann

Band 55: Jan Eric Borchert
Operatives Innovationsmanagement in Unternehmensnetzwerken
Gestaltung von Instrumenten für Innovationsprojekte
ISBN 3-86537-984-2

Band 56: Andre Daldrup
Konzeption eines integrierten IV-Systems zur ratingbasierten Quantifizierung des regulatorischen und ökonomischen Eigenkapitals im Unternehmenskreditgeschäft unter Berücksichtigung von Basel II
ISBN 978-3-86727-189-9

Band 57: Thomas Diekmann
Ubiquitous Computing-Technologien im betrieblichen Umfeld
Technische Überlegungen, Einsatzmöglichkeiten und Bewertungsansätze
ISBN 978-3-86727-194-3

Band 58: Lutz Seidenfaden
Ein Peer-to-Peer-basierter Ansatz zur digitalen Distribution wissenschaftlicher Informationen
ISBN 978-3-86727-321-3

Band 59: Sebastian Rieger
Einheitliche Authentifizierung in heterogenen IT-Strukturen für ein sicheres e-Science-Umfeld
ISBN 978-3-86727-329-9

Band 60: Ole Björn Brodersen
Eignung schwarmintelligenter Verfahren für die betriebliche Entscheidungsunterstützung
Untersuchungen der Particle Swarm Optimization und Ant Colony Optimization anhand eines stochastischen Lagerhaltungs- und eines universitären Stundenplanungsproblems
ISBN 978-3-86727-777-5

Band 61: Jan Sauer
Konzeption eines wertorientierten Managementsystems unter besonderer Berücksichtigung des versicherungstechnischen Risikos
ISBN 978-3-86727-858-4

Band 62: Adam Melski
Datenmanagement in RFID-gestützten Logistiknetzwerken
RFID-induzierte Veränderungen, Gestaltungsmöglichkeiten und Handlungsempfehlungen
ISBN 978-3-86955-041-1

Cuvillier Verlag Göttingen

Nonnenstieg 8 • 37075 Göttingen

Göttinger Wirtschaftsinformatik

Herausgeber: Prof. Dr. J. Biethahn† • Prof. Dr. L. M. Kolbe • Prof. Dr. M. Schumann

Band 63: Thorsten Caus
Anwendungen im mobilen Internet
Herausforderungen und Lösungsansätze für die Entwicklung und Gestaltung mobiler Anwendungen
ISBN 978-3-86955-399-3

Band 64: Nils-Holger-Schmidt
Environmentally Sustainable Information Management
Theories and concepts for Sustainability, Green IS, and Green IT
ISBN 978-3-86955-825-7

Band 65: Lars Thoroe
RFID in Reverse-Logistics-Systemen
ISBN 978-3-86955-902-5

Band 66: Stefan Bitzer
Integration von Web 2.0-Technologien in das betriebliche Wissensmanagement
ISBN 978-3-86955-918-6

Band 67: Matthias Kießling
IT-Innovationsmanagement
Gestaltungs- und Steuerungsmöglichkeiten
ISBN 978-3-95404-104-6

Band 68: Marco Klein
HR Social Software
Unternehmensinterne Weblogs, Wikis und Social Networking Services für Prozesse des Personalmanagements
ISBN 978-3-95404-247-0

Band 69: Malte Schmidt
Migration vom Barcode zur passiven RFID-Technologie in der automobilen Logistik
Exemplarische Untersuchung am Beispiel eines Automobilherstellers
ISBN 978-3-95404-441-2

Band 70: Janis Kossahl
Konzeptuelle Grundlagen zur Etablierung einer Informationsplattform in der Energiewirtschaft
Ein Beitrag zur Energiewende aus der Perspektive der Wirtschaftsinformatik
ISBN 978-3-95404-524-2

Cuvillier Verlag Göttingen
Nonnenstieg 8 • 37075 Göttingen

Göttinger Wirtschaftsinformatik

Herausgeber: Prof. Dr. J. Biethahn† • Prof. Dr. L. M. Kolbe • Prof. Dr. M. Schumann

Band 71: Stefan Friedemann
IT-gestützte Produktionsplanung mit nachwachsenden Rohstoffen unter Berücksichtigung von Unsicherheiten
ISBN 978-3-95404-606-5

Band 72: Arne Frerichs
Unternehmensfinanzierung mit Peer-to-Peer-gestützter Mittelvergabe
ISBN 978-3-95404-624-9

Band 73: Ullrich C. C. Jagstaidt
Smart Metering Information Management
Gestaltungsansätze für das Informationsmanagement und für Geschäftsmodelle der Marktakteure in der Energiewirtschaft
ISBN 978-3-95404-696-6

Band 74: Sebastian Busse
Exploring the Role of Information Systems in the Development of Electric Mobility
Understanding the Domain and Designing the Path
ISBN 978-3-95404-727-7

Band 75: Christoph Beckers
Management von Wasserinformationen in der Fleischindustrie
Analyse von Sytemanforderungen zur produktspezifischen Ausweisung von Water Footprints
ISBN 978-3-95404-809-0

Band 76: Hendrik Hilpert
Informationssysteme für die Nachhaltigkeitsberichterstattung in Unternehmen
Empirische Erkenntnisse und Gestaltungsansätze zur Datengrundlage, Erfassung und Berichterstattung von Treibhausgasemissionen
ISBN 978-3-95404-908-0

Band 77: Simon Thanh-Nam Trang
Adoption, Value Co-Creation, and Governance of Inter-Organizational Information Technology in Wood Networks
ISBN 978-3-7369-9031-9

Band 78: Stefan Gröger
IT-Unterstützung zur Verbesserung der Drittmittel-Projekt-Bewirtschaftung an Hochschulen - Referenzprozessgestaltung, Artefakt-Design und Nutzenpotenziale
ISBN 978-3-7369-9077-7

Cuvillier Verlag Göttingen

Nonnenstieg 8 • 37075 Göttingen

Göttinger Wirtschaftsinformatik

Herausgeber: Prof. Dr. J. Biethahn† • Prof. Dr. L. M. Kolbe • Prof. Dr. M. Schumann

Band 79: Johannes Schmidt
Demand-Side Integration Programs for Electric Transport Vehicles unter Berücksichtigung von Unsicherheiten
ISBN 978-3-7369-9123-1

Band 80: Christian Tornack
IT-gestütztes Nachfolgemanagement in Großunternehmen
ISBN 978-3-7369-9161-3

Band 81: Shanna Appelhanz
Tracking & Tracing-Systeme in Wertschöpfungsnetzwerken für die industrielle stoffliche Nutzung nachwachsender Rohstoffe
ISBN 978-3-7369-9207-8

Band 82: Henning Krüp
IT Corporate Entrepreneurship – Identifying Factors for IT Innovations in Non-IT Companies
ISBN 978-3-7369-9253-5

Band 83: Andre Hanelt
Managing the Digital Transformation of Business Models – An Incumbent Firm Perspective
ISBN 978-3-7369-9254-2

Band 84: Björn Pilarski
Mobile Personalinformationssysteme
Empirische Erkenntnisse und Gestaltungsansätze zum Einsatz mobiler Anwendungen im Personalmanagement
ISBN 978-3-7369-9291-7

Band 85: Everlin Piccinini
Digital Transformation of Business - Understanding this Phenomenon in the Context of the Automotive Industry
ISBN 978-3-7369-9323-5

Band 86: Matthias Eisel
Analyzing the Range Barrier to Electric Vehicle Adoption - The Case of Range Anxiety
ISBN 978-3-7369-9379-2

Cuvillier Verlag Göttingen

Nonnenstieg 8 • 37075 Göttingen

Göttinger Wirtschaftsinformatik

Herausgeber: Prof. Dr. J. Biethahn† • Prof. Dr. L. M. Kolbe • Prof. Dr. M. Schumann

Band 87: Gerrit Remané
Digital Business Models in the Mobility Sector: Using Components and Types to Understand Existing and Design New Business Models
ISBN 978-3-7369-9544-4

Band 88: Thierry Jean Ruch
Consumerization of IT –
Studies to Explore the Phenomenon and Implications for IT Management, Information Security, and Organizational Security
ISBN 978-3-7369-9558-1

Band 89: Carolin Ebermann
Die Förderung von nachhaltigem Mobilitätsverhalten durch erhöhte User-Experience und den Einsatz von Informationssystemen
ISBN 978-3-7369-9568-0

Band 90: Sebastian Zander
Interorganizational Information Systems for the Efficient Utilization of Renewable Resources - Insights from Networks in the Wood Industry
ISBN 978-3-7369-9584-0

Band 91: Ilja Nastjuk
The Dark and the Bright Side of Digitalization -
The Case of Sustainable Mobility
ISBN 978-3-7369-9586-4

Band 92: Aaron Mengelkamp
Informationen zur Bonitätsprüfung auf Basis von Daten aus sozialen Medien
ISBN 978-3-7369-9628-1

Band 93: Alfred Benedikt Brendel
Applied Design Science Research in the Context of Smart and Sustainable Mobility
The Case of Vehicle Supply and Demand Management in Shared Vehicle Services
ISBN 978-3-7369-9685-4

Band 94: Markus Mandrella
IT-Based Value Co-Creation in Inter-Organizational Networks
Theory Integration, Extension, and Adaptation to the Wood Industry
ISBN 978-3-7369-9695-3

Cuvillier Verlag Göttingen
Nonnenstieg 8 • 37075 Göttingen

Göttinger Wirtschaftsinformatik

Herausgeber: Prof. Dr. J. Biethahn† • Prof. Dr. L. M. Kolbe • Prof. Dr. M. Schumann

Band 95: Benjamin Brauer
Persuasive User-Centric Green IS
Exploring the Role and Paving the Way of Information Systems to Induce Pro-Environmental Behavior Change
ISBN 978-3-7369-9764-6

Band 96: Sebastian Hobert
Empirische Erkenntnisse und Gestaltungsansätze zum Einsatz von Wearable Computern im Industriesektor
ISBN 978-3-7369-9794-3

Band 97: Björn Hildebrandt
Digitalization of Mobility - Understanding the Transformational Impacts of Pervasive Digital Technologies on Business Models in the Mobility Sector
ISBN 978-3-7369-9827-8

Band 98: Jasmin Decker
Micro Learning und Mobile Learning in Unternehmen – Empirische Erkenntnisse und Gestaltungsempfehlungen zum Einsatz mobiler Lernanwendungen
ISBN 978-3-7369-9835-3

Band 99: Jan Moritz Anke
IT-gestützte Lern- und Assessmentmodule für nachhaltiges Wirtschaften
Empirische Erkenntnisse und Gestaltungsansätze zum Einsatz IT-gestützter Lern- und Assessmentmodule
ISBN 978-3-7369-9986-2

Band 100: Daniel Leonhardt
Organizing for Digital Innovation – The Role of the IT Function
ISBN 978-3-7369-7060-1

Band 101: Schahin Tofangchi
Towards a Theory for Designing Machine Learning Systems for Complex Decision Making Problems
ISBN 978-3-7369-7200-1

Band 102: Stephan Diederich
Designing Anthropomorphic Conservational Agents in Enterprises: A Nascent Theory and Conceptual Framework for Fostering a Human-Like Interaction
ISBN 978-3-7369-7216-2

Göttinger Wirtschaftsinformatik

Herausgeber: Prof. Dr. J. Biethahn† • Prof. Dr. L. M. Kolbe • Prof. Dr. M. Schumann

Band 103: Bernd Herrenkind
Driving the Future Diffusion of Mobility
Investigating User Acceptance of Autonomous Driving in Shared Mobility Services
ISBN 978-3-7369-7214-8

Cuvillier Verlag Göttingen

Nonnenstieg 8 • 37075 Göttingen

www.ingramcontent.com/pod-product-compliance
Ingram Content Group UK Ltd.
Pitfield, Milton Keynes, MK11 3LW, UK
UKHW021652190726
13853UKWH00001B/218

9 783736 972582